D1447181

Practical tips for facilitating research

PRACTICAL TIPS FOR LIBRARY AND INFORMATION PROFESSIONALS

This series provides a set of practical guides for the busy professional in need of inspiration. Sourced from experienced library and information practitioners, grounded in theory, yet not overwhelmed by it, the information in these guides will tell you what you need to know to make a quick impact in a range of topical areas of professional interest.

SERIES EDITOR: HELEN BLANCHETT

Subject specialist (scholarly communications), JISC

After qualifying and working as a librarian in her early career, Helen worked for Jisc Netskills for 13 years providing training and working on a diverse range of projects across various sectors and then as librarian in the liaison team at Newcastle University. She has a keen interest in all aspects of information and digital literacy, and in supporting staff and students in their development.

PRACTICAL TIPS FOR LIBRARY AND INFORMATION PROFESSIONALS
SERIES EDITOR: HELEN BLANCHETT

Practical tips for facilitating research

Moira J. Bent

facet
publishing

© Moira J. Bent 2016

Published by Facet Publishing
7 Ridgmount Street, London WC1E 7AE
www.facetpublishing.co.uk

Facet Publishing is wholly owned by CILIP: the Chartered Institute
of Library and Information Professionals.

Moira J. Bent has asserted her right under the Copyright, Designs
and Patents Act 1988 to be identified as author of this work.

Except as otherwise permitted under the Copyright, Designs and
Patents Act 1988 this publication may only be reproduced, stored
or transmitted in any form or by any means, with the
prior permission of the publisher, or, in the case of reprographic
reproduction, in accordance with the terms of a licence
issued by The Copyright Licensing Agency. Enquiries
concerning reproduction outside those terms should be sent to
Facet Publishing, 7 Ridgmount Street, London WC1E 7AE.

British Library Cataloguing in Publication Data
A catalogue record for this book is available from
the British Library.

ISBN 978-1-78330-017-4 (paperback)
ISBN 978-1-78330-109-6 (hardback)

First published 2016

Text printed on FSC accredited material.

Typeset from author's files in 10/13 pt Palatino Linotype and
Myriad Pro by Facet Publishing Production.
Printed and made in Great Britain by CPI Group (UK) Ltd,
Croydon, CR0 4YY.

Every purchase of a Facet book helps to fund CILIP's
advocacy, awareness and accreditation programmes
for information professionals.

Contents

List of figures

Series Editor's introduction

Helen Blanchett, Jisc, UK

This series provides a set of practical guides for the busy professional in need of inspiration. Sourced from experienced library and information practitioners, grounded in theory, yet not overwhelmed by it, the information in these guides will tell you what you need to know to make a quick impact in a range of topical areas of professional interest.

Each book takes a tips-based approach to introduce best practice ideas and encourage adaptation and innovation.

The series is aimed at experienced library and information professionals looking for new ideas and inspiration, as well as new professionals wanting to tap into the experience of others, and students and educators interested in how theory is put into practice.

Practical Tips for Facilitating Research

The changing nature of the research environment, involving increased competition and demand for wider dissemination and impact, provides challenges for librarians, but also opportunities. Roles are evolving, with activities being driven more by researcher requirements, which in turn requires more engagement with researchers.[1] New specialisms are also emerging,[2] such as that of data librarians. This book aims to provide practical tips for librarians wishing to survive the 'crisis in research librarianship',[3] demonstrate value and shape new roles in the research process.

Moira J. Bent has a wealth of experience working with researchers in her library role, and indeed as a researcher herself. When looking for an author to write this book she was an obvious choice.

Moira has previously written about providing effective library services for researchers[4] and explored information literacy throughout a researcher's life.[5] As a leading expert in information literacy, Moira co-authored the SCONUL Seven Pillars of Information Literacy.[6] She was an advisor on the information literacy lens on the Vitae's Researcher Development Framework[7] and co-authored the Informed Researcher booklet.[8]

While supporting researchers has long been part of an academic librarian's job, Moira feels strongly that librarians have a role beyond 'support' – that we can play a vital role as a partner in the research process. While this book is intended to provide practical advice, ideas and tips, it may also change how you think about your role.

As well as incorporating her own tried and tested examples, Moira has gathered together ideas from practitioners around the world and added her own reflections.

I'm grateful to her for writing this book to capture and share her years of experience.

References

1. Auckland, M. (2012) *Re-skilling for Research: an investigation into the role and skills of subject and liaison librarians required to effectively support the evolving information needs of researchers.* A report conducted for RLUK. Available at: www.rluk.ac.uk/wp-content/uploads/2014/02/RLUK-Re-skilling.pdf.
2. Cox, A. M. and Corrall, S. (2013) Evolving Academic Library Specialties, *Journal of the American Society for Information Science and Technology*, **64** (8), 1526–42.
3. Anderson, R. (2011) The Crisis in Research Librarianship, *The Journal of Academic Librarianship*, 2011, doi:10.1016/j.acalib.2011.04.001.
4. Webb, J., Gannon-Leary, P. and Bent, M., (2007) *Providing Effective Library Services for Research*, London, Facet Publishing.
5. Bent, M. et al. (2007) Information Literacy in a Researcher's Learning Life: the Seven Ages of Research, *New Review of Information Networking*, **13** (2), 81–98.
6. Bent, M. and Stubbings, R. (2011) The SCONUL Seven Pillars of Information Literacy, Core Model for Higher Education. Available at: www.sconul.ac.uk/sites/default/files/documents/coremodel.pdf.
7. Vitae (2012) Information Literacy Lens on the Vitae's Researcher Development Framework. Available at: https://www.vitae.ac.uk/vitae-publications/rdf-related/information-literacy-lens-on-the-vitae-researcher-development-framework-rdf-apr-2012.pdf.
8. Vitae (2012) The Informed Researcher. Available at: https://www.vitae.ac.uk/vitae-publications/guides-briefings-and-information/the-informed-researcher-vitae-2012.pdf.

Acknowledgements

Writing a book is a great adventure, but it's not one which can be undertaken alone, even if there's only one name on the cover. Patience and understanding are required from all those around you and I've had these in abundance from my family, friends and colleagues. I'd like to thank my husband, Adam, for all the weekends he's given up when we could have been out and about and for the endless cups of tea and continuous supply of Toblerone he provided. The rest of the family (especially Henry) have provided a welcome change from research and writing, have listened to me politely and, along with my friends, have been unfailingly positive and supportive. Special mention must be made of my close colleagues at Newcastle, especially Jenny Campbell and Yvonne Davison for their daily encouragement and friendship. Further afield, I have been overwhelmed by the willingness of people in libraries all around the world to share their ideas and experiences with me and special thanks is due to you all for responding to my call for contributions so enthusiastically. Most of the book comprises suggestions and case studies from both experienced and newly qualified librarians; my role has been to organize them into a coherent framework and provide some context. I hope I have acknowledged you all individually in the tips with which you are associated. I was 'persuaded' to write the book by the series editor, Helen Blanchett, whose ideas underpin the format of the book and I'm very grateful, Helen, for your reassurance and guidance to keep me on track. A final mention must be made of Pippin, our cat, who diligently sat on every piece of paper and created a constant, furry, companionable barrier between me and my computer screen.

Moira J. Bent

SECTION 1

Introduction

1.1 Introduction

This is a practical book consisting of ideas and suggestions for library and information staff working with researchers, garnered from librarians all around the world. Inevitably, as the author is based in an English university, it has a UK HE bias, but the concepts and tips will often be transferable to different situations and countries. The aim is not so much to give you a definitive answer but to set you on the path to finding your own solutions.

The book has been developed using a mind map to gather tips into natural chapters and very much reflects the interests of the contributors. Hence, you will not find a detailed theoretical exposition; there are other books in existence that do this very well and they are listed in the further reading; this book aims to raise awareness of issues and suggest ways to begin to address them.

We all know that librarians love to share and this book is a shining example of sharing in practice. Over the last year, at conferences and meetings, via e-mail and social media, I have explained what I was doing and asked for contributions. This is the result and you may well recognize a comment or idea in the following pages. I have tried to acknowledge everyone who has helped and apologize now if I have inadvertently missed someone. In this respect, therefore, the tips are self-selecting, representing the main interests and discussions prevalent at the time of writing.

1.2 My story

I'm a Faculty Liaison Librarian at Newcastle University and I've spent many years working with researchers at all levels, as well as researching into different aspects of information literacy and research workflows.

When I moved from a 'new' teaching-focused university to a Russell Group university over 16 years ago my job description said I was responsible for 'research support' but when I asked my new colleagues what that meant in practice, no one could give me a simple definition. This led us at Newcastle University to initiate a research project to find out what our researchers needed from us, resulting in our original library web pages for researchers, which we called ResIN: Research Information at Newcastle (Bent, 2004). For a few years they were very successful and acted as a model for several other university libraries.

In the ResIN project, we'd asked researchers what they wanted but it wasn't until I started research for a book with Jo Webb and Pat Gannon-Leary in 2007 that I realized I still didn't really know much about the research community and what it was they actually did, and so our next major piece of research involved getting to know researchers better and building on that knowledge to look at how we might develop our relationships (Webb, Gannon-Leary and Bent, 2007).

More recently, work on resources such as the *SCONUL Seven Pillars of Information Literacy: Research Lens* (Bent and Stubbings, 2011) and the *Informed Researcher* booklet (Bent et al., 2012), as well as conversations with colleagues, has led me to the realization that a publication gathering together all the good ideas I've come across into a practical resource might be a useful addition to the literature. The outcome is this book; I hope you find it useful.

1.3 About the book

What is the relevance of libraries and library staff to modern researchers, and just who are these people, anyway? Research takes place in many different contexts, performed by a wide variety of individuals. This book draws on my own research to highlight the complexity encompassed by the terms 'research' and 'researcher' and to demonstrate how this understanding can help library and information staff operate more effectively within a research environment. It proposes that interacting effectively with information is at the heart of all research; consequently library and information professionals have a key role to play in facilitating the development of researchers who are able to operate confidently and successfully in the information world.

I've been a practitioner researcher in libraries for many years and I always try to apply the pedagogic theories of librarianship and information science to my daily practice. However, when you're working full-time 'doing the job', it's not easy to find the time to step back and reflect on what you're doing and it's even more difficult to find the time to read the theories and to keep up to date on current and new practices from around the world. As a National Teaching Fellow in the UK I've been fortunate to be able to travel widely and to network with colleagues from many different countries. I'm constantly amazed and motivated by the exciting and innovative ideas I hear and read about, some of which I'm able to apply to my own practice, others to which I can only aspire. Quite often, a chance remark from a colleague can lead to a change in practice or a new service development, or even initiate a changed strategy, but as practitioners we may not have time to document any of this process – we are far too busy implementing it.

This book, therefore, is an attempt to bridge the gap between theory and practice, grounding the very practical ideas garnered from library and information staff around the world in current research in the library and information science discipline in order to assist LIS staff in developing and managing their role in the research environment. It offers innovative tips and reliable best practice to enable both new and experienced practitioners to evaluate their current provision and develop their service to meet the evolving needs of the research community. Somebody has a good idea. It works. We all want to replicate that – why reinvent the wheel? The suggestions from practitioners from many different countries have been supplemented by ideas found during the course of my own research, as well as my personal experience of liaising with the research community for over 20 years and numerous conversations with individuals. For this reason, it doesn't aim to be comprehensive and to address every single aspect of how librarians engage with researchers; rather, it is built up from the 'wisdom of the crowd' and so focuses on the issues that contributors felt most concern them. Many of the tips were contributed by librarians in a liaison or relationship management role in higher education libraries, and so are likely to be of most interest to those in a similar position, although a lot of the suggestions can be adapted to different environments. I am very grateful to all those who have taken the time to contribute their ideas and to share their documentation and resources, making the book truly international in scope. Whenever possible, tips and ideas are acknowledged and attributed, so you can follow them up directly with the contributor if you wish. However, some respondents preferred to remain anonymous, whilst other tips are derived from a myriad of chance conversations over time and in these cases a direct attribution has not been possible. Inevitably, many examples are also drawn from my own experience and from the library in which I work.

1.4 Context

Universities, libraries and researchers are constantly changing. As Parker (2012) puts it, we are moving away from the 'cosy' library, with traditional users and services, to the 'scary' library, with a much more diverse user population and with both collections and users increasingly off-site. Changes in approaches to higher education research in many countries mean that university research programmes are no longer defined solely in altruistic terms of the public good; the focus has shifted to economic legitimacy

(Hansson and Johannesson, 2013). Governments around the world, recognizing the vital importance of information and data in their strategic planning, are investing in national research information infrastructures and in this setting universities, with their central role in the generation of knowledge, are major stakeholders. League tables such as those of *The Times* in the UK, the Shanghai Jiao Tong and the Australian ERA are examples of national benchmarking exercises for research.

How do libraries fit into the picture? Over the last few years, many libraries, especially in the UK, have focused attention on undergraduate students. The introduction of fee-paying students in the UK has led to a much more customer-focused approach, with league tables and student surveys lending further weight. However, we must not forget that the strategic directions of many universities revolve around research and the merit of universities at a global level is judged mainly on research performance. Universities need to be able to compete in world ranking tables in order to attract high-quality research students and staff; they need to maximize their investment to increase their research impact worldwide. Research is valued by universities as a mark of esteem but is also expected by government as a source of income for future research. This focus on output leads to an increased demand for performance measures and metrics. What evidence is there that the library is adding value to research outcomes? 'The paradox may be that the more library services are integrated with academic activity the more difficult it will become to determine a direct relationship.'(Research Libraries UK, 2012)

More recently, research-specific drivers, such as raised awareness of open access, research excellence exercises and the increased acceptance of the need to share research data have added an extra dimension to research workflows, often leaving researchers feeling ill-equipped in their own research landscape.

In this environment what is the role of libraries and librarians? Are we purely information givers or do we need to rethink our function and realize our capacity for knowledge enhancement rather than service delivery? What do we mean by 'research support services'? Is supporting researchers the same as supporting research? In some cases, we may even be confined by traditional expectations and patterns of scholarly behaviour. Hansson and Johannesson (2013) ask 'how is it possible to make academic librarians achieve in the processes surrounding research and how do identities influence attitudes of librarians in their work amongst scholars?', whilst Corrall and Lester (2013) envisage librarians moving into 'more specialized, higher-end roles' that are 'aligned with institutional concerns and have the potential to enable strategic repositioning on campus'; an opportunity, rather than a threat.

1.5 Terminology

The original title proposed for this book was 'Practical Tips for *Supporting Research*'. Why was the title changed? Many of us use the word 'support' when we refer to our work with researchers – we see it in job titles such as 'research support librarian' and even in the title of my own aforementioned book (Webb, Gannon-Leary and Bent, 2007). However, it can be argued that by using a word such as *support*, we immediately set ourselves apart from our research community. Definitions of support include phrases such as:

- To bear the weight of, especially from below.
- To hold in position so as to keep from falling, sinking, or slipping.
- To act in a secondary or subordinate role to a leading performer.
- To aid the cause, policy, or interests of.

Farlex, 2014

One of the issues with using this terminology is that we immediately place ourselves in a secondary role, so that we are in a position which is 'academic-related'; we aren't viewed as academics. This immediately sets limits on what we are able to achieve in our interactions with researchers; both we and the researcher are defining our places within the scholarly information environment.

If we focus on the idea of providing support, librarians are seen as purely providing a service, rather than enhancing or creating knowledge in our own right, reinforcing our position as a service department, rather than a more dynamic, knowledge creation entity. This can lead to quite a restricted view of librarians as information givers, something we are very good at and should be very proud of, but can we realize our capacity to be more than this? Perhaps it is time for us to re-evaluate the identity which has been assigned to librarians in our relationships with researchers, both by ourselves and others. Over the last few years many librarians have done this very successfully in other aspects of our role, especially as teachers, when, for example, integrating information literacy into the undergraduate curriculum gains equal recognition with teaching staff in this arena. We don't seem to have quite the same approach when thinking about our role in the research activities of our organizations and I think this can be a real barrier to us in establishing our position within our research community. Do we need a new language for describing how we assist scholars carrying out novel research, articulating the ways in which we contribute to improving research productivity?.

In summary, support is essential for success but is outside the process, secondary and supplementary, often underneath, underpinning and invisible. Is this how we want our relationships with researchers to be perceived? The debate is neatly summarized by Hall (2010), when she makes the point that a research scientist is someone who is him-/herself a researcher in a science discipline, but a research librarian is seen as someone who helps others conduct research, rather than a researcher in his/her own right. Perhaps 'research liaison librarian' is a more accurate description?

I believe that starting with the terminology, we can, little by little, start to change perceptions about who we are and what we are about. Instead of the 's' word, we can use terms such as facilitating, engaging, participating, collaborating and sharing. They all imply a more active role in the research process and hence an integral involvement in the research community of practice, in addition to the service level provision which libraries traditionally supply to all users. This, therefore, is an opportunity for librarians to develop their research role from a support service to a project partner.

1.6 Structure of the book

As the title suggests, the book is not designed to be read from cover to cover, but to be dipped into as a source of ideas and inspiration for those library staff seeking new ways to facilitate research within their organizations. It does not aim to provide a comprehensive approach to library services for researchers, but to identify common opportunities and offer practical suggestions and approaches; the structure is designed to help readers identify issues and possible solutions quickly and easily. Where appropriate, reference is made to in-depth research on the topic in order to contextualize the point and a comprehensive bibliography is provided at the end of the book, but in general the focus is on very practical ways in which librarians can engage with their research community and truly facilitate the research process.

Many of the tips suggested here may address situations which are familiar to you, but perhaps a concept has been approached in a novel way, or the technique adapted to a different situation. The majority of the ideas come from real situations and are accompanied by advice or comment from those who have tried them. Not all may be relevant to you; others you may need to adjust to your particular situation. Some are quite small, specific suggestions which can be easily adopted while others describe a general approach or even a reorganized library service.

For simplicity, the tips have been grouped under eight main headings:

- landscapes and models
- structures and strategies
- places and spaces
- library staff roles
- collections
- specific interventions in the research process or lifecycle

- teaching approaches
- information literacy skills workshops and programmes.

Inevitably, there is overlap between the sections. Open access, for example, can be considered as part of the publication process in the research workflows section but can also be addressed in the information literacy skills section with regard to ethics and awareness-raising and again within library strategy when determining how the library facilitates the institutional repository. The book's contents pages list all the individual tips.

1.7 How to use the book

The book is designed to be dipped into for ideas and inspiration, rather than to be read from cover to cover. Section 2 summarizes the context of each chapter and you may find it helpful to read this before dipping into the tips themselves.

Each suggestion is described from the perspective of the originator where possible and includes a description of the tip, practical advice for adopting it, things to think about, links and further reading if available.

🖒 Best for

For each tip, suggestions have been made for situations, activities or audiences for which the tip might be most applicable in its current form. However, this should not preclude the use of ideas within the tip in different circumstances; the aim of the book is to encourage re-use and developments of the concepts described.

★ Examples from practice

Wherever possible, personal stories and anecdotes have been used under this heading to bring the tips to life and to demonstrate how they have been used in different situations. Where contributors have been generous enough to share resources these have been included as good practice examples. Recommendations and advice from contributors have also been included. Links to online materials have been provided as appropriate.

⚠ To think about

This feature highlights the experiences of the originators of the tips, identifying potential pitfalls and suggesting issues which may need further thought if the tip were to be adopted.

1.8 A note about references

At the end of each tip you will find any specific citations referred to in that tip, along with additional relevant further reading and links. The bibliography at the end of the book includes all the citations and further reading, together with some more general references which may be of interest. Please note that all links were correct at the time of writing.

1.9 References and further reading

Anderson, R. (2011) The Crisis in Research Librarianship, *The Journal of Academic Librarianship*, **37** (4), 289–90.

Bent, M. (2004) ResIN: Research Information at Newcastle University Library, *SCONUL Focus*, **32**, 28–30.

Bent, M., Gannon-Leary, P., Goldstein, S. and Videler, T. (2012) *The Informed Researcher*, London, Vitae, www.vitae.ac.uk/researcherbooklets. (Accessed 25.5.15)

Bent, M. and Stubbings, R. (2011) *The SCONUL Seven Pillars of Information Literacy: research lens*, London, SCONUL, www.sconul.ac.uk/sites/default/files/documents/researchlens.pdf. (Accessed 25.5.15)

Corrall, S. and Lester, R. (2013) The Researcher's View: context is critical. In Watson, L. (ed.), *Better Library and Learning Spaces: projects, trends and ideas*, London, Facet Publishing, 183–92.

Farlex (2014) *The Free Dictionary*, www.thefreedictionary.com/support. (Accessed 29.12.14)

Hall, H. (2010) Promoting the Priorities of Practitioner Research Engagement, *Journal of Librarianship and Information Science*, **42** (2), 83–8.

Hansson, J. and Johannesson, K. (2013) Librarians' Views of Academic Library Support for Scholarly Publishing: an every-day perspective, *The Journal of Academic Librarianship*, **39** (3), 232–40.

Parker, R. (2012) What the Library Did Next: strengthening our visibility in research support. In *VALA 2012*, Melbourne, Australia, VALA, www.vala.org.au/direct-download/vala2012-proceedings/435-vala2012-session-1-parker-paper-file. (Accessed 4.1.16)

Research Libraries UK (2012) *Value and Impact*, www.rluk.ac.uk/strategicactivity/strategic-strands/redefining-research-library-model/foundations/impact/. (Accessed 4.1.16)

Webb, J., Gannon-Leary, P. and Bent, M. (2007) *Providing Effective Library Services for Research*, London, Facet Publishing.

SECTION 2

Section summaries

You may find it helpful to read these section summaries to put the tips into context before dipping into the tips themselves.

2.1 Landscapes and models (Section 3)

It may seem contradictory to begin a practical tips book with a section on theory, but a clear understanding of the context against which we operate is essential if librarians wish to truly engage with their research community. A consideration of the different environments or landscapes through which researchers move can provide a helpful perspective. Landscapes can be personal and internal or objective and external, but they will all overlap to a greater or lesser extent to create an individual research landscape which influences the outcome of any research.

For example, the prevailing *political landscape* will influence funding, organizational decision-making, opportunities for 'blue sky' research over economic necessity and thus ultimately the general direction of the research. A country's *higher education landscape* situates university research within a broad educational environment, with considerations such as the research/teaching nexus, parity of esteem and the pedagogy of research. *Commercial research landscapes* may focus on commercial viability, trials, licences and ethics, to suggest just a few elements.

Within an *organizational landscape* researchers may function individually and in teams, within and across disciplines and sectors, priorities changing with the objectives of their employer. At an individual level, researchers operate within their own *information literacy landscape* (Bent, 2008), influenced by their attitudes and behaviours towards information, as well as their personal abilities. The wider *information landscape* provides the context for this, including as it does aspects of quantity and quality of information, access, language and availability.

An individual research landscape therefore, is a complex blend of different external factors and individual attributes and the picture is further complicated when additional definitions, models and frameworks are introduced. Even seemingly straightforward terms such as 'research' and 'researcher', which seem self-explanatory, can mean different things in different situations. Can undergraduates completing an essay be thought of as doing research? They might argue so, but it is certainly different to research undertaken by a postdoc, for example.

By unpicking these concepts and relating them to recognized frameworks and models, a more holistic approach to working with the research community can be developed. In order to achieve this, we need to be aware of all the current frameworks, theories and landscapes relating to research which pertain in our individual situation.

This section touches on a few ideas but there are many more which will be equally relevant.

References and further reading
Bent, M. (2008) *Information Literacy Landscape*, Moira's Info Lit Blog, www.moirabent.blogspot.co.uk/p/information-literacy-landscape.html.
Coonan, E. M. (2011) Navigating the Information Landscape, *The Serials Librarian*, **61** (3–4), 323–33.

2.2 Structures and strategies (Section 4)

In many countries research is now defined, not in terms of the public good or the furthering of knowledge, but of 'economic legitimacy' (Hansson and Johannesson, 2013). In such a market-orientated approach, where performance measures for research are focused on producing an output, what are the implications for the library? We need to be able to deliver the expertise, services and resources that will be differentiators in research lives, so the focus needs to shift from the library and what librarians do to the needs of the scholars. However, the challenge for many libraries, especially in universities, is to tackle the 'rigidity of the university system' and its attitude to the role of the library (Hansson and Johannesson, 2013). How can we manage the ways we respond to external drivers so that our libraries remain of vital importance within our organizations? Luce (2008) suggests librarians can take an active role as convenors amongst different stakeholders, developing a 'new paradigm of collaboration and partnership'.

This approach involves the library management team and the organization itself recognizing the shifting roles and opportunities librarians are subject to. It may result in a total staff restructure, perhaps with jobs redefined by functional tasks, or be a combination of smaller, softer step changes. This section highlights some of the ways in which a research library might develop new or different strategies to cope within such a fluctuating space.

References and further reading

Hansson, J. and Johannesson, K. (2013) Librarians' Views of Academic Library Support for Scholarly Publishing: an every-day perspective, *The Journal of Academic Librarianship*, **39** (3), 232–40.

Luce, R. E. (2008) A New Value Equation Challenge: the emergence of eresearch and roles for research libraries. In Council on Library and Information Resources (ed.), *No Brief Candle: reconceiving research libraries for the 21st century*, Washington, DC, Council on Library and Information Resources, 42–50.

2.3 Places and spaces (Section 5)

This section suggests ways to attract researchers into the library building as well as ideas for librarians to reach out, both physically and virtually, to the research community. It's about the places and spaces in which to engage with the research community.

> *'I try to meet all new heads of department and heads of research groups – one lady was very difficult to pin down and when we finally met she made it clear that she felt the library had no place in her life. She told me she never used it, as everything she needed was free. I discovered that she always worked on campus and was obviously making use of many electronic library resources, but I couldn't make her understand that she only had access to them because we were providing them for her.' (Jennifer Peasley, La Trobe University, Australia).*

Jennifer's experience is not uncommon; as the virtual library provides most resources, certainly in STEM subjects, researchers have little need to visit the physical library building at all and the library as a place becomes much less visible. If researchers are no longer coming to us we need to be ever more enterprising in devising opportunities to engage.

2.4 Library staff roles (Section 6)

Section 6 addresses the importance of library staff being perceived as equals in the research environment, of being proud of who we are and what we contribute to the research process, of not being self-effacing or reluctant to get involved. Key to this idea is that of terminology, of dispensing with words such as 'support' and instead, using ideas such as 'engage' and 'facilitate'.

Rather than being 'research support', librarians are now describing themselves as 'research partners', 'research liaison librarians' or simply 'research librarians'. Our position in the world of research is determined by our own perceptions of what we can contribute as much as it is by the expectations and opinions of researchers themselves.

Partnering, engaging, facilitating: this is easy to say in the abstract, but in practice how can it be achieved? Much relies on staff confidence in their abilities as well as experience and the development of relevant skills and expertise. However, this is not a quick fix: time is needed for LIS staff to learn and develop and yet more time to demonstrate to researchers where we fit into their world and to be accepted in these more complex roles. Libraries need an increasingly diverse and talented staff (Lowry et al., 2009) with a range of new skills and competencies (Puente, 2010). This section addresses some of the ways in which this might be accomplished.

References and further reading

Lowry, C. B., Adler, P., Hahn, K. and Stuart, C. (2009) *Transformational Times: an environmental scan prepared for the ARL Strategic Plan Review Task Force*, Washington, DC, www.arl.org/focus-areas/statistics-assessment/1203-transformational-times-an-environmental-scan-prepared-for-the-arl-strategic-plan-review-task-force.Voouy-mLSUK (Accessed 4.1.16)

Puente, M. A. (2010) Developing a Vital Research Library Workforce, *Research Library Issues: a bimonthly report from ARL, CNI, and SPARC*, **272**, 1–6.

2.5 Collections (Section 7)

The strength of any research library is the depth of its collections, be they physical or electronic holdings. Researchers place a high value on quality book and journal collections and they still feature prominently in descriptions of libraries. However, as the amount of information available has increased exponentially in recent years, libraries can no longer afford either resources or space to store everything that may be needed. National and legal deposit libraries provide essential back-up services but the reputation of a university research library rests on the uniqueness of its assets and their importance and relevance to the research business of the institution.

Managing collections effectively is therefore a key contribution to the research process and is not a passive role. There is still a place for active, systematic collection building, although perhaps in a more discerning way than might have been common in the past, when size of the collection was an indication of quality. Exploiting and promoting available resources and ensuring researchers know how to access them is of paramount importance.

Modern collection development is about ensuring that we create hybrid libraries that contain, or enable access to, many forms of resources, finding ways in which to stay relevant when scholars turn to Google first. This section includes ideas for exploiting and developing research collections.

2.6 Specific interventions in the research process or lifecycle (Section 8)

While Section 5 identifies some of the places and spaces in which to engage with researchers, this section considers some opportunities for library mediation within the research lifecycle or process itself. Inevitably there is overlap, as what you do may be influenced by where you do it, but the focus in this section is on opportunities for engagement at different stages of a researcher's research and learning life. Interventions may involve providing specific information or resources, working with researchers for a specific outcome, engaging with the research community to learn about their research, advising on dissemination, or something else entirely. The chances that arise will be dependent on the combination of landscapes within which the researcher and librarians are operating, the different contexts that apply and the prevailing organizational culture. Although no two libraries will be exactly the same and the research community will have individual characteristics, there are similarities and key stages within the lifecycle that lend themselves to contribution from libraries.

2.7 Teaching approaches (Section 9)

Only a relatively small number of librarians who teach have formal teaching qualifications and there are still some library and information science courses that do not include this aspect of the role. Consequently, many librarians tasked with this activity shy away from it altogether or revert to the safety of a training role. Although very useful and indeed often essential, training is easy; it's purely about explaining how to do something or showing someone how something works. Training can be delivered via a workbook or an online activity very safely from the trainer's perspective. Teaching, however, is different. It's about education, about learning, about crossing thresholds and dealing with troublesome knowledge (Meyer and Land, 2003). Librarians who truly teach, therefore, are developing more information literate researchers; we are challenging researchers to reflect on their place in the information world and to consider how they can develop as 'informed researchers' (Bent et al., 2012)

This approach can seem daunting at first, but in reality there are few librarians who don't embrace the concepts underlying information literacy, even if they may use different terminology to describe it. Translating these ideas into teaching researchers is the tricky part but librarians need to have the confidence that their message is important and believe that training is not sufficient. In actuality, teaching and training are inextricably linked; for example, when demonstrating a database, the training part comprises how the database works (click here and this happens), the teaching part is about the critical approach a researcher takes in choosing this specific resource, hence understanding about the world of information available, the understanding of the search strategy and the evaluation of the results.

Having a teaching qualification or following a basic course on teaching skills is invaluable for librarians who teach. Developing an understanding of pedagogy will underpin your teaching and help you to understand why different approaches have different levels of success. In addition, you'll learn many practical skills about dealing with small and large groups, presentation tips and the use of technology, to name just a few. Becoming a reflective teacher will help you to become a more authoritative teacher too.

> *'It's useful to know how to construct and conduct a session, how to keep a group engaged and also to reflect on your experience. It also gives you confidence that you're not just floundering, but actually know what you're doing and why.' (Karen McAulay, Royal Conservatoire of Scotland)*

In some organizations, a teaching qualification is a requirement for all staff who deliver classes.

Teaching well is all about preparation, knowing your topic and knowing your class, planning for the unexpected, but there are always new ideas and new approaches – no one ever stops learning to teach. The tips in this section describe just a few ideas of different ways in which library staff might approach teaching researchers.

References and further reading

Bent, M., Gannon-Leary, P., Goldstein, S. and Videler, T. (2012) *The Informed Researcher*, London, Vitae, www.vitae.ac.uk/researcherbooklets. (Accessed 25.5.15)

Meyer, E. and Land, R. (2003) *Threshold Concepts and Troublesome Knowledge: linkages to ways of thinking and practising within the disciplines*, Edinburgh, www.ed.ac.uk/etl/docs/ETLreport4.pdf.

2.8 Information literacy skills workshops and programmes (Section 10)

Section 9 considered approaches to teaching situations and the different methods that can be used. This section focuses on the content, with practical ideas on material that can be used and adapted. Various stages of the research lifecycle offer opportunities for educating researchers and librarians have approached them in different ways. It's not always easy to underpin a training session with a more holistic approach because, as Kroll points out, 'researchers prefer easy solutions that are adequate and not optimal' (Kroll and Forsman, 2010). Finding a balance between adequate and optimal relies on understanding the audience, their values and pressures and addressing these issues, whilst at the same time raising their awareness of issues they may never have considered before.

> 'For example, PhD students often struggle with their relationship with their supervisor, whether and when to publish or talk at conferences, fulfilling teaching and other commitments, motivation and self esteem.' (Beth Hall, Bangor University)

If you are able to identify such pressure points and relate the content of a teaching session to them, participants are much more likely to engage and to understand the messages you are trying to convey.

In 2014, a query posed to the *Lis-researchsupport* mailing list by Helen McEvoy from Salford University elicited a wide range of examples of titles of workshops currently being delivered in the UK. They included: article processing charges, appraising data, bibliometrics, citation searching, collaboration tools, communicating your research, copyright, IPR, data management planning, ethics, searching, impact, open access, plagiarism, referencing, referencing tools, RDM, social media and more. Some of these are represented in this section, others are listed here as inspiration.

References and further reading
Lis-researchsupport is available at www.jiscmail.ac.uk/.
Kroll, S. and Forsman, R. (2010) *A Slice of Research Life: information support for research in the United States*, www.oclc.org/content/dam/research/publications/library/2010/2010-15.pdf. (Accessed 4.1.16)

Acknowledgements
Jo Webb and Pat Gannon-Leary (co-authors of previous works); Karen McCaulay, Royal Conservatoire of Scotland; Beth Hall, Bangor University; Jennifer Peasley, La Trobe University, Australia.

SECTION 3
Landscapes and models

3.1 Ensure you understand what 'research' is

INTERACTING WITH INFORMATION is at the very heart of the research process and as interacting with information is what librarians do, it's clear that we have a pivotal role in facilitating research. However, perhaps it's not as simple as it sounds. For anyone involved in facilitating the research process, our challenge is to identify opportunities for successful interventions and to develop strategies to implement them. In order to do that, we need to have a clear understanding of who researchers are, what research is all about and where in the research environment we can add value.

The first step, therefore, is to ensure you have a clear idea in your mind of what research is all about. Researchers describe what they do in a variety of ways. Some may see it as developing new theories based on existing evidence, others as collecting and interpreting new data. There is general agreement, however, that research is systematic or methodical and involves discovering, revising or interpreting facts and ideas. In some cases, this can be seen as a holistic activity, the term 'research' encompassing a broad understanding of the whole research lifecycle. Others interpret it more specifically as a linear or cyclical process or set of transferable skills. Depending on the situation, research may be firmly grounded within a discipline, but more commonly now can be multi- or interdisciplinary. Similarly, researchers can work independently or as part of a team. Researchers may undertake research in order to develop or contribute new knowledge or to provide a different understanding of existing material; however, the outcomes are only made meaningful if they are shared with a wider audience. This is a key issue in terms of knowledge transfer. In summary, we can say that research is a process of investigation leading to new insights, effectively shared.

👍 Best for:

- gaining a clearer understanding of what research entails so that you are better able to facilitate it.

★ Examples from practice

If you work in a small, specialized library, research in your organization may be a very tightly defined process: in fact, the whole aim or ethos of the business. In a university setting, research is generally understood to be an activity distinct from teaching, carried out by expert researchers. Doctoral and masters students are also considered to be researchers, however, and even undergraduate students carry out research as part of their studies, as do students in secondary education. It's important therefore to relate your concept of research to the context in which it is happening.

⚠ To think about

What kinds of research take place in your organization? Can you identify similarities and differences which might affect how you can facilitate the process? Don't make assumptions that everyone is talking about the same thing; remember that even though you may have a clear understanding of what research is, others may be interpreting it differently. Can you work towards a shared understanding, perhaps even making a clear statement on your web pages or documentation?

References and further reading

Webb, J., Gannon-Leary, P. and Bent, M. (2007) *Providing Effective Library Services for Research*, London, Facet Publishing.

3.2 Ensure you understand who researchers are

IN ORDER TO engage effectively with researchers, we need to understand what drives and motivates them, what their academic ambitions are, for example, and how these are affected by institutional imperatives and even by political pressures. We tend to consider researchers as one homogeneous group and it's true that researchers themselves may share some common characteristics; they tend to be questioning and passionate about the subject of their investigation. Many are keen to make connections and work across boundaries, while others are more inward-looking and immersed in a very narrow field of interest. However, when considering how we might work with researchers and facilitate their research it's important to remember that there are also many differences to consider. It's naïve to assume researchers are all the same. A 'one size fits all' approach is doomed to failure. One of the key differences is that of discipline. In general, for example, we might conclude that scientific researchers usually (but not always) work collaboratively and tend to focus on collecting new quantitative data, whereas a humanities researcher is more likely to be collecting qualitative data. An arts-based researcher may be more likely to be working with existing material and looking for new insights. However, even this distinction is a very simplistic view.

Other factors to consider are the age and experience of researchers and how this affects their ability to undertake practical tasks, as well as to network and disseminate their findings. Although researchers may be motivated by passion for their subject, funding is also a key driver. Some researchers are employed to undertake a specific piece of work, perhaps in a commercial or industrial situation, while others are motivated by the desire to achieve a higher qualification. Some researchers are self-funded and need to work outside the research environment to pay their way, others may be funded by grants or governments and have an obligation to report back to a funding body of some kind. In different parts of the world there is a range of doctoral qualifications and study modes and different terminology may be used, and so even the experience of studying for a PhD may be very different.

Researchers may be located within a university or other academic research centre, or in an industrial or commercial enterprise, may be part of a large research group or may work independently. Whatever their situation, few researchers today have the luxury of being able to pursue blue sky research without considering a practical application or outcome. Of course, as individuals all researchers will have their own personal preferences; their learning/research style, research habits and attitudes will all affect how they interact with information and consequently with information professionals.

Researchers, therefore, can be viewed as existing in a series of landscapes. The contextual landscape includes where they are situated, the institutional structure and strategies and the motivations and pressures of their situation, whereas the research landscape relates to the discipline, the local, national and global communities of practice and the research lifecycle and processes. Their own personal researcher landscape, whilst set within a recognizable framework of a research lifecycle, will be distinct from that of another researcher as it depends on their personal research behaviours and habits. In addition, each researcher will be moving through his or her own information literacy landscape (Bent, 2008), taking into account his or her attitudes and behaviours relating to information, and this in turn can be viewed within a wider information landscape which comprises the wide variety of information and data available to him or her.

Taking this into account, it's safe to assume that the views of researchers are likely to differ from those of librarians when thinking about priorities (RIN, 2006); in fact, researchers' experiences and perceptions of libraries may not be altogether positive and this will impact on how they can benefit from the library services and resources.

⚐ Best for:

■ understanding researchers, their differences and motivations

■ ensuring your approach is appropriate to each individual situation.

★ Examples from practice

It can be helpful to use the 'Seven ages of research' model (Bent, Gannon-Leary and Webb, 2007) to think about the different stages of a researcher's life. This model, developed in 2007 and focusing on researchers in universities, defines the seven ages as:

1 masters students
2 doctoral students
3 contract research staff
4 early career researchers
5 established academic staff
6 senior researchers
7 experts.

As researchers follow their research journey through the different ages, meeting new milestones along the way, their experience and attitudes change and develop. Those at the start of their career, students undertaking a masters or doctoral course of study, may not be committed to a lifetime in research, seeing their research as a means to an end. They are often moving from a structured learning environment to a self-organized research setting with different levels of control, which take time to adapt to. Certainly in the UK, doctoral training programmes mean that the skills and competencies they are expected to develop are well defined. Their approach tends to be highly influenced by a supervisor or mentor, which can have an impact on how they view libraries and information resources, not to mention the staff. Frequently research students have to balance conflicting demands, perhaps holding down another job or developing teaching skills. In terms of interacting with information they are still mainly consumers rather than producers and they ought to be very familiar with key resources.

Researchers in ages 3 and 4 have often moved beyond student positions to paid contracts, though rarely to permanent tenure, short-term contracts being most common. At this stage of their career researchers tend to be situating themselves within their discipline, establishing their credentials and starting to make a name for themselves, both locally within the organization and within their wider research community. These are the people who pick up all the extra little tasks within their work environment; they are probably balancing a teaching workload as well as trying to maintain their research profile, they may be starting to supervise research students and also need to learn about management and administration. Writing research proposals and funding bids, thinking about income generation, developing skills in teaching and supervising all become part of everyday life. At the same time, they need to keep up to date with research in their topic and start to publish and disseminate their own work. This broader academic landscape, with all the consequent time pressures, often means that their interaction with information shifts from a systematic to pragmatic approach.

By the time researchers move into the later ages of the model they are developing a significant role in research leadership and administration. They are well known both internally and within the wider research community. These are the people who are leading research teams, heading up research centres and projects, and are involved in mainstream university management. Many senior researchers supervise and examine theses and some may be involved in passing on their knowledge by contributing to research methods courses. It is likely that they will be on the editorial boards of journals and involved in refereeing and peer review of journal articles and conference submissions. As plenary conference speakers, experts in the seventh age are those who define their field.

⚠ To think about

Whilst the ideas and the model described above can be helpful in increasing your understanding of who researchers are, they are only a general guide and approach. All researchers are individuals, with different backgrounds and experiences that colour their behaviour. Any activities designed to engage with researchers must be flexible enough to take this into account. Figure 3.1, the Information Literacy Landscape diagram (Bent, 2008), demonstrates this extra layer of complexity by identifying some of the different influences on an individual's levels and perceptions of information literacy.

Remember that people in the middle age of research have not necessarily 'done it all' previously in their career and may have quite basic needs.

In recent years, many university libraries have become very focused on undergraduate needs, developing flexible collaborative learning spaces, sometimes at the expense of more traditional scholarly study space. Does your library still have that wow factor of a large research library? What can you do to attract the research community back to the library?

Consider whether you need to develop a differentiated approach to engaging with the research community and, if so, how you might publicize it. For example, an open programme of workshops enables researchers to be self-selecting, relying on them to identify their needs. An alternative is to approach individuals or groups and tailor activities specifically to their situation.

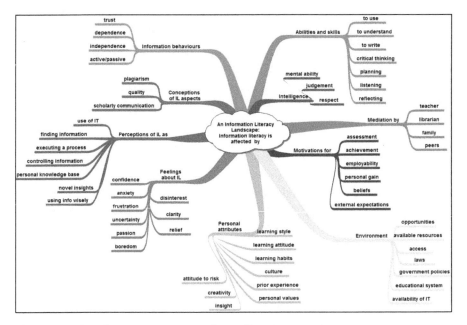

Figure 3.1 *The Information Literacy Landscape (from Bent, 2008)*

References and further reading

Bent, M. (2008) *Information Literacy Landscape*, Moira's Info Lit Blog, www.moirabent.blogspot.co.uk/p/information-literacy-landscape.html. (Accessed 24.5.15)

Bent, M., Gannon-Leary, P. and Webb, J. (2007) Information Literacy in a Researcher's Learning Life: the 7 ages of research, *New Review of Information Networking*, **13** (2), 81–99.

Research Information Network (2006) *Researchers' Use of Academic Libraries and Their Services*, www.rin.ac.uk/system/files/attachments/Researchers-libraries-services-report.pdf. (Accessed 4.1.16)

3.3 Make reference to researcher development models when appropriate

IN UNIVERSITIES, STRUCTURED training and development programmes for postgraduate students are increasingly common. Whereas in the past they have been internally devised, many are now derived from national models for researcher development. Models can play a useful role in aiding practitioners in implementing training and development programmes.

One example is the Researcher Development Statement (RDS) and associated Researcher Development Framework (RDF) produced in the UK by Vitae, a body 'dedicated to realizing the potential of researchers through transforming their professional and career development'(Vitae, 2015), shown in Figure 3.2. The RDF identifies the knowledge, behaviour and attributes of successful researchers. It helps them 'maximize their potential and get the most out of their career by developing these attributes'. In essence, the RDF is a tool that can be used by researchers to help them plan their personal development within four domains: knowledge and intellectual abilities, personal effectiveness, research governance and organization and engagement, influence and impact. Within each domain, subdomains describe in more detail the qualities to which a researcher might aspire.

During the development of the RDF, librarians in the UK worked closely

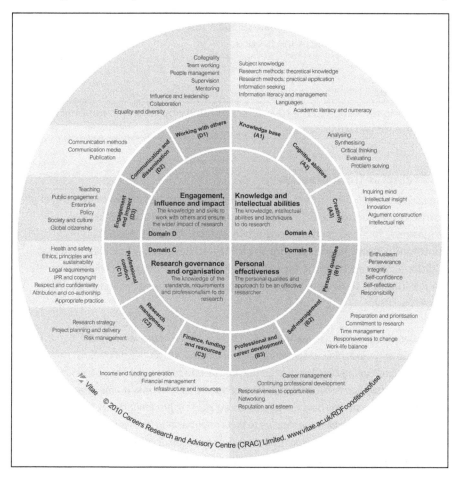

Figure 3.2 *The Researcher Development Framework (Vitae © 2010 Careers Research and Advisory Centre (CRAC), www.vitae.ac.uk/researchers-professional-development/about-the-vitae-researcher-development-framework, reproduced with permission)*

with Vitae to produce documentation relating to the information aspects of the framework. The information literacy (IL) lens provides a bridge between the RDF and SCONUL's Seven Pillars of Information Literacy, highlighting how information literacy is part of the professional development of researchers. Using the Seven Pillars approach of identifying understanding and abilities, the lens picks out key IL attributes within each domain of the RDF, enabling library staff to demonstrate to researchers where they can add value to researcher development.

The booklet *The Informed Researcher* (Bent et al., 2012) expands on the RDF lens by providing researchers with a guide to information literacy aspects of the RDF. It includes a quiz, so that researchers can assess their current understanding and abilities, along with suggestions of ways in which they might wish to extend their skills. All the Vitae materials are available for re-use under Creative Commons licences.

🖒 Best for:

■ ensuring relevance to the research community by linking to national models of researcher development.

★ Examples from practice

The Postgraduate Researcher Development Programme at Newcastle University is structured around the RDF, enabling library staff to produce a library programme focused on the Informed Researcher booklet. A Blackboard Community, using headings from the Informed Researcher booklet, provides additional resources for the face-to-face workshops which are delivered at regular intervals to researchers in the Science, Agriculture and Engineering (SagE) Faculty:

> *The informed researcher: Interacting with information is at the very heart of your research but you may place different emphasis on it at different stages of your research career. The Library and Writing Development Centre provide advice for researchers at all stages, aiming to help you to become an 'informed researcher'. Our programme of workshops for SagE PhD students will help you if you're a new student, just embarking on your PhD, or if you're in the later stages and starting to think about writing up or publishing your research. The Informed Researcher programme has been developed in the context of the Researcher Development Framework (RDF) which you can use to record how the workshops have contributed to your development as a researcher and plan for your future continuing professional development. The Vitae booklet 'The Informed Researcher' will also help you to identify areas on which to focus.' (Newcastle University Library, 2015)*

⚠ To think about

In order to be germane to individual researchers, it is important to link library activities to models and frameworks with which they are familiar. However useful and comprehensive a framework may seem to be from your perspective, unless it is easily recognizable to researchers themselves they are unlikely to engage.

References and further reading

Bent, M., Gannon-Leary, P., Goldstein, S. and Videler, T. (2012) *The Informed Researcher*, London, Vitae, www.vitae.ac.uk/researcherbooklets. (Accessed 25.5.15)

Vitae (2012) *Information Literacy Lens on the Vitae Researcher Development Framework Using the SCONUL Seven Pillars of Information Literacy*, https://www.vitae.ac.uk/vitae-publications/rdf-related/information-literacy-lens-on-the-vitae-researcher-development-framework-rdf-apr-2012.pdf. (Accessed 4.1.16)

Vitae (2015) *Realising the Potential of Researchers*, www.vitae.ac.uk. (Accessed 25.5.15)

3.4 Keep up to date with information literacy models and theories

A VARIETY OF guidelines, standards and models is available around the world, all aiming to help practitioners to promote the development of information literacy amongst their communities. Models have been criticized over the years for their limitations, often relating to weaknesses in structure and approach, as well as their separation from educational theory. More recent models have responded by providing a more holistic perspective. Such frameworks can provide a useful baseline against which to develop information literacy activities for researchers. It may be that the prevailing national model can be comprehensively adopted but it is also possible that strengths and ideas will need to be adapted from different sources. Flexibility is essential, however, to adapt to local singularities as well to take account of changes and developments since the models were devised.

No study of information literacy theory is complete without reference to some of the key literature that has defined the field in recent years. Christine Bruce's *Seven Faces of Information Literacy* (Bruce, 1997) and her more recent *Six Frames* (Bruce, Edwards and Lupton , 2006) are essential background reading.

👍 Best for:

■ providing a framework for information literacy development to underpin your researcher development programmes.

★ Examples from practice

SCONUL Seven Pillars, UK

The SCONUL Seven Pillars of Information Literacy (see Figure 3.3) comprises a core model that describes the attitudes and behaviours as well as skills and competencies that define an information literate person. The core model is refined by a series of lenses that use the terminology of a specific community, such as researchers.

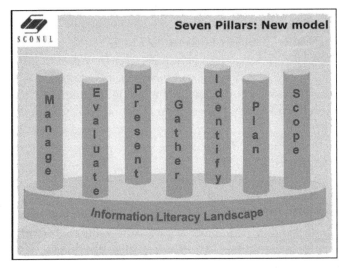

Figure 3.3
The SCONUL Seven Pillars of Information Literacy (CC BY)

Developing as an information literate researcher is a continuing, holistic process with often simultaneous activities or processes which can be encompassed within the Seven Pillars of Information Literacy. Within each 'pillar' a researcher can develop from 'novice' to 'expert' as they progress through their research life, although, as the information world itself is constantly changing and developing, it is possible to move down a pillar as well as progress up it. The expectations of levels reached on each pillar may be different in different contexts and for different ages and levels of researcher and is also dependent on experience and information need. Any information literacy development must therefore also be considered in the context of the broad information landscape in which an individual operates and their personal information literacy landscape.

Bent and Stubbings, 2011

By using vocabulary from the research community, the Seven Pillars lens provides a practical tool which links into other documentation from the UK researcher development community, such as the Vitae Researcher Development Framework (Vitae, 2012).

ANCIL, UK

A New Curriculum for Information Literacy (ANCIL) is aimed at the undergraduate curriculum in higher education, but nevertheless provides a useful framework. ANCIL divides information literacy into ten aspects or 'strands' that encompass the whole process of study and research. Students need to develop their skills, behaviour and attitudes in each strand in order to perform at their best and become autonomous learners. ANCIL materials are available for re-use with a Creative Commons licence. Figure 3.4 shows the ten strands represented, with the learner at the centre developing from key information skills through more advanced information handling to learning to learn. Additional materials on the ANCIL website include, for example, Resources for Supervisors, with materials on academic writing and the use of language.

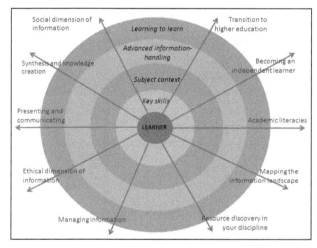

Figure 3.4 *ANCIL Spider (https://newcurriculum. files.wordpress.com/2012/ 07/ancil_spider_2012.jpg, reproduced with permission)*

ACRL Framework for Information Literacy for Higher Education

A revision of the Information Literacy Competency Standards in the USA, the new Framework for Information Literacy for Higher Education from the Association of College and Research Libraries (ACRL) includes six core concepts, based on the theory of threshold concepts (see Tip 3.5):

- Concept 1: Authority Is Constructed and Contextual
  Information resources reflect their creators' expertise and credibility, and are evaluated based on the information need and the context in which the information will be used. Authority is constructed in that various communities may recognize different types of authority. It is contextual in that the information need may help to determine the level of authority required.
- Concept 2: Information Creation as a Process
  Information in any format is produced intentionally to convey a message and is

shared via a selected delivery method. The iterative processes of researching, creating, revising, and disseminating information vary, and the resulting product reflects these differences.
- Concept 3: Information Has Value
  Information possesses several dimensions of value, including as a commodity, as a means of education, as a means to influence, and as a means of negotiating and understanding the world. Legal and socioeconomic interests influence information production and dissemination.
- Concept 4: Research as Inquiry
  Research is iterative and depends upon asking increasingly complex or new questions whose answers in turn develop additional questions or lines of inquiry in any field.
- Concept 5: Scholarship as Conversation
  Communities of scholars, researchers, or professionals engage in sustained discourse with new insights and discoveries occurring over time as a result of varied perspectives and interpretations.
- Concept 6: Searching as Strategic Exploration
  Searching for information is often nonlinear and iterative, requiring the evaluation of a broad range of information sources and the mental flexibility to pursue alternate avenues as new understanding is developed.

Association of College and Research Libraries, 2015

UNESCO MIL Assessment Framework

The UNESCO Global Media and Information Literacy (MIL) Assessment Framework provides 'a conceptual and theoretical framework for MIL, and introduces the rationale and methodology for conducting an assessment of country readiness and existing competencies on MIL at the national level. It also includes practical steps for adaptation of its recommendations at national level.' Although aimed at national initiatives rather than individuals, the framework provides useful background information and ideas.

⚠ To think about

Models and standards need to be updated and amended regularly if they are to stay aligned to developments in technology and with new directions of educational thought, such as the debates around terminology for digital and metaliteracies, for example.

Models can provide a useful framework to contextualize your approach to developing information literate researchers but can rarely be adopted wholesale. Their language and terminology may not be appropriate for your situation or community; some aspects may be more or less relevant. Consider whether you can adapt or tailor parts of such models to help inform your planning. You may wish to explain to a research group that your approach is backed up by national or internationally accepted models, or you may prefer to use them less visibly.

References and further reading

Association of College and Research Libraries (2015) *Framework for Information Literacy for Higher Education*, www.ala.org/acrl/standards/ilframework. (Accessed 25.5.15)

Bent, M. and Stubbings, R. (2011) *The SCONUL Seven Pillars of Information Literacy: research lens*, London, SCONUL, www.sconul.ac.uk/sites/default/files/documents/researchlens.pdf. (Accessed 4.1.16)

Bruce, C. (1997) *The Seven Faces of Information Literacy*, Adelaide, Auslib Press.

Bruce, C., Edwards, S. and Lupton, M. (2006) Six Frames for Information Literacy Education: a conceptual framework for interpreting the relationships between theory and practice, *ITALICS*, **5** (1), 1–18.

Coonan, E and Secker, J. (2011) *A New Curriculum for Information Literacy*, https://newcurriculum.wordpress.com/project-reports-and-outputs. (Accessed 25.5.15)

Martin, J. (2013) Refreshing Information Literacy: learning from recent British information literacy models, *Communications in Information Literacy*, **7** (2), 114–27.

UNESCO (2013) *The UNESCO Global Media and Information Literacy (MIL) Assessment Framework: country readiness and competencies*. [Online.] Available at: http://unesdoc.unesco.org/images/0022/002246/224655e.pdf. (Accessed 30.7.15)

Vitae (2012) *Information Literacy Lens on the Vitae Researcher Development Framework Using the SCONUL Seven Pillars of Information Literacy*, www.vitae.ac.uk/vitae-publications/rdf-related/information-literacy-lens-on-the-vitae-researcher-development-framework-rdf-apr-2012.pdf. (Accessed 4.1.16)

3.5 Learn about threshold concepts

THIS BRIEF DISCUSSION considers two concepts close to my heart, information literacy and threshold concepts. The SCONUL Seven Pillars model (Bent and Stubbings, 2011) states that 'Information literate researchers will demonstrate *an awareness of how they gather, use, manage, synthesise and create information and data in an ethical manner and will have the information skills to do so effectively'*. In this description, information literacy is an umbrella term which encompasses concepts such as digital, visual, media, academic and data literacies, to name but a few. The model also understands information literacy to be a complex concept, involving, as well as the development of specific skills, the development and change of learning attitudes and learning habits.

As soon as we start to consider changing attitudes and understanding, we need to address the idea of threshold concepts. For those who haven't come across the idea before, Meyer and Land (2003) suggest that in order to progress in our learning and research we need to cross thresholds, moving from our old way of understanding or perceiving something to a new way. Once we've crossed that threshold, we can't go back to the old way of understanding. They suggest that threshold concepts involve 'troublesome knowledge' (Perkins, 1999) – a great term for expressing the fact that accepting a new idea can be challenging and that learning may not be comfortable. Crossing a threshold implies moving from a safe to a riskier space, and so learning requires stepping into the unknown. We may exist in a state of liminality for a while, oscillating between known and unknown, old and new. 'Getting it' can be instant, or can be a gradual process.

The theory of threshold concepts is particularly pertinent to information literacy for researchers. Information literacy is an often misunderstood term, both within information science and in the wider teaching, learning and research environment. In fact, the words are much less relevant than grasping a clear understanding of the concept, perhaps crossing the threshold from perceiving it as skills and training to understanding it in a more holistic way. There are also different communities to be considered in terms of threshold concepts. It's not just about challenging researchers to become more information literate; administrative staff, library staff and university leaders all have thresholds to cross so that we all have a similar understanding.

However, much more exciting than this metacognitive understanding of IL is some research which has recently been published in the USA, which is seeking to identify a set of threshold concepts which will aid our understanding of how learners develop within their information literacy landscape (see, for example, Hofer et al., 2013). This research and the resulting Framework (Association of College and Research Libraries, 2015) (see Tip 3.4) has the potential to transform the ways in which we approach information literacy development in learners, challenging us to consider how learners understand concepts such as authority, format and the conversation of scholarship and hence how we can help them to cross their personal thresholds to develop as truly information literate researchers.

🖒 Best for:

■   understanding how to design activities that take account of difficult
concepts so that researchers are able to become more information literate.

⚠ To think about

What relevance might the theory of threshold concepts have to the ways in
which you engage with researchers? The ACRL standards highlight specific
points within a learning journey at which thresholds in understanding of
information can be crossed. Can you identify some common misconceptions
that researchers hold about the library or information in general which you want
to correct? For example, do you find yourself thinking 'if only "they" could
understand that not all information is freely available'? Developing a clear
understanding of how information is published is a common threshold concept
for researchers. You might start by equating them with learning outcomes, but
be aware that a threshold concept involves a shift in understanding, whereas
some learning outcomes relate to specific skill development. Once you have
identified some threshold concepts relevant to your research community,
consider the ideas of 'troublesome knowledge' and liminality. By their very
nature, thresholds are challenging and can make people feel uncomfortable.
How difficult will it be to encourage researchers to approach and cross these
thresholds? What can you do to mitigate the process? Personally, I find that
having an understanding of threshold concepts in the learning process has
helped me to better understand why some activities are more successful than
others and to start to design teaching that takes account of these pressure
points. For librarians, perhaps moving from the idea of 'supporting' researchers
to a more equitable engagement position might be seen as a threshold concept?

References and further reading

Association of College and Research Libraries (2015) *Framework for
Information Literacy for Higher Education*,
www.ala.org/acrl/standards/ilframework. (Accessed 18.4.15)

Bent, M. and Stubbings, R. (2011) *The SCONUL Seven Pillars of Information
Literacy: research lens*, London, SCONUL.

Hofer, A., Brunetto, K. and Townsend, L. (2013) A Threshold Concepts
Approach to the Standards Revision, *Communications in Information
Literacy*, **7** (2), 108–13, www.comminfolit.org/index.php?journal=
cil&page=article&op=view&path%5B%5D=v7i2p108.

Meyer, E. and Land, R. (2003) *Threshold Concepts and Troublesome Knowledge:
linkages to ways of thinking and practising within the disciplines*, Edinburgh,
www.ed.ac.uk/etl/docs/ETLreport4.pdf.

Perkins, D. (1999) The Many Faces of Constructivism, *Educational Leadership*, **57** (3), 6–11.

3.6 Think about research lifecycles

A LIFECYCLE IS GENERALLY understood to be a series of events or stages in a process, the cyclical nature of which means they will be repeated. When considering the process of research, it is possible to view it as a lifecycle, but the perspective from which it is seen will depend upon your original position. A researcher may give a different description of a research lifecycle to that of a librarian, for example, and different elements of research may have their own specific lifecycles or lenses.

It can be helpful, when engaging with researchers, to plan interventions at different stages of the research lifecycle but in order for this to be successful, the model used must be recognizable to all concerned. Once this is agreed, such a visual representation is a useful tool against which to describe activities. As Jaguszewski says, 'if we aim to enhance scholar productivity we must participate in the entire lifecycle of research' (Jaguszewski and Williams, 2013). Corrall and Lester (2013) talk about 'the knowledge creation cycle of scholarly research workflows' and considering research as a knowledge creation process is a helpful way to identify opportunities for librarians to contribute.

Although a circular model of the research lifecycle is most common, linear versions are also used. In North Carolina, librarians devised 22 opportunities for interventions along a continuum where 'the library is poised to be a partner through the entire research process not just a bookend' (Vaughan et al., 2013).

In addition to mapping interventions to the research lifecycle it can be used to map library staff skills and development and highlight gaps in library activities that need to be addressed. In *Redefining the Research Library Model* Brewerton (2013) identifies 13 steps in the research process: conceptualizing, seeking, managing, data collection, data discovery, sharing, analysing, writing, compliance, preservation, quality, commercialization and emerging technology. He then goes on to try to match librarians' skill sets to the 13 steps to identify gaps. This is a useful approach when planning a staff development programme to enable library staff to better understand the research process.

👍 Best for:

- providing a visual representation of the research process to help identify opportunities for engagement
- making engagement immediately relevant to researchers.

★ Examples from practice

There are many similar versions of research lifecycles available in the literature and a myriad of both simple and complex diagrams to choose from on Google. The following links are to specific examples of lifecycles used in differing ways.

Jisc research lifecycle

Although described as a general research lifecycle model, in fact the Jisc model (see Figure 3.5) concentrates on data. In the Jisc lifecycle, *Ideas* refers to finding resources, reading and literature searching. *Partners* collates tools such as social media to help find partners for collaboration. *Proposal writing* focuses on data management plans. *Simulate, experiment, observe* is about managing big data, while *Manage the data* is also about data management plans. Data analysis is addressed in *Analyse data,* while *Share data* concerns curation and repositories.

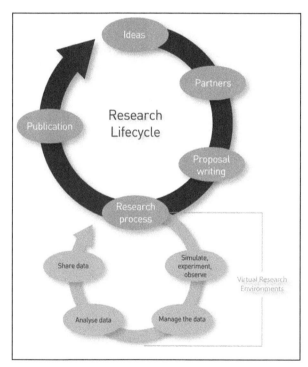

Figure 3.5 *The Jisc research lifecycle (www.jisc.ac.uk/ whatwedo/campaigns/res3/ jischelp.aspx)*

UK Data Archive

The UK Data Archive lifecycle, shown in Figure 3.6, describes the following processes:

Creating data

■ design research
■ plan data management (formats, storage, etc.)

- plan consent for sharing
- locate existing data
- collect data (experiment, observe, measure, simulate)
- capture and create metadata.

Processing data

- enter data, digitize, transcribe, translate
- check, validate, clean data
- anonymize data where necessary
- describe data
- manage and store data.

Analysing data

- interpret data
- derive data
- produce research outputs
- author publications
- prepare data for preservation.

Preserving data

- migrate data to best format
- migrate data to suitable medium
- back-up and store data
- create metadata and documentation
- archive data.

Giving access to data

- distribute data
- share data
- control access
- establish copyright
- promote data.

Re-using data

- follow-up research
- new research
- undertake research reviews
- scrutinize findings
- teach and learn.

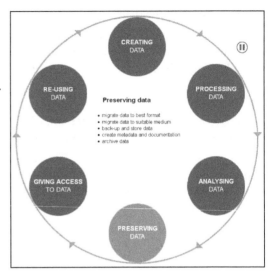

Figure 3.6 *The UK Data Archive lifecycle (© UK Data Archive, University of Essex, www.data-archive.ac.uk/create-manage/life-cycle, reproduced with permission)*

DCC data curation lifecycle

The Digital Curation Centre's Curation Lifecycle Model (Figure 3.7) is an overview of the stages required for successful curation and preservation of data. It can be used to plan activities within your organization to make sure you have considered all the different steps and one of its strengths is that it can used in different ways by different people.

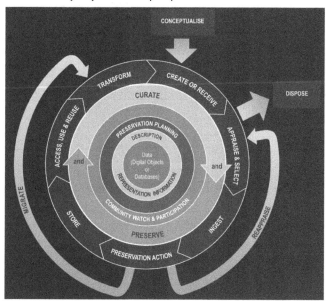

Figure 3.7 *The Digital Curation Centre: curation lifecycle model (www.dcc.ac.uk/resources/curation-lifecycle-model, CC BY)*

University of Western Australia (UWA) research data management lifecycle

Housed on the Library website, the UWA's model (Figure 3.8) has clear links to research data management plans.

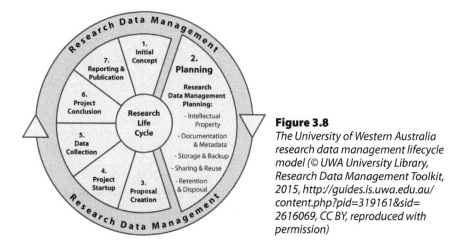

Figure 3.8
The University of Western Australia research data management lifecycle model (© UWA University Library, Research Data Management Toolkit, 2015, http://guides.is.uwa.edu.au/content.php?pid=319161&sid=2616069, CC BY, reproduced with permission)

Oregon State University Library

This model (Figure 3.9) situates data management within the broader context of the whole research lifecycle.

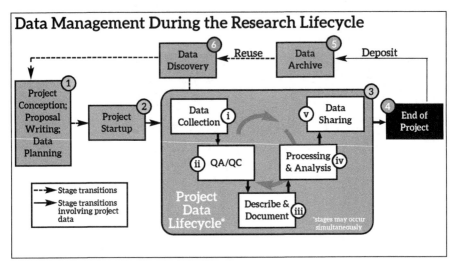

Figure 3.9 *Oregon State University research lifecycle (http://guides.library.oregonstate.edu/ lifecycle, CC BY)*

Library adaptations of the research lifecycle

Vaughan (Vaughan et al., 2013) describes the University of Pittsburgh's Research Lifecycle model for library services (Figure 3.10), in which they identify five key opportunities: Idea development, Funding, Proposal, Conducting and Disseminating.

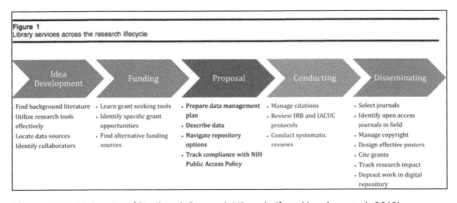

Figure 3.10 *University of Pittsburgh Research Lifecycle (from Vaughan et al., 2013)*

Loughborough University Library's research lifecycle (Figure 3.11) is now used by other sections of the university.

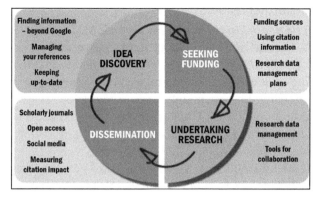

Figure 3.11 *Loughborough University Library Research Lifecycle (Loughborough University Library, 2015 www.lboro.ac.uk/services/library/research, reproduced with permission)*

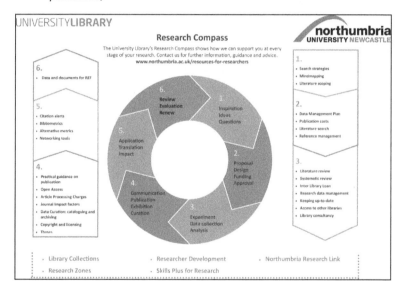

Figure 3.12 *Research Compass, Northumbria University Library (reproduced with permission)*

The University of Northumbria is piloting a Research Compass (Figure 3.12) as a way of demonstrating how the library's services and resources are relevant at different stages of the research journey.

⚠ To think about

It can be very helpful to have a visual representation to demonstrate your offering. How simple or complex does it need to be to be both relevant and informative without being overwhelming?

References and further reading

Ball, A. (2012) *Review of Data Management Lifecycle Models*, http://opus.bath. ac.uk/28587/1/redm1rep120110ab10.pdf. (Accessed 1.5.15)

Brewerton, A. (2013) *RLUK: Redefining the research library model: workforce survey findings*, www.rluk.ac.uk/strategicactivity/strategic-strands/ redefining-research-library-models. (Accessed 4.1.16)

Corrall, S. and Lester, R. (2013) The Researcher's View: context is critical. In Watson, L. (ed.), *Better Library and Learning Spaces: projects trends and ideas*, London, Facet Publishing, 183–92.

Jaguszewski, J. M. and Williams, K. (2013) *New Roles for New Times: transforming liaison roles in research libraries*, Washington, DC, www.arl.org/nrnt.

King's College Library Research lifecycle, www.kcl.ac.uk/library/researchsupport/index.aspx.

Sferdean, F. (2014) *Research Lifecycle Model at UM*, https://mlibrarydata. wordpress.com/2014/02/28/research-lifecycle-model. (Accessed 1.5.15)

Vaughan, K. T. L., Hayes, B. E., Lerner, R. C., McElfresh, K. R., Pavlech, L., Romito, D., Reeves, L. H. and Morris, E. N. (2013) Development of the Research Lifecycle Model for Library Services, *Journal of the Medical Library Association*, **101** (4), 310–14.

Acknowledgements

Helen Young, Loughborough University; Northumbria University Library.

3.7 Research assessment

Not everything that counts can be counted, and not everything that can be counted counts.

Cameron, 1963, 13

A KNOWLEDGE-BASED SOCIETY is fundamental for sustainable economic and social development and as researchers are creators of new knowledge their contribution to a country's prosperity is key. Assessment of university-based research is therefore an important concern for a variety of different stakeholders, not least governments and funding bodies, and the issue is tackled in different ways around the world. Tied as it is to funding, success in research assessment exercises is central to any university's vision for future success and is of paramount importance to the organization's continued wellbeing. No wonder then that so much attention is given to preparation for research evaluation practices in different countries. However, there is no easy solution, there is no simple way to assign numbers to all aspects of research and research output. The co-existence of different models to assess university-based research appears to be inevitable.

Most assessments rely on some quantitative measures of research impact, attempting to discover what differences the research outcomes have delivered. The most common measures are based on impact factors of journals, devised from international databases such as Web of Science from Thomson Reuters.

In the academic community, especially outside the science and medical disciplines, there is much concern that these measures are questionable and do not accurately reflect the true situation. One attempt to address this is the *San Francisco Declaration on Research Assessment* (DORA) (2012), initiated by the American Society of Cell Biology and other scholarly publishers, which says:

> There is a pressing need to improve the ways in which the output of scientific research is evaluated by funding agencies, academic institutions, and other parties. . . . The outputs from scientific research are many and varied, including: research articles reporting new knowledge, data, reagents, and software; intellectual property; and highly trained young scientists. Funding agencies, institutions that employ scientists, and scientists themselves, all have a desire, and need, to assess the quality and impact of scientific outputs. It is thus imperative that scientific output is measured accurately and evaluated wisely.

In the UK, a recent report (Wilsdon, 2015) commissioned by HEFCE (The Higher Education Funding Council) recommended that institutions sign up to DORA but so far relatively few institutions have done so. Another document, the Leiden Manifesto, was published in *Nature* in 2015 (Hicks et al., 2015). The Manifesto presents ten principles of best practice in metrics for research assessment, namely:

- Quantitative evaluation should support qualitative, expert assessment.
- Measure performance against the research missions of the institution, group or researcher.
- Protect excellence in locally relevant research.
- Keep data collection and analytical processes open, transparent and simple.
- Allow those evaluated to verify data and analysis.
- Account for variation by field in publication and citation practices.
- Base assessment of individual researchers on a qualitative judgement of their portfolio.
- Avoid misplaced concreteness and false precision.
- Recognize the systemic effects of assessment and indicators.
- Scrutinize indicators regularly and update them.

Although such a detailed knowledge of these documents and debates may initially appear to be outside the scope of many librarians' roles, it is nevertheless imperative that we are aware of the debates and issues that can have such a major impact on the lives of the researchers with whom we are working.

👍 Best for:

- understanding the importance of research assessment exercises to the research community
- identifying how the library might contribute to research assessment exercises.

★ Examples from practice

The UK

In the UK the Research Excellence Framework (REF) replaced the Research Assessment Exercise (RAE) in 2014. Similar assessments of academic research excellence have been conducted in the UK approximately every five years since 1986 and the results are used to allocate research funds to universities. The REF evaluated research on the quality of research outputs as before, but also took into consideration the wider impact of the research. The UK is the first country to attempt to allocate funding based on the wider societal impact of research.

> The primary purpose of REF 2014 was to assess the quality of research ... the four higher education funding bodies will use the assessment outcomes to inform the selective allocation of their grant for research to the institutions which they fund, with effect from 2015–16.
>
> REF, 2014

As impact may not occur immediately, the REF took into account case studies based on research that predated the impact by up to 15 years.

Australia

In Australia, the Australian Technology Network of Universities (ATN) and the Group of Eight (Go8) undertook a joint trial exercise, the Excellence in Innovation for Australia (EIA) Trial, in 2012 to assess the impact of research produced by the Australian university sector. The pilot focused around types of impact, defined as socio-economic objectives, for example an impact on defence, or an impact on the economy.

Europe

The Expert Group on Assessment of University-based Research was established in 2008. It aimed to evaluate the main assessment and ranking systems in existence and to identify key parameters to be assessed.

> In its quest for excellence, the European Commission must and will encourage, promote and support every effort to understand and monitor the quality of research at universities.
>
> Janez Potočnik, Foreword to European Commission Expert Group on Assessment of University-Based Research, 2010

The USA
STAR METRICS is a

> federal and research institution collaboration to create a repository of data and tools that will be useful to assess the impact of federal R&D investments.
>
> STAR, 2015

⚠ To think about
As research evaluation is such a key part of the university's business, how best can the library contribute and add value to the process? Consider how a more in-depth knowledge of the debates and issues surrounding metrics can help in conversations with the research community. Some of the tips in later chapters suggest specific ways in which librarians can assist with such assessment exercises.

References and further reading

Cameron, W. B. (1963) *Informal Sociology: a casual introduction to sociological thinking*, New York, NY, Random House.

Cozzens, S. E. (2007) Death by Peer Review? The Impact of Results-Oriented Management in U.S. Research. In Whitley, R. and Gläser, J. (eds), *The Changing Governance of the Sciences: the advent of research evaluation systems*, Dordrecht, Springer, 225–42.

European Commission Expert Group on Assessment of University-Based Research (2010) *Assessing Europe's University-Based Research* (EUR 24187 EN), Brussels, http://ec.europa.eu/research/science-society/document_library/pdf_06/assessing-europe-university-based-research_en.pdf. (Accessed 15.5.15)

Hicks, D., Wouters, P., Waltman, L., de Rijcke, S. and Rafols, I. (2015) Bibliometrics: The Leiden Manifesto for research metrics, *Nature*, **520** (7548), 429–31.

League of European Research Universities (2012) *Research Universities and Research Assessment*,

www.leru.org/index.php/public/publications/category/position-papers/.
(Accessed 4.1.16)

REF (2014) *REF 2014*, www.ref.ac.uk/about. (Accessed 15.5.15)

San Francisco Declaration on Research Assessment (2012)
www.ascb.org/dora/. (Accessed 4.1.16)

STAR METRICS (2015) *Science and Technology for America's Reinvestment*
(STAR), www.starmetrics.nih.gov. (Accessed 25.5.15)

Wilsdon, J. et al. (2015) *The Metric Tide: Report of the Independent Review of the
Role of Metrics in Research Assessment and Management,*
doi: 10.13140/RG.2.1.4929.1363.

SECTION 4
Structures and strategies

4.1 Collaborate with other sections of the organization

TOO OFTEN IN large organizations we can operate in a silo, looking at things from the safe perspective of our own experience and understanding. This can be especially true of the library, which has a clearly defined position. However, when considering how we might engage with researchers, it helps to consider which other sections of the institution might be trying to do the same thing and to see if there are synergies that you can exploit. A large university is likely to have a central research office, for example; do you know what they do and what their role is? The Research Information Network, as long ago as 2010, recommended closer liaison between libraries and other central bodies within the university (Research Information Network, 2010). What about the careers service – do they contribute to the research experience? Does the staff development section provide courses for research staff? Are there administrators and managers in faculties and departments specifically tasked with a research role? Does the IT section provide specific software or infrastructure for researchers?

By contacting staff in different sections, you may be able to identify duplication of effort or work together to provide a more holistic package of opportunities for researchers. A joined-up approach may involve some compromise and will certainly take time and energy to develop but your researchers will reap the benefits of a more rounded approach. Being more aware of who the key people are across the organization and knowing what their priorities are and what they are working on will help you to plan and inform your own activities.

In order to build these kinds of relationships we must have something to offer other sections as well as the research community, and as a minimum that can be a co-ordinating or signposting role, bringing together scattered or fragmented sections, explaining who does what and raising visibility. This is something many libraries already do unofficially, so formalizing collaboration will make it easier for both researchers and staff to identify different responsibilities and lead to a more streamlined approach.

🖒 Best for:

- building links across the organization
- ensuring support is co-ordinated and not duplicated
- making best use of the institution's resources.

★ Examples from practice

Lancaster University

Tanya Williamson describes how she has liaised with other sections of the university to put together joint initiatives:

'I was appointed in April 2014 as part of an effort to improve support for research and researchers. As well as getting to know my colleagues in the Library, it became apparent early on that I needed to get to know other people across campus who were also developing support and training opportunities for researchers. There didn't seem to be an existing relationship between the Library and many of our 'partners' across campus. We wanted to start a series of 'Research Bites' talks that we'd heard about at Stirling, Aston and Sheffield, but needed input from others. I sent a speculative e-mail to the general inboxes of our staff development unit, Organisation and Educational Development (OED), and the Research Support Office (RSO) and Information Systems Services (ISS), suggesting we may have a similar goal, and asking whether anyone would like to work together. I quickly received very positive responses and an invitation to meet. It transpired that they were also at the start of this journey, and looking to develop a Research Development Programme (RDP), aimed at early–mid-career research staff. The Library and OED are now in regular conversation about how the Research Bites programme fits with the more substantial content of the RDP. We are sharing our ideas and programmes as they develop, and trying to tie together the content using the Vitae Researcher Development Framework. We have regular contributions from colleagues in the other services, with a much broader range of topics than we could hope to deliver based on the knowledge of Library staff alone. So far our conversations have been open and positive, without any sense of competition or possessiveness between our efforts. We have been able to make suggestions to one another, and the Library will benefit from the departmental connections of OED in particular. The Library serves all segments of the "research community", so I think we make a good hub to pull these connections together.' (Tanya Williamson, Lancaster University, UK)

Staff meetings

Loughborough University Library has a regular agenda item on its research team meetings called 'news from the research office', to which staff from the university's research office can send items. Library staff also go to the research office meetings and find the opportunities for personal contacts and serendipity invaluable.

Another library has started opening up its internal meetings to colleagues from across the university; so, for example, staff from the IT service and the teaching development service now regularly attend library research group meetings and similarly library staff have a presence in the other section meetings. All staff are enjoying the benefit of learning from colleagues with different viewpoints and expertise.

⚠ To think about

Before you contact other sections of your organization, have a clear idea of what you want to discuss and what you can offer to them.

> *'Don't be afraid of reaching out across services and asking novice questions. I've found that colleagues are very happy to be contacted and work together across services, especially if you approach the meetings with an open mind and something to offer.' (Tanya Williamson, Lancaster University)*

References and further reading

Research Information Network (2010) *Research Support Services in UK Universities*, London, http://soas.ac.uk/careers/earlycareerresearchers/file69090.pdf. (Accessed 4.1.16)

Acknowledgements

Helen Young, Loughborough University; Tanya Williamson, Lancaster University.

4.2 Develop the library as a publisher

THE EXISTENCE OF university presses is testament to the fact that many universities have engaged with publishing for many years and library publishing services are on the rise (Dixon, 2014). In the survey undertaken on behalf of the Association of American University Presses, 77% of librarians who responded believed that they should be involved in publishing.

Although the concept of the library as a publisher has been around since before the internet, the ease of access to free open source software to publish digitally means that many more libraries can get involved. However, a strategic decision needs to be made about whether the library should be directly involved in open access journal publishing on behalf of its researchers. This is still a major undertaking, involving investment of time, money and expertise, but in the current open access environment it can be an excellent way of demonstrating the library's commitment to open access in a practical and pragmatic way, especially for niche areas of research. The library can offer a secure central location for the journal content and archive, whilst the researchers should be responsible for the editorial content, peer review and general management of the journal. As well as offering a showcase for the organization's research, this role further establishes the library as the leader in terms of open access expertise (see tips 8.16–8.19). Existing print titles can also be digitized, offering new avenues for existing research output, and you can even consider adding different media, such as audio or video streaming content and links to data. However, some of the additional services offered by publishers, such as copy-editing and typesetting, may be more challenging to provide.

Rather than setting up a separate university open access journals service, some libraries, such as Huddersfield University, overlay journals onto their institutional repositories, creating a virtual journal by drawing content directly from the repository.

Managing and allocating ISBNs and DOIs on behalf of the institution is another way in which libraries can contribute to the publishing process and, of course, managing the institutional repository is an excellent demonstration of the library's commitment.

👍 Best for:

- engaging with researchers and the publication process
- demonstrating expertise in the publishing process.

★ Examples from practice

Utrecht University Library
Utrecht University Library provides a publishing platform, Uopen, for editors who wish to create a new open access journal, as well as offering advice for editors who may wish to transition their journal to open access: www.uu.nl/en/university-library/publishing/open-access-at-utrecht-university/publishing-services-uopen-journals.

Open Journal Systems

The University of Edinburgh and the University of St Andrews both use Open Journal Systems (OJS) to provide a platform for staff and students to publish OA journals. St Andrews also provide useful information in the form of a checklist for individuals wishing to start a journal using OJS, listing all the different issues to be considered around content, customization, processes and policies. The St Andrews Open Journals Set Up form, Figure 4.1 (available under a CC licence) covers the following headings, with additional columns for details to be added.

Journal Element
Journal Manager/Managing Editor
University staff member overseeing the project
Publisher (School or Dept responsible for journal content)
Other sponsor(s)/ supporting organisation(s)
Date of project initiation

Journal Description
Journal Title
Journal abbreviation/acronym
Short description (introduction for journal homepage)
Proposed language(s) of the journal
Does the journal already exist in print?
Does the journal already exist online? (Give existing URL)
Proposed file formats (e.g. PDF, HTML)
Will the proposed journal also be distributed in print?
ISSN Print:
ISSN Online:
Main contact name
Contact address
Contact e-mail
Technical support contact
Standard e-mail signature
Role(s) of main contact
Other named contacts/roles
Keywords (for journal indexing)

Figure 4.1 *University of St Andrews Journal Hosting Service: OJS Journal set-up form*
(Continues on next page)

Policies and 'about' the journal
Focus and Scope: What is the journal about? What do you wish the journal to achieve? Is there a strong ideological or disciplinary base?
Review Policy: Describe criteria/principles/time taken for decisions, etc.
Open Access: Will your online journal be completely open access? Will open access be delayed for some content?
Subscription Policy: Will some issues require subscription or registration? Will you offer print subscriptions?
Copyright Policy: Will authors retain copyright and grant you a licence to publish? Do you require authors to transfer copyright to the publisher? [You will need a short statement for the journal web pages and a full author agreement].
Do you require authors to clear 3rd party copyright for online use? Will your submissions contain images? Are there additional legal issues to consider?
Do you plan to use Creative Commons as an 'end user' licence?
Do you require a 'Competing interests' statement in author guidelines?
Journal history (for 'About' section)

Processes and Functionality
Do you want to use DOIs? (Digital Object Identifiers to uniquely identify online content)
Do you need a new ISSN?
Do you want an additional long-term preservation option for your journal?
Do you want to use OJS to manage the review process?
Guidelines for Reviewers: Do you have documented criteria and instructions for reviewers? Do you want to create review forms in OJS?
Guidelines for Authors: Do you have instructions, formatting guides, templates, etc., for author submissions?
Submission Checklist: Which elements of author guidelines should submitters be asked to tick, e.g. correct file format, citations, style?
Indexing terms for content
Scheduling: Please note frequency and identification, e.g. vol/iss or number/year
What sections will your journal have, e.g. Articles, Reviews, Letters?
Do you want to be able to add Announcements/News?
List editorial board or team(s) to be shown under 'People'
Other information for 'About the journal'
Note additional editorial roles

Figure 4.1 *Continued*

Customisation
Do you have a logo? Should this be on the homepage only or every journal page?
Do you current issue to appear on homepage? [sic]
Footers – do you want ISSN or any other statement?
Do you want additional links in the navigation bar?
Will you use a standard theme or use CSS for customisation? (note – you will need extra technical support for CSS)
Information sections – see default text for Readers, Librarians and Authors
Other functionality controlled by **Journal Manager**
Other functions controlled by **Editor**

Content
Do you have existing content to be uploaded to OJS? We may be able to help with an initial batch of content.
Do you want to be able to upload content in future without going through review/editing processes?
Is there 3rd party content, e.g. images that can't be included?
Do you need a storage area for administrative files, e.g. copyright forms, licences, redacted files?
Do you want content to be archived in our institutional repository?

Figure 4.1 *Continued*

The University of St Andrews Journal Hosting Service: OJS Journal set-up form by University of St Andrews Library is licensed under a Creative Commons Attribution 4.0 International Licence. OJS is free open source software which is widely used for OA journal publishing.

Similarly, Northampton University Library is involved with the development of Northampton Open Journals, a collection of open access online journals, edited and maintained by members of the University of Northampton. The site is currently under development: http://journals.northampton.ac.uk.

Other examples include University College London Press, the UK's first open-access university press for monographs, officially launched in June 2015: www.ucl.ac.uk/ucl-press.

Library Publishing Coalition

The Library Publishing Coalition was formed in the USA in 2014, bringing together 61 academic libraries. Working co-operatively, they can broker collective purchasing arrangements for resources, develop advocacy and awareness of library publishing and provide learning opportunities for professionals to develop requisite skills: www.librarypublishing.org/about-us.

Strategies for success

The *Library Publishing Services: strategies for success* report (Mullins et al., 2012) has a series of recommendations of best practice for libraries wishing to develop publishing services, including:

- Develop meaningful impact metrics for library publishing services.
- Establish editorial quality and performance criteria.
- Develop return-on-investment justifications for funding library publishing programmes.
- Create a shared repository of policies, tools, and templates.
- Develop centrally hosted software solutions for publishing platforms.
- Articulate the particular value delivered by library publishing programmes.

⚠ To think about

Is publishing a journal really as easy as just making scholarly content available digitally? Is a hosting service the same as a publishing service? What added value do commercial publishers give that you need to take into consideration? For example, how will you build a trusted brand – is the institution's name sufficient? What about marketing and raising awareness of the journal – how can you make it more discoverable by search engines? It's unlikely that potential readers will come directly to your website, so consideration needs to be given to visibility if researchers are to be persuaded to participate and contribute. Assignment of metadata and an understanding of web discovery tools is an essential part of publishing a journal. Bear in mind that some level of technical expertise is helpful, as well as dedicated server space and well thought-through maintenance and back-up to ensure stable, long-term access.

Many researchers wish to publish their work in established, traditional journals in their discipline and will need strong motivation to consider a less established university operation. What can you do to address these fears? In addition, for some traditional university libraries, the challenge may be about challenging the rigidity of the university system and its attitude to the role of the library.

References and further reading

Barker, A. (2015) The Liverpool Scene – University Library and University Press as Partners', *SCONUL Focus*, **63**, 18–20.

Brown, A. (2013) *Library Publishing Toolkit*, IDS Project Press.

Dixon, D. (2014) Complementary Skills, Resources, and Missions: best practices in developing library-press collaborations, poster presented at

the Library Publishing Forum, Kansas City, MO, 2014,
  doi: http://dx.doi.org/10.7710/2162-3309/lpf.1005. (Accessed 26.5.15)
Mullins, J. L., Rust, C., Ogburn, J. L., Crow, R., Ivins, O., Mower, A., Nesdill,
  D., Newton, M. P., Speer, J. and Watkinson, C. (2012) *Library Publishing
  Services: strategies for success: final research report (March 2012)*, SPARC,
  http://docs.lib.purdue.edu/purduepress_ebooks/24.
Price, G. (2014) Library as Publisher: capacity building for the library
  publishing subfield, *Journal of Electronic Publishing* **17** (2),
  www.infodocket.com/2014/05/27/new-article-library-as-publisher-
  capacity-building-for-the-library-publishing-subfield. (Accessed 28/3/15)
UKSG (2014) *Webinar on the Library as Publisher*,
  www.uksg.org/libraryaspublisher. (Accessed 28.7.15)

Read more on the debate around libraries as publishers on the Scholarly
  Kitchen blog: http://scholarlykitchen.sspnet.org/2014/12/01/whats-going-
  on-in-the-library-part-1-librarian-publishers-may-be-more-important-
  than-you-think. (Accessed 28/3/15)

Open Journal systems, http://pkp.sfu.ca/?q=ojs.
University of Edinburgh open-access journals, http://journals.ed.ac.uk.
University of St Andrews open access journals,
  www.st-andrews.ac.uk/library/services/researchsupport/journalhosting.

More links on OA publishing on the SPARC website,
  http://sparceurope.org/open-access.

4.3 Define library staff roles and library structures

AROUND THE WORLD, there are several ways in which university library staff who engage with researchers are organized. The more traditional model is that of the subject specialist who offers a comprehensive liaison service to researchers in one or more subject areas. This approach is taken to its extreme in the example of embedded librarians working directly in research teams (see Tip 5.9) The danger of this model is that it can stretch the abilities of staff to the limit, as they have to take on ever more new knowledge and develop an expanded collection of skills to continue to work effectively. In practice this may lead to an inconsistent service as some staff find it easier to develop new abilities whilst others prefer the traditional, comfortable role.

More recently two newer approaches are gaining popularity. Some libraries (York, Manchester, University College Dublin, Northumbria) have completely reorganized their staff into functional teams, identifying key library operations, such as collection management, services for teaching and learning and services for researchers. At Northumbria University, for example, the

Research Support Team comprises three sub-teams: research skills, collection development and scholarly publications. Teams can be closely aligned to university strategies and so are a very visible demonstration of how the library is responding to institutional change. Such research teams include specific, often newly designated, jobs such as bibliometrician, data manager and publications manager. This enables staff to concentrate on gaining a deeper knowledge of their specialism and to provide very detailed assistance on their area of expertise. It does, however, risk the loss of some of the informal networking and personal touch offered by the subject specialists.

A combination of the two previous approaches offers a hybrid model, retaining the very valuable expertise and networking provided by subject liaison staff and pairing these disciplinary experts with functional specialists. Specialist roles can have a different person specification and will attract staff with different expertise and not necessarily with a library background or qualifications. Loughborough University Library has subject liaison teams but staff also have a functional responsibility.

> 'The advantage of subject staff is that they can go to department meetings as a matter of course and often see opportunities for engagement in unexpected places.'
> (Helen Young, Loughborough University)

Newcastle University Library also retains academic liaison librarians but is also developing specialist roles around open access and research data management to work alongside the more traditional functions.

👍 Best for:

- considering how different roles and job functions can assist with researcher engagement.

★ Examples from practice

University of York
The following is contributed by Michelle Blake (Head of Relationship Management, Information Directorate) and Janette Colclough (Research Support Manager, Information Directorate).

In 2013 the Relationship Management team within the University of York Information Directorate (consisting of Library, IT and Archives Services) began a programme of change to meet the challenges of the new University Information Strategy, taking into account the environment of increased fees for students, the competitive research grants environment and demonstrating the Library's value and impact.

Conversations with staff raised concerns about how any one person could address all the areas of activity identified from the new Information Strategy. It became clear that a realignment of staff was required. The aim of this realignment was to refocus the Relationship Management team into three functional teams.

Structure

The previous structure was centred around subject clusters of Academic Liaison Librarians. In addition, a team of IT trainers and support staff formed part of the Relationship Management team. Figures 4.2 and 4.3 show the changes to the structure before and after.

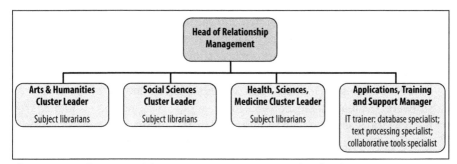

Figure 4.2 *York University Library, previous structure (reproduced with permission)*

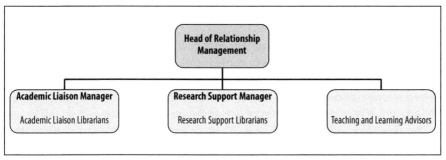

Figure 4.3 *York University Library, structure from January 2014 (reproduced with permission)*

The functional teams

1 **Relationships and Engagement: Academic Liaison**

The focus of this team is to strengthen relationships with academic departments to ensure consistent delivery of services across departments. In addition, the Information Directorate wanted to ensure collaborative working with other areas of the University. The ethos of the team focuses on collaborative working to ensure that all departments receive a consistent and high level of service at all times. This means that although each team member will be the named contact point for a number of specified departments staff are required to deliver services across all departments. While the Liaison team delivers teaching they are not expected to create the teaching materials (except to tailor them for a specific subject area). Liaison Librarians need a broad overview of all services in order to be able to deliver a comprehensive service to their department (much like a sales rep might have).

2 **Teaching and Learning**
The increase in student fees coupled with the University's new teaching strategy created the need to reassess how we supported teaching and learning. The rise of the importance of digital literacy has meant that pedagogic skills work, for both staff and students, is a priority for the University and is an area where the Information Directorate can visibly add value. The team brings together a mix of staff from Library and IT backgrounds who have a remit for supporting formal teaching activities based around a skills framework as well as support in the use of some software. The team are responsible for creating, delivering and evaluating the training and learning materials produced by the Information Directorate for use across both academic and support departments. Staff work collaboratively with colleagues in other support services who deliver training, including Academic Liaison Librarians, and academic colleagues.

3 **Research Support**
This is an area of strategic importance for both the University and the Information Directorate. It has become increasingly important owing to cuts in research funding, the open access agenda and the REF, as well as requirements from research funders such as research data management. The Research Support team was established during the realignment of staff in January 2014 and contains four staff, a Research Support Manager and three Research Support Librarians. The three Research Support Librarians each support one of the team's specialist areas (open access, research data management and copyright). The team manager undertakes the line management of the team members, maintains an overview of the team's work and represents the team within the Information Directorate and beyond. As well as providing support in the specialist areas listed, the team also provide more general support to researchers and postgraduate research students via training activities and enquiry work.

There are a number of channels that users can use to contact the team.

Webpages outline the areas of responsibility the team have and a dedicated e-mail address can be used. In addition, the team work within the wider Relationship Management team and are often 'connected' to users via Academic Liaison Librarians; for example, an academic or researcher will get in touch with their Liaison Librarian and will be connected to a member of the Research Support team.

Pros of having a Research Support team

- Having dedicated staff to resource research support work has proved vital, e.g. RDM, open access, both of which have significant funder compliance issues.
- A separate team gives staff the opportunity to develop the expertise required in these specialist areas.
- The expertise developed means that staff are credible when engaging with the wider University.
- A dedicated team has meant there has been time to forge new relationships with other support services. These relationships have proved invaluable, e.g. the University's research office (Research and Enterprise), departmental research managers, departmental research chairs.
- The new team have been able to take advantage of new opportunities as they arise. For example, York was able to put in a successful bid to be part of the Jisc-ARMA ORCID pilot.
- The team have had space to develop new external relationships/partnerships, e.g. working with other research support librarians in the local White Rose partnership and beyond.

Cons of having a Research Support team

- A separate team does have the risk of potential double handling/loss of relationships.
- There may be some uncertainty initially about who is responsible for some activities: for example, some aspects of support for postgraduate research students.
- There is a danger of staff becoming isolated in specialist roles.
- A small specialist team can make it difficult to provide cover when staff are on leave.
- Risk of damaging other activities if staffing is not balanced across all areas of activity.

UCD Library, University College Dublin

Contributed by Julia Barrett, Research Services Manager, and Peter Hickey, Head of Client Services.

The reorganization

In 2012 UCD Library introduced a new organizational structure, significantly realigning services and roles, amalgamating teams and introducing two new units, 'Research Services' and 'Planning and Administration'. In creating the Research Services Unit UCD Library identified the need to treat these services as core library activities, recognizing that the former project-led approach limited long-term development and growth.

The key driver of change was to ensure that UCD Library services were aligned with and supported the aims and ambitions of the 2009–2014 UCD Strategic Plan, 'Forming Global Minds'. UCD Library undertook a strategic planning process in 2009–2010 which informed its 2010–2014 Strategic Plan. This plan articulated the Library's mission and vision and identifies five strategic objectives. To enable realization of these objectives, and also to accommodate the aggressive changes to Library budget and staffing resulting from public sector austerity measures, all Library units and administration were reviewed and reorganized.

Research Services Unit

The Research Services Unit was established by bringing staff from disparate library units together with a new focus on the support of the UCD Research Strategy. Two new developmental opportunities were identified for librarians to express an interest in, Bibliometrics Librarian and GIS and Mapping Librarian. The current team comprises ten staff. The recruitment process currently being undertaken for a Data Manager will bring the number to 11. The Research Services Unit is responsible for developing and delivering specialist and innovative services to researchers in UCD, within the overall Research Lifecycle. Services include:

- UCD Digital Library (http://digital.ucd.ie)
- Research Repository UCD (http://researchrepository.ucd.ie)
- Mapping and geospatial services (http://libguides.ucd.ie/gisguide)
- Bibliometrics support (http://libguides.ucd.ie/bibliometrics)
- Data services, including research data management http://libguides.ucd.ie/data
- Management and operation of the Irish Social Science Data Archive, a national service (www.ucd.ie/issda).

Impact

The development of the unit has enabled UCD Library to have more impact in university business relating to research activities, in particular having a clear go-to manager and team of experts. The creation of expert librarians has been a clear success of the overall reorganization with the vesting of specialist responsibility to individuals. This has given librarians the permission and scope to develop expertise, to speak with authority and to make informed decisions on behalf of the library. While formerly staff typically developed competencies in a range of fields, it was often in relation to their specific faculty needs or in a personal-interest capacity. This tended to lack the strategic university perspective and all too frequently diffused impact, with the absence of clear go-to contacts. Across the units this allocation of responsibility for delivering on specialist leads has enabled the library to engage at higher levels as those expert competencies are increasingly acknowledged and valued across the university and national communities. Through the new Bibliometrics Service, UCD Library provides training and support around issues related to bibliometrics and raising research impact. This service is provided to individual researchers (career promotions, support for funding applications, etc.), Schools and Research Institutes (funding application, benchmarking, etc.). This service is very popular with Schools and Institutes conducting unit quality reviews and external accreditations. With the GIS service, UCD Library has been able to take a lead in catalysing the interest of a broad group of stakeholders with an interest in geographic information systems and the development of university-level services.

Consultancy
In its reorganization UCD Library recognized the challenges of a delivery service model for some of its research and teaching services. The development of experts allows the Library to offer consultancy services and advice for mapping/GIS, creating digital collections, research data management, increasing research impact, funding applications. The consultancy advisory model potentially allows the library to increase the impact of its services and expertise. UCD Library also operates one commercial information service, called Archinfo (see Tip 4.5).

Practical example
The key strength of library-based research services is the ability to transcend university strategic objectives and to see differing needs. A key concern in arts and humanities disciplines is the focus on bibliometrics as key university determinants of impact. In presentations on research services our college liaison librarians encountered some strong opposition to the concept of open access. The Library Research Services Manager and Research Repository Librarian met directly with the Arts College Research Committee and their open and honest discussion of the positives and negatives actually led to increased engagement and a rise in submissions to the Research repository.

Figure 4.4 and 4.5 illustrates the reorganization carried out at UCD and the resulting structure.

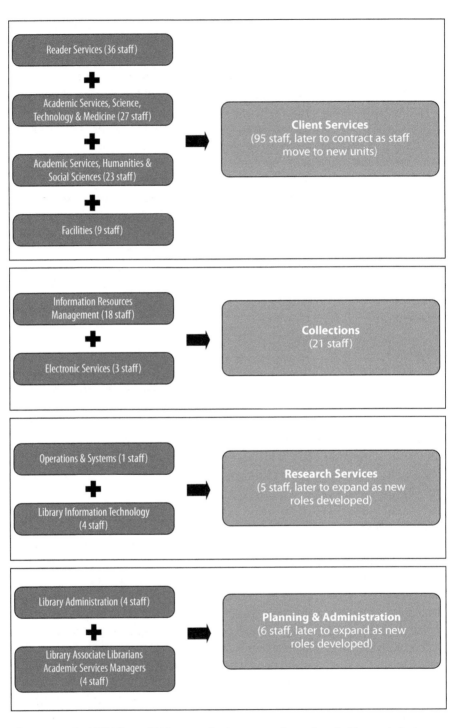

Figure 4.4 *The UCD Library 2012 reorganization process (reproduced with permission)*

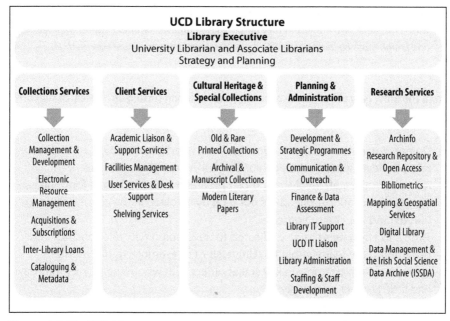

Figure 4.5 *The UCD Library structure since reorganization (reproduced with permission)*

⚠ To think about

From UCD

Building relationships is the key determinant for the success. Many of the services that are being designed and delivered require specialist skills that no single person may have. Collaborating with specialists across the campus helps in the provision of co-ordinated services, reduces fragmentation and helps to integrate services at campus-wide level.

It is through these connections that a library is able to demonstrate the value and relevance of its services. It is important to get onto relevant committees (formal) but equally crucial to regularly meet key people individually (informal and formal). It is through these conversations that one can outline benefits that help to meet overall UCD objectives, design joint approaches and negotiate and agree respective roles.

> 'One of the positive things to come out of our new structure is that the individual specialists feel they have a remit to make things happen in their area in a way the liaison librarians didn't.' (Peter Hickey, UCD)

> 'We find that the specialists can go into a School as a neutral voice, giving impartial advice, so it's more of a conversation and not seen by staff as being imposed by the university. For

example, when my colleague went into the Arts Faculty they started off by saying the IR wasn't for them, but afterwards they became very enthusiastic about depositing their work and I think that's because of the way it was presented to them.' (Peter Hickey, UCD)

From the University of York: advice for others considering setting up a research support team

- Do not expect too much too soon. Staff will need time to adjust to their new roles, to develop new relationships and learn new specialist skills.
- Remember the staff involved and be prepared to give staff time for upheaval, trauma and change. Colleagues not directly involved in the change need to understand the change process.
- Time and effort need to be dedicated to developing new relationships and positioning the team within the University. For example, departmental research administrators are key stakeholders with whom the Library may have had little contact previously.
- Do not over-commit, as services need to build up over a period of time. The York team, for example, have yet to explore potential bibliometric services.
- It is important to try to ensure that when staff are in specialist roles a basic understanding exists elsewhere so that there is no single point of failure.
- Communication is, of course, vital. This particularly applies to internal communication, to ensure that all staff understand the roles of the new team and how they relate to their own area.
- It is difficult to do things in isolation within your own library. It is important to look at the whole structure and to see how the constituent parts will work together.
- Take account of the wider structures at your own institution – your teams need to understand the environment in which they are operating.
- Just because something works in one institution does not mean it will work in another. The structure, history and context is important.
- In a multi-team model a number of different staff will be working with academic departments. Think carefully about how your communication works with other library teams. At the University of York, a customer relationship management solution has been adopted to record the various conversations with academic and support departments to ensure a co-ordinated response and that people are aware of all activity taking place.

Acknowledgements

Michelle Blake (Head of Relationship Management, Information Directorate) and Janette Colclough (Research Support Manager, Information Directorate),

University of York, UK; Julia Barrett, Research Services Manager, and Peter Hickey, Head of Client Services, UCD, Ireland; Northumbria University Library, UK.

4.4 Develop a research data management strategy (see also Tips 8.10 and 8.11)

RESEARCH DATA MANAGEMENT (RDM), in essence, involves the initial planning for collection or creation of the data, its organization and analysis, storage and access, discoverability and dissemination. All of these activities align closely with more traditional information literacy activities and so it's easy to draw a parallel with the work librarians are used to undertaking.

Research data varies between disciplines; in sciences it may consist of numerical data, whereas in social sciences it may be more qualitative, text-based data. Whatever the form, good practice in managing research data has always been central to high-quality research, but with developments in open access there is increasing recognition that data, as well as written work, should be open, able to be shared and re-used. In many countries, the drivers for open data now come from funders and government bodies; in the UK, for example, several of the research councils expect preservation and availability of research data for up to ten years after completion of the work.

Research organizations and universities have therefore been developing systems and strategies for managing their data for several years and libraries are well placed to contribute to this activity, along with other sectors such as the IT department, research office and the researchers themselves. Indeed, as activity has grown, libraries may often have become involved in a piecemeal, opportunistic way and many excellent initiatives have resulted.

At a strategic level, however, developing a policy on research data management that clearly articulates the library's role is essential. The policy will serve to raise awareness of the potential contribution LIS staff can make in this arena, as well as managing expectations. Librarians have skills in creating and managing metadata, cataloguing and curating digital information, advocacy, researcher development, open access publishing, copyright and intellectual property issues which can all contribute to an effective institutional strategy but need to be expressed in a formal way. Once such a policy is in place library staff at all levels need to be aware of it, so that they can disseminate it effectively.

👍 Best for:

■ raising awareness of the potential contribution library staff can make to managing research data

■ getting involved with the research community.

★ Examples from practice

SCONUL Briefing for Library Directors

In the SCONUL *Research Data Management Briefing* (Taylor, 2015) the library is identified as one of the components of the holistic RDM system illustrated in Figure 4.6.

Senior university managers	Funding and resources	Repository systems	Policy, strategy and governance	IT services
Senior academic staff	Online advice and guidance	RDM tools	Active data storage and backup	University library
Senior support services managers	Archiving, presentation and sharing data	Metadata	Training programmes	Research office
	Research teams	Principal investigators	Research systems	

Figure 4.6 *Holistic RDM system (Taylor, 2015)*

In the document, Taylor (2015, 9) describes an example of an RDM service based on the research lifecycle to help librarians to define the parameters of an RDM service. It highlights opportunities for libraries to contribute at different stages: for example, in identifying existing data sources, advising on compliance, managing metadata, data citation, data hosting and archiving. As well as providing links to current examples of good practice, the briefing identifies some of the knowledge and competencies required if librarians are to engage in this kind of activity, so it can also be used to develop staff training programmes.

Good practice examples

The University of Leeds data management policy is hosted on the library website. As well as summarizing the university's position, it includes clear links to other relevant policies such as confidentiality and anonymization, data protection, data storage and security, ethical review, ethical review policies and guidelines, information security policies, good research practice and ethics, professional integrity in research and safeguarding data – storage, back-up and encryption.

The University of Manchester Library Research Data Management web page is clearly linked to the university's RDM policy statement, as well as to tools for data management planning and data storage.

Jisc documents

The Jisc RDM Quick Guide has a self-assessment tool, CARDIO, to enable organizations to:

> ... collaboratively assess data management requirements, activity and capacity, build
> consensus between data creators, information managers and service providers,
> identify practical goals for improvement in data management provision and support,
> identify operational inefficiencies and opportunities for cost saving, make a
> compelling case to senior managers for investment in data management support.
>
> Jisc, 2015

It includes case studies as examples of good practice and provides links to published data management policies from around the UK. Links to a wide variety of tools and training resources make this an essential resource for data managers and librarians alike.

The Jisc document *Directions for Research Data Management for UK Universities* (Brown et al., 2015) usefully highlights key topic areas and issues with suggestions for action. Although not solely aimed at library policies it does have a strong library focus.

⚠ To think about

Ensuring that the library has sufficient staff with appropriate skills is key to a successful RDM strategy; expecting existing staff to change direction and add such a complex additional set of skills to their remit is challenging. Conversely, bringing in a whole new team may not be appropriate. Consider what extra skills staff will need, how they can be supported and how new staff with different skills can integrate with existing teams to provide a holistic offering.

References and further reading

The Digital Curation Centre has a range of useful How To guides aimed at developing a RDM service. Find them at www.dcc.ac.uk/resources/developing-rdm-services.

Akers, K. G., Sferdean, F. C., Nicholls, N. H. and Green, J. A. (2014) Building Support for Research Data Management: biographies of eight research universities, *International Journal of Digital Curation*, **9** (2), 171–91.

Brown, S., Bruce, R. and Kernohan, D. (2015) *Directions for Research Data Management in UK Universities*, London, www.fosteropenscience.eu/ sites/default/files/pdf/1240.pdf. (Accessed 30.4.15)

Burrows, T. and Croker, K. (2012) Supporting Research in an Era of Data

Deluge: developing a new service portfolio within information services at the University of Western Australia, paper presented at VALA, 6–9 February, Melbourne, Australia, www.vala.org.au/vala2012-proceedings/vala2012-session-1-burrows. (Accessed 12.3.15)

Cox, A. M. and Pinfield, S. (2013) Research Data Management and Libraries: current activities and future priorities, *Journal of Librarianship and Information Science*, **46** (4), 299–316.

Jisc (2015) *Institutions and Managing Research Data*, www.jisc.ac.uk/guides/research-data-management. (Accessed 1.9.15)

Taylor, C. (2015) *Research Data Management: briefing for library directors*, www.sconul.ac.uk/sites/default/files/documents/SCONUL RDM briefing.pdf.

Tenopir, C., Birch, B. and Allard, S. (2012) *Academic Libraries and Research Data Services: current practices and plans for the future.* An ACRL White Paper (4), www.ala.org/acrl/files/content/publications/whitepapers/Tenopir_Birch_Allard.pdf.

University of Leeds data management policy, https://library.leeds.ac.uk/research-data-policies.

University of Manchester Library Research Data Management web page, www.library.manchester.ac.uk/services-and-support/staff/research/services/research-data-managment/.

4.5 Generate income from research activity

MOST LIBRARIES RELY on their organization, be it a university, a company or a public body, to provide the bulk of the library budget. Traditionally, additional income has been generated from charges for overdue or lost books, from copying and scanning, occasionally as payment for use of facilities and as internal charges for specific activities, such as service teaching. Facilities such as cafés, binding and reproduction and digitization also provide opportunities for additional income. Substantial income may also be derived from donations and libraries across the globe are investigating opportunities for fundraising, although acknowledging that this can only ever be a minor contribution to the overall budget.

More recently, librarians who contribute to research projects and proposals have been able to charge a fee for their contribution, perhaps levying a fee for literature searches or involvement in systematic reviews, as is the case at the University of Northumbria in the UK (Tip 8.6). If library staff are able to engage with researchers at the early stages of a research proposal, it may also be possible to cost in funding for library staff time or resources for the project.

Libraries with large digitized collections of archives usually make them freely available, but income can be generated by charging for higher-quality images of special collections, especially if they are rare or unique images.

Providing a more formal commercial service, either within the organization or for external researchers, is another option, although this can be much more complex in terms of licensing of resources. The effective marketing of such a service is essential. Some libraries deliberately target a market sector, for example the local engineering research community, offering a package of services such as specialist advice, physical access and negotiated access to some electronic resources. As well as providing a useful service, this kind of activity can raise the profile of the library within the community and can facilitate other networking and collaboration opportunities.

🖒 Best for:

- raising the profile of the library and demonstrating the value of specific services
- generating income from services which it might otherwise not be possible to provide
- facilitating networking and collaboration opportunities
- benefiting the local community.

★ Examples from practice

Archinfo

University College Dublin (UCD) Library in Ireland operates a specialized commercial information service called Archinfo, established in 1988 and operating as a spin-off company. This service offers mapping and research services to architectural practices, planners, consulting engineers and local authorities. As well as being profitable this service supports a targeted community with specific products not easily accessible elsewhere.

Just over 100 architectural practices around Ireland are members of Archinfo (before the economic downturn this figure was in the region of 280). These companies pay an annual membership fee and this entitles them to avail of additional services, such as book loans, inter-library loans, historic map searches, research and reference enquiries – there is an additional fee for some of these services. Non-members are offered a pay-as-you go service whereby they can purchase Ordnance Survey maps. Archinfo is self-funded, so all salaries and expenses are paid by the income Archinfo generates.

Archinfo, 2014

⚠ To think about

What are the benefits of developing a commercially viable service? Are you motivated by income generation or is this an additional benefit of a service for the local community? Will the amount of income generated offset the costs of setting up and running the service? Does attributing a monetary value to an expert service help to demonstrate the value the library can offer to research projects?

References and further reading

Archinfo (2014) Available at: www.archinfo-richview.com/index.html. (Accessed 1.5.15)

Boadi, B. Y. (2006) Income-generating Activities: a viable financial source for African academic libraries?, *The Bottom Line,* **19** (2), 64–77.

Cuillier, C. and Stoffle, C. J. (2011) Finding Alternative Sources of Revenue, *Journal of Library Administration,* **51** (7–8), 777–809.

Acknowledgements

Peter Hickey, UCD Library.

SECTION 5

Places and spaces

5.1 Host research events in the library

ONE WAY OF attracting researchers into the library is to host regular events for them to attend. The library is a neutral space in the organization and can be an ideal venue for events organized by and for researchers. Such events don't need to have a specific link to the library and its resources, it's sufficient that they bring researchers into the space and raise the profile of the library as a scholarly venue. These events may be organized and run by library staff, as with information literacy workshops, but they can equally be owned by the research community and just facilitated by library staff. Facilitation can simply take the form of providing a space, but can also extend to providing refreshments (always a draw) or to helping with the administrative tasks, such as promoting the event, maintaining a list of attendees, etc. Events may be part of a regular programme to which researchers have to apply for space, for example a Library World Café, or you may simply identify a suitable space and advertise it as available for research-focused meetings. If there are any LIS staff who are also active researchers this is an excellent opportunity for them to participate on a level playing field with other researchers in the organization, potentially altering perceptions amongst researchers about who they are and what they do. Such events are also useful for both raising awareness of the library and for learning more about current research activity.

One of the benefits of this kind of activity is that researchers will start to see the library in a different light, not just as a provider of information, but as a key part of their research life. It is surprising what a difference such a subtle change in emphasis can make in terms of changing perceptions of the library from a purely supporting role to being a more integral part of the research lifecycle.

If the library includes a research commons or specific research zone, then this kind of activity may be common practice, but even without such a specific facility it's possible for the library to become the accepted place for research-focused events.

👍 Best for:

- becoming part of your research community and a more integral part of the research process
- changing perceptions of library staff.

★ Examples from practice

Liverpool John Moores University Library, UK

The library service at Liverpool John Moores University (LJMU) hosts regular Research Café events, circulating between their three libraries. Up to four participants volunteer to talk about their research in a relaxed and informal setting, followed by questions and discussion. Booking isn't required and all staff, students and alumni are welcome to attend. Researchers are encouraged to speak via their graduate schools and the event is publicized across the university. Cakes are provided!

> 'At Christmas we take the Research Café out into the wider community and invite more experienced researchers to present their work. Our most recent Christmas Special took place in the public library, where our speakers covered the seasonally appropriate subjects of excess, shyness and exercise.' (Jan Burrell, LMU University)

Following the event a photograph and summary presentations are hosted on the library website.

⚠ To think about

It's important to identify your role in this kind of meeting clearly . To generate a sense of ownership, it's best for them to be initiated and run by the research community, but inevitably reminders have to be sent by the LIS team to the organizers and the administration and organization is also done via the library.

> 'As the research community is a fluid population, it is hoped that this will enable the Research Workflows Community of Practice to grow and develop even if the original participants have moved on.' (UK librarian)

Providing a small amount of refreshment helps encourage attendance, though it isn't essential.

> 'We offer food at our workshops but we find that often folks don't eat much. It's more about changing the atmosphere of the event.' (Helen Young, Loughborough)

Think about who the audience for the event is. Can you extend it to final year/masters students for example, or past employees or alumni? Is there scope for involving the local community?

References and further reading

Liverpool John Moores Research Cafés: an example of how the cafés were
  promoted: https://lineupnow.com/event/research-cafe-. (Accessed 20.1.16)
Liverpool John Moores Research cafés: YouTube recordings:
  https://www.youtube.com/playlist?list=PLD-
  jFJJqLKxKvqu278STa81qZPcaXGmG6. (Accessed 20.1.16)

Acknowledgements

Jan Burrell, LJMU Library Services and Graduate School.

5.2 Engage distant researchers in real time

NOT ALL PHD STUDENTS are based close to their home university. Many conduct their original research in the field; others choose a specific distance learning degree which allows them to study from home. Even those based locally may have personal commitments, such as job and families, which make it difficult to participate fully in university life. With such a disparate research community it can be difficult to foster a sense of community, to engage with researchers who may be in different parts of the globe and to offer an equitable experience to them.

Online solutions to this issue are becoming more common. Information literacy lectures and workshops can be recorded and made available, videoconferencing and webinar software can be employed to run real-time sessions and even regular online chat can help. If your organization makes use of a virtual learning environment such as Blackboard or Moodle, consider whether you can interact with the research community in this environment, perhaps using the chat or whiteboard facilities at a regular time each week.

In an attempt to provide parity of experience for distant researchers some university libraries have extended their face-to-face consultation booking service for postgraduates to encompass different media, for example using Skype, Lync or similar software, to book virtual face-to-face meetings. Even booking a phone conversation so that the researcher is discussing his or her queries in real time with a named individual can help to make a distant researcher feel more valued and adds a personal touch that merely engaging with online resources can't replicate. The personal touch, knowing with whom you are talking, can be vital for an isolated researcher. Whilst general queries might be fielded by an enquiries team, getting to know an individual or small team within the library is very comforting and helps to build better relationships.

👍 Best for:

- engaging with PhD students, both locally and at a distance
- providing equity of service to all the research community
- building relationships and fostering community.

★ Examples from practice

Concurrent seminars and webinars

The University of Leicester runs a regular Thesis Forum, in which existing or recently graduated PhD students talk about common aspects of their PhD experience. It is run as a simultaneous seminar and webinar using Adobe Connect with a microphone and webcam, and a projector in the seminar room so that all can see. The session is also recorded and made available later, but only within the community, so that speakers feel more able to speak freely. The sessions work well, with participants from all over the world giving very positive feedback on how the experience makes them feel part of the research community.

Skype research interviews

A university library in Australia liaises with a research community spread over a very wide geographical area and even encompassing different time zones, making it difficult for many of them to visit the library. In order to mitigate the effect of distance, the library invites researchers (mainly, but not exclusively, postgraduate students) to book an initial research interview with their research librarian at the start of their research. Whenever possible the interviews are carried out via Skype so that both participants can see each other and discussion centres around the topic of the research and the ways in which the librarian and the library can offer help. Each interview is followed with an informative e-mail, summarizing the key content of the discussion, and a further e-mail is sent two months later to maintain contact with the researcher. Where Skype is not possible, interviews are carried out over the phone.

> 'It is quite time-consuming to talk to each researcher individually and we've been talking recently about trying to get small groups together on Skype, but I think we'd lose a lot of the personal contact that is set up with this approach and folks do really seem to appreciate the effort we go to.' (Australian librarian)

⚠ To think about

Having control of the space and the equipment can help ensure success of an online session; if you are reliant on technical support from elsewhere this could jeopardize the smooth running of the event. For this reason, it is recommended that you train staff well in the use of the equipment and test it well before every session.

Confidence is also important. Think about how you will cope if the technology does let you down. Have a back-up plan so that participants still gain value from the interaction.

References and further reading

Leicester Thesis forum,
    www2.le.ac.uk/departments/gradschool/current/thesis-forum.
Gannon-Leary, P., Fontainha, E. and Bent, M. (2011) The Loneliness of the Long Distance Researcher, *Library Hi Tech*, **29** (3), 455–69.

Acknowledgements

Helen Steele, University of Leicester.

5.3 Develop research zones

WITH THE RECENT focus on undergraduate students and learning spaces, many university libraries have developed as very successful, exciting, dynamic learning places. Do these spaces work equally well for researchers, or might there need to be more differentiation? Does the status of researchers entitle them to special spaces, or is anyone who is working hard at their own level also entitled to think of themselves as a researcher? Opinions vary on this and libraries around the world have dealt with it in different ways. Some libraries provide separate, closed access spaces for researchers, with additional services and privileges, such as coffee machines, lockers and access to the library's research team. Specialist software, for use only by researchers, can also be made available if the access to the space is restricted. Other libraries may identify research space with walls, screens, furniture or signs but do not physically restrict access, relying on the space itself to create the research ambience. Alternatively, some libraries treat all study space as research space and expect users to respond accordingly. Each approach has merits and drawbacks and may depend on the individual organization and the recognition given to research within it. Much has been written about the design of spaces for researchers. For example Freeman (2005), Beard and Bawden (2012) and Corrall (2014) all provide useful context for a deeper investigation of this topic.

The research commons concept is a more sophisticated development of a research zone, combining traditional quiet study with collaborative social space in a technology-rich, multifunctional space, usually in partnership with other sections of the university, to provide complementary expertise. This one-stop-shop space for researchers is often in a prime location, highly visible and clearly differentiated, indicating that researchers 'need to be separate from undergraduates as they are engaging in knowledge creation at a different level' and that they will be 'inspired by a creative and contemplative atmosphere' (Corrall and Lester, 2013). For library staff looking to develop closer working relationships with researchers, the research commons provides an ideal location. The detailed task force report from Ohio State University Library is a helpful working document (Black et al., 2013).

👍 Best for:

- defining specific library spaces for researchers to demonstrate the library's commitment to the research community
- creating a creative and contemplative atmosphere.

★ Examples from practice

Research zone at Northumbria University
The University of Northumbria Library in the UK has a dedicated Research Zone in the library, accessible to postgraduate research students and university staff. It operates with swipe cards and includes a breakout zone for coffee and a bookable research room. Individual workstations, interactive whiteboards and other collaborative tools are provided. The Library's Research Support team is located adjacent to the space and ran a Christmas tea party for regular users in the breakout room in 2014.

> 'Having a dedicated space for researchers gives them an identity and a separate space away from other students who they may also teach. We have a breakout room where they can relax, have a coffee and make phone calls – a place for them to rest away from their study area.' (Suzie Kitchen, Northumbria University)

The Edge, Duke University Library
Duke University Library in the USA has a space called The Edge, 'a collaborative space for interdisciplinary, data-driven, digitally reliant or team-based research'. It's a physical space in the Library which provides resources and expertise, including such things as data and visualization software, a digital studio, workshops, project rooms and presentation spaces.

University of Cape Town

The access controlled Research Commons opened in the main library at the University of Cape Town, South Africa, in 2008, mirroring the undergraduate Knowledge Commons and enabling staff to offer 'specialized support in both specific subject domains and research skills' (Daniels, Darch and de Jager, 2010). A detailed investigation of the effectiveness of the facility concluded that it has been successful in facilitating the creation of new knowledge and that it is popular with the research community, contributing to the development of the community of practice. However, scalability is of concern, both in practical economic terms but also whether the community feel would still be effective on a larger scale.

Wolfson Research Exchange, University of Warwick

The University of Warwick Library in the UK opened its Research Exchange in 2008, offering an opportunity for the research community to come together to share and create ideas. Partly in response to feelings of isolation amongst postgraduate researchers, who expressed a desire for a dedicated space distinct from the undergraduate student body, the Exchange provides a variety of different spaces: informal seating for discussions and small group activities, traditional study space and access to technology (Carroll, 2011).

⚠ To think about

By restricting access to parts of the library to specific groups of users you may leave yourself open to criticism. Policies for access need to be clearly defined and advertised.

The development of a research commons offers additional benefits in terms of closer working relationships with other sections of the university that also work with researchers, potentially leading to a much richer provision for the research community.

Does such a space need to be housed within existing library space, or might it be better located elsewhere, closer to the research community?

References and further reading

Beard, C. and Bawden, D. (2012) University Libraries and the Postgraduate Student: physical and virtual spaces, *New Library World*, **113** (9/10), 439–47.

Black, B., Connell, T., Dotson, D., Efkeman, T., Leach, B., Mandernach, M. and Reese, T. (2013) *Research Commons Task Force Findings and Recommendations*, http://library.osu.edu/staff/administration-reports/RCTFReport.pdf. (Accessed 27.5.15)

Carroll, D. (2011) Fostering a Community of Scholars at the University of

Warwick: The Wolfson Research Exchange, *New Review of Academic Librarianship*, **17** (1), 78–95.

Corrall, S. (2014) Designing Libraries for Research Collaboration in the Network World: an exploratory study, *Liber Quarterly*, **24** (1), 17–48.

Corrall, S. and Lester, R. (2013) The Researcher's View: context is critical. In Watson, L. (ed.), *Better Library and Learning Spaces: projects, trends and ideas*, London, Facet Publishing, 183–92.

Daniels, W., Darch, C. and de Jager, K. (2010) The Research Commons: a new creature in the library?, *Performance Measurement and Metrics*, **11** (2), 116–30.

Freeman, G. T. (2005) The Library as Place: changes in learning patterns, collections, technology and use. In *Library as Place: rethinking roles, rethinking space*, Council on Library and Information Resources, www.clir.org/pubs/reports/pub129/freeman.html.

Other examples of Research Commons initiatives (of many) include:

- University of Washington Research Commons, USA http://commons.lib.washington.edu.
- Kelvin Smith Library, Case Western Reserve University, USA, http://library.case.edu/ksl/aboutus/researchcommons.
- New York University Bobst Library Research Commons, USA, http://guides.nyu.edu/content.php?pid=169930&sid=1431162.
- Sussex Research Hive, UK, www.sussex.ac.uk/library/research/hive.
- The Edge, Duke University, USA, http://library.duke.edu/edge.

Acknowledgements
Northumbria University Library.

5.4 Host research exhibitions in the library

WHY DO EXHIBITIONS in the library always have to focus on library collections? If you have the luxury of space, identifying a specific area within the library that can be used for highlighting current research can be a useful way of engaging with the research community. If the space is large enough to contain physical artefacts, perhaps sculptures or engineering structures, as well as research output such as copies of papers, books and reports, this can make the exhibition space very visually appealing. Research groups can be encouraged to bid for the space; an element of competition can make use of the space more attractive. Alternatively, a regular programme of exhibitions, with allocated slots for the research community, will enable researchers to plan ahead and work towards the event. Tying the library's resources into the exhibition by highlighting 'find out more' or 'further reading' opportunities will not only engage library staff in learning more about the current research taking place within the organization but can raise awareness amongst the research group of additional resources for their research.

Smaller-scale activities, such as regular poster exhibitions, can be a less demanding, cheaper approach. Many researchers produce posters for conferences and might welcome the opportunity to display them locally afterwards. If your university has annual poster displays for postgraduate research students, or even poster competitions for undergraduates, consider whether the work can also be displayed in the library.

⚑ Best for:

■ encouraging researchers into the library
■ making the library part of the research community
■ promoting the benefits of the library in widening access to research outputs
■ building relationships between the library and the research community.

★ Examples from practice

University of Western Australia
The science library at the University of Western Australia has an exhibition space that has housed racing cars developed by an engineering research group (Figure 5.1). They have also used images provided by their scientists to decorate the walls of their group study rooms.

Figure 5.1
*Exhibition space,
University of Western
Australia science library*

Nailing the thesis

'Nailing the thesis' is a tradition in several universities in Sweden and in many the ceremony is held in the library. At Umea University in Sweden the tradition is for doctoral students who have completed their thesis to nail a copy of the thesis to a noticeboard in the library as a public declaration that they have completed their research. See Tip 8.23 for more details.

Durham University Library

Durham University Library in the UK worked with students on an archaeology masters course to house an exhibition of artefacts found in the local river. The students researched the objects and curated the exhibition, which was located in a prime exhibition space in the library. The exhibition was launched at a Friends of the Library evening, attended by local residents and academic staff, and the students talked about both discovering the items and the process of curating them. This activity has led to a very rich relationship between the library and the department.

⚠ To think about

Mounting exhibitions can be time-consuming and requires expertise that individual research groups may not have. If LIS staff can provide this, working closely with researchers to develop the display, this can enrich the relationships. However, it will demand a consistent, ongoing level of investment of both time and money from the library and so is not to be entered into lightly. A poorly curated exhibition will reflect badly on all concerned. Having fewer, high-quality exhibitions each year may be more effective.

References and further reading

For further information about the UWA Science Library exhibition see www.news.uwa.edu.au/uwa-motorsport-aug2014.

For more information about nailing the thesis see https://internwebben. ki.se/en/nailing-and-distribution, and https://m.youtube.com/watch?v= ONuJ2_8z6PI ('Usually, we don't sing . . .').

Acknowledgements

Therese Erixon, Umea University Library, Sweden.

5.5 Get involved with local research conferences and events

MANY UNIVERSITIES AND large organizations hold both internal and externally facing conferences, bringing together experts from around the institution as well as from further afield. If you work in a large university, it is likely that researchers at your institution will be involved in organizing and hosting discipline-specific conferences within the university. Although at first glance they may appear to be very discipline-specific, it is worth considering whether the library might have something to offer. The conference can be an opportunity for you to learn more about what researchers are doing, to listen to their concerns and to become more aware of what their priorities are. It's a great way to meet researchers in their own environment

If the conference has sponsor stalls, you can offer to provide a library stall, especially useful for internal conferences, where you can promote specific events, workshops and resources.

Perhaps you can provide library goodies for the delegate bags, or if the conference has a specific theme, can you create a book display or leaflet highlighting relevant resources?

Are there ways in which the library can contribute to the specific topic of the event, perhaps by providing a small, relevant exhibition at the conference itself, or in some way contiguous to it? Having recently been involved in organizing the LILAC conference at my own university, I know at first hand how much conference organizers welcome any additional help to make their event stand out. It may be that there is a local conference team who provide regular support for conferences; they will be able to advise you about impending activities so that you can follow up any which seem appropriate.

External delegates at conferences may wish to visit the library during their stay, and so if you are able to offer a special package for visiting delegates (even if it's just 'show your delegate badge to gain access to the library') that can also raise the profile of the library and will be welcome to the conference organizers, who will be keen to showcase their local facilities. If you know when the event is happening you can ensure that any library reception staff are aware of potential visitors.

Alternatively, you might contribute a few PowerPoint slides highlighting relevant library collections or interesting facts about the library; these could be displayed at the start of the conference to entertain delegates as they settle in.

🖒 Best for:

- raising the profile of the library within the research community
- meeting researchers in their own environment
- developing a better understanding of what research is happening and what researchers' priorities are.

★ Examples from practice

University of Central Lancashire, UK

The University of Central Lancashire (UCLan) holds a two-day conference for their early career researchers at which they can present posters or a short presentation. Library staff attend the conference and network with the researchers, chatting about their work and offering advice on resources and personal consultations.

> 'Meeting in person is far better than an e-mail, also showing an interest in their individual research engages them.' (Annette Ramsden, UCLan)

University of Northumbria Library, UK

Northumbria University Library staff attended their university's Research Conference, providing a stall focusing on ORCID sign-up as well as offering breakout workshops on specific topics.

> 'This worked well for us and we'll do it again. Going to where the researchers are and meeting them in their space made us more visible.' (Suzie Kitchen, Northumbria University)

Loughborough University Library, UK

Loughborough University Library staff attend the university's Research Conference every year, providing a stall with a range of free gifts. As well as providing information about the library, it is used as an opportunity to find out more about researchers' views.

> 'The past two years we have held a sort of raffle, where one year, to tie into the conference theme, we asked people who came to stand to give us their views on open access (e.g. do you prefer green or gold) and then we drew out a couple of forms at the end of the conference and they won either the green Easter egg or the gold Easter egg (it was held in March). This year we asked them to tell us about their research and whether they would like to meet with their academic librarian for a one-to-one chat about their research needs – again we popped all the forms into a basket and some people won chocolates and a posh notebook.' (Helen Young, Loughborough University)

Newcastle University Library, UK

Newcastle University Library developed a modest exhibition and accompanying LibGuide on Alan Turing to run alongside a short conference on Turing held in the School of Computing Science to celebrate the Turing Centenary in 2012 (see Figure 5.2). Visitors to the event were encouraged by researchers to visit the exhibition in the library as part of their experience and some even contributed to the online guide afterwards. Although the exhibition itself was small, it was valued by the research group and has resulted in a much closer working relationship with them since then. The following e-mail from a senior member of academic staff to a national society demonstrates the value placed on this kind of work:

Figure 5.2 Turing exhibition at Newcastle University

'Dear Professor [x]

In connection with our seminar 'Alan Turing: Computing Pioneer' tomorrow the University Library here has prepared a small exhibition of materials and an online resources guide. Details are at http://libguides.ncl.ac.uk/turing.

My colleague Brian Randell wondered if it would be appropriate to include the link on the Alan Turing Year web pages.

Dr J. L. Lloyd BSc PhD CITP FBCS, School of Computing Science'

In a similar way, the library contributed to an event to celebrate the life of Sir Joseph Swan, inventor of the lightbulb. Again, an online guide was created and his descendants visited the library to view various artefacts held within the library's Special Collections: http://libguides.ncl.ac.uk/c.php?g=130245&p=850694.

⚠ To think about

Finding out about conferences and when they are happening can be difficult and time-consuming. Is there a conference organizing team within your organization who you can make contact with?

Can you create a leaflet explaining what the library can offer to conferences that can be sent to local organizers?

If the service proves popular, will you be able to maintain it?

Even if you aren't a subject expert, there should be some aspect of research that you can pick up on and ask about. Demonstrating that you have listened to/read the work of any researchers you are engaging with will mean you are more likely to be remembered.

What capacity do you have to engage with research conferences in this way? Could the library invest in a small, relatively secure travelling exhibition case? What kind of materials might you display – current books, rare materials (or facsimiles) from your archives, copies of research papers?

Does the exhibition need to be specifically tailored for the conference or would a fairly generic display of 'treasures' suffice?

References and further reading

The Joseph Swan guide is available at
   http://libguides.ncl.ac.uk/c.php?g=130245&p=850501.
The Turing Centenary Guide is available at http://libguides.ncl.ac.uk/turing.

Acknowledgements

Suzie Kitchen, Northumbria University Library.

5.6 Be a secret shopper

MOST LIBRARIANS ENJOY visiting other libraries, looking for examples of good practice and for ideas which they can emulate. However, if you visit another library as a researcher yourself, putting yourself in their shoes, you may have a very different experience and this can help you to reflect on your own practice. Preparation for such a visit is very important. There may be aspects of your own library's provision for researchers that you wish to develop, and so plan ahead for the kinds of questions you might ask and the types of provision you want to look for. Once you have a framework in place, you can utilize it at relatively short notice if the opportunity arises.

Alternatively, rather than being a secret shopper yourself in other libraries, you can recruit researchers from within your organization to act as secret shoppers in your own library. This can be done in a very light-touch way, perhaps by giving new or inexperienced researchers a task to complete and asking about their customer journey. Engaging researchers in your own research in this way can also be helpful in changing their perceptions of your role – you are also a researcher as well as helping them to learn about the library themselves in a different way.

👍 Best for:

- gaining a better understanding of the researchers experiences
- identifying development opportunities and new ideas.

★ Examples from practice

The librarian who suggested this Tip says:

'It's all about empathy. It is beneficial to visit other libraries as a researcher, not least because it puts you on the receiving end of library query-handling and the library user experience in general. If you leave a library muttering, "They're all so LIBRARIANLY" – and that's not really a compliment – stop and ask yourself what exactly you disliked about the experience. Were they welcoming? Were they keen to help? Were they heavy on rules and procedures? Did you feel as though you were being restricted in some way for no apparent reason? As a librarian myself, I totally understand the need for rules and policies, but as a researcher, I can also understand that libraries need to take care not to appear obstructive.'
(Karen McCaulay, Royal Conservatoire of Scotland)

⚠ To think about

Before you visit another library as a secret shopper, decide what you hope to achieve. You will experience this library as an external researcher – are you looking for approaches you can adopt in your own situation? Perhaps you will be able to identify processes and procedures which are common in your own library, but seeing them through the eyes of a researcher, rather than a librarian, can cause you to reflect on their efficacy.

Consider also the ethical issues of this situation. If, as a secret shopper in another library, you have a poor experience, will you pass that information on? If you are recruiting secret shoppers from within your research community, what do you need to say to your own LIS staff?

References and further reading

Kocevar-Weidinger, E., Benjes-Small, C., Ackermann, E. and Kinman, V. R. (2010) Why and How to Mystery Shop Your Reference Desk, *Reference Services Review*, **38** (1), 28–43.

Acknowledgements

Karen McCaulay, Royal Conservatoire of Scotland.

5.7 Become an embedded librarian

THE TERM 'EMBEDDED LIBRARIAN' is relatively new, but the concept itself is not; as long ago as 1985, Neway (1985) investigated how librarians could move from being passive providers to being proactive members of research groups. Carlson and Kneale (2011) describe embedded librarianship as 'taking a librarian out of the context of the traditional library and placing them in a setting that enables close co-ordination and collaboration with researchers'. In this context, librarians might be involved in collating data as it is produced, making data available, literature searching and dissemination and in joint funding bids. Being located in an academic department allows a librarian to have a much closer relationship with stakeholders.

However, as McCluskey (2013) points out, even when a librarian is integral to the research team, the role relates to information searching and management, rather than research itself. Drewes and Hoffman (2010) consider that it's both the physical and the metaphysical location of librarians that defines them as embedded: librarians (and researchers) perceiving them as an insider in the research community. Librarians may be integrated into the research community on multiple levels, in different arenas, both physically and virtually and in different ways with different groups. As with so many aspects of engagement with the research community, there is no simple model to follow.

An embedded librarian is not the same as a departmental librarian; this long-standing model of providing branch libraries in academic departments relates much more to physical stock and space, whereas an embedded librarian, as part of the research team, will not have a physical library location at all.

An embedded librarian should be seen as a partner in a research enterprise. For many librarians this may be uncomfortable or challenging – certainly it is an expensive approach for the library. In practice librarians may struggle to find enough to do and the relationship also requires a big shift in perception from researchers. An ideal embedded librarian has been described as being creative and flexible, possessing excellent interpersonal skills and having a capacity to thrive in traditional and non-traditional settings (Kesselman and Watstein, 2009). David Shumaker details many issues that need to be taken into account in his book, *The Embedded Librarian* (Shumaker, 2012).

🖒 Best for:

- providing highly tailored services to specific research groups
- changing perceptions of librarians and their role
- engaging with the research community.

★ Examples from practice

Helsinki University Library, Finland

Helsinki University Library used an approach called 'knotworking', described as a 'boundary crossing, collective problem solving way of organizing work' (Engeström et al., 2012). The idea is to identify a specific problem, or knot, and then for researchers and librarians to work through it together, so that 'continuity is connected to the object, not the people'. This innovative approach involves commitment from all those involved and ensures that a true partnership develops as the collaborators work towards a solution.

Sheffield Hallam University Library, UK

Melanie Gee describes her role embedded within a research team:

> 'My job title is "Researcher (Information Scientist)": my role is a "tame" information professional within a research centre. I have been in this role for four years. Initially this service was bought in from the university's Learning and Information Services so I was line-managed by an Information Specialist (academic librarian) in the Learning Centre, although I was based in the research centre myself. Just over a year ago my line management transferred within the research centre, and I am now line-managed by a professor in the centre.
>
> The role is something of a cross-over between "academic librarian offering a service" and "researcher bringing in money": I am involved in research projects, by virtue of doing literature searches for input to project proposals and for actual funded projects; I am increasingly becoming involved more deeply, e.g. at the moment I am undertaking a realist review myself in order to feed into an evaluation. I am also involved in training for staff and PhD students, in literature searching, reference management, information management, bibliometrics, choosing where to publish, etc. – some of which overlaps a little with what is offered centrally, but the training I provide is a little more in-depth and tailored to the research group I support. I also handle some fairly basic enquiries about e.g. our reference management software (RefWorks) or getting hold of the full text of papers, just by virtue of being to hand.
>
> I am now pretty well established in the research centre and have a steady stream of work (often too much work!), but I found that my reputation had – not unreasonably – to be earned.' (Melanie Gee, Sheffield Hallam University)

⚠ To think about

Developing an embedded librarian model must be a strategic decision for the library. Staff who remain based in the library need to be aware of the concept and understand what you are doing so that they can also contribute; being embedded does not mean being isolated from other librarians.

Persuading researchers of the value of including a librarian in their team is one of the most common concerns. Changing perceptions of roles may take a long time. To justify this approach you need to be able to demonstrate what an embedded librarian can add to the research outputs in terms of value.

If you are aiming to be an embedded librarian think about how you can truly be a team player and what your role in the team will be.

'Having the confidence to question what researchers say they want can be difficult at first. When I first started in the job I tended not to question what the researcher was asking me to do – I would just create the search strategy, run the searches and deliver the results, which were of course exactly what they asked for, but often running to several thousand results when what the researcher really wanted was a couple of hundred. It was a bit soul-destroying to realize, months down the line, that the researchers were so overwhelmed by the volume of results, that they had not engaged with them at all and reverted to doing their own Google searches instead!' (Melanie Gee, Sheffield Hallam University)

References and further reading

Carlson, J. and Kneale, R. (2011) Embedded Librarianship in the Research Context: navigating new waters, *College and Research News*, March, 167–70.

Dewey, B. I. (2004) The Embedded Librarian, *Resource Sharing & Information Networks*, **17** (1–2), 5–17.

Drewes, K. and Hoffman, N. (2010) Academic Embedded Librarianship: an introduction, *Public Services Quarterly*, **6** (2–3), 75–82.

Engeström, Y., Kaatrakoski, H., Kaiponen, P., Lahikainen, J., Laitinen, A., Myllys, H., Rantavuori, J. and Sinikara, K. (2012) Knotworking in Academic Libraries: two case studies from the University of Helsinki, *Liber Quarterly*, **21** (3/4), 387–405.

Kesselman, M. and Watstein, S. (2009) Creating Opportunities: embedded librarians, *Journal of Library Administration*, **49** (4), 383–400.

McCluskey, C. (2013) Being an Embedded Research Librarian: supporting research by being a researcher, *Journal of Information Literacy*, **7** (2), 4–14.

Neway, J. (1985) *Information Specialist as Team Player in the Research Process*, Westport, CT, Greenwood Press.

Shumaker, D. (2012) *The Embedded Librarian: innovative strategies for taking knowledge where it's needed*, Medford, NJ, Information Today.

Acknowledgements

Hanna Voog, Helsinki University Library; Melanie Gee, Sheffield Hallam University.

5.8 Go on tour

I**T'S OFTEN ONLY** in informal discussions that library staff are able to publicize all the ways in which they can facilitate the research process but as more and more material becomes available electronically researchers have less need to visit the physical library and opportunities for serendipitous conversations between library staff and researchers become fewer. From a researcher's perspective all may be well; researchers often operate in a 'satisficing' mode, finding what is quick and easy to satisfy an information need, and they may well believe that is all the library offers. It's easy to see how relationships can become more distant. If researchers are no longer visiting library spaces, then it makes sense that librarians need to spend more time in research spaces, but this is not as simple as it sounds. Librarians are busy people too – we don't have time to wander around our organizations in the hope of connecting randomly with researchers; if we are to go 'on tour' this needs to be planned in a more strategic way.

Researchers and research groups will have regular meetings, either within the group or at a departmental and organization level, and it's crucial that the library is represented at such gatherings: if not attending every one, then at least with the expectation of being present occasionally. Research administrators may be able to facilitate entry to such a group and it helps to present them with a specific reason for attending, even something as vague as ensuring all researchers are aware of new resources and developments in the library. Never attend such a meeting without something to say; people will soon start to value your contribution and expect your presence if you can contribute in a positive way.

> 'Offer to present at the School's seminar series on scholarly publishing.' (Nicola Foxlee, University of Queensland, Australia)

Attending meetings, however, only puts you into contact with a small number of representative researchers, and so you need other strategies to reach the wider group. One possibility might be to devise an informal 'tour schedule' and publicize this ahead of time, noting where you will be, what kinds of questions you can answer and what you hope to achieve. Badging this as a tour, mobile librarian or pop-up library can give it a brand which people can remember and relate to and will raise the profile of the library too.

Alternatively, make a list of all the key research groups and contact them directly, explaining that you want to come and meet them to find out more about their research, tell them what's happening in the library and discuss ways you can work together. This could become an annual event, raising expectations amongst researchers that the library often has something new to offer.

👍 Best for:

- making services more visible and convenient for researchers
- contacting the research community and building relationships.

★ Examples from practice

Library Research Forum

'We have been doing our Library Research Forum events for the last few years and now academics seem to expect them. We work out a programme in the summer months, usually June and July, with a mix of short talks and consultation desk sessions, and we hold them in different places around the campus. So one week there may be a session in the engineering department on finding your h-index one day and the next day we'll just set up a laptop in the coffee area and answer questions on anything. The next week we might be in the history department with a talk about archive materials and also the help desk. We try to make it varied and check with the different departments about when will be best for them, though anyone can come to any talk – they are advertised on posters and leaflets and we do get engineers coming to the archives talk, for example.' (Librarian, German University)

Welcome events

Staff at one university library always attend the postgraduate welcome events in the Faculties, setting up a stall with free pens and notepads to attract visitors and providing information about the workshops and other ways in which they can help new research students with their research. The informal atmosphere enables relaxed conversations and encourages students to sign up for the programme of workshops offered by the library. In addition, for academic staff induction events, library staff set up a similar stall, with material tailored to the different level of staff attending.

⚠ To think about

If you plan to go on tour make sure you consult with researchers and administrators over the best times and locations to maximize impact. Publicity is vital, whether by e-mail, social media, posters or leaflets, and a reminder a few days before is useful too.

Don't be discouraged if attendance is small initially:

'We made the decision right from the start to plan a whole summer programme and to repeat it the next year, even though sometimes only a few people came at the start. We *reckoned it would take some time for people to get to know what it was all about so we perseveredsevered. It was hard to justify sometimes but now people even ask when we are starting and seem to look forward to it and come back each year. It seems now that they are suggesting things we might do, too, and that is good, as it feels they are owning it themselves.' (Librarian, German University)*

5.9 Join virtual research communities

SUBSEQUENT TO THE development of virtual learning environments (VLE) has been the development of virtual research environments (VRE). In essence, a VRE, or virtual research community, is an online space in which researchers can operate collaboratively. Similarly to a VLE, a VRE may offer space to host documents, collaborative tools such as blogs and wikis and resources to help, for example, with writing and publication. Some VREs are institution-specific and hosted behind firewalls, whilst others are more open.

Jisc define a VRE as 'a set of online tools and other network resources and technologies interoperating with each other to facilitate or enhance the processes of research practitioners within and across institutional boundaries'(JiscInfoNet, 2014).

Libraries have worked with VLEs for many years, so translating similar practices across to a VRE is not difficult. However, often this simply comprises links to resources and in a research environment there are other opportunities for engagement. Librarians can contribute to the development of the environment itself, advising on the use of metadata to enhance discoverability (Carlson and Yatcilla, 2010). As members of the community we can engage in debates, actively suggest resources and practices and advise on specific issues as they arise.

The main problem can be discovering where the researchers are in the first place. Are they operating within a VRE and if so which one(s)? If your organization provides a local facility, it may be possible to find out how it is being used and to get a list of research groups involved.

Social media tools such as LinkedIn and ResearchGate also operate as VREs for some researchers, so registering with these will also enable you to see how researchers are communicating and, as a minimum, can raise your own profile within the community.

🖒 Best for:

- meeting researchers in their own space
- building relationships with researchers
- making services more visible and accessible for researchers.

★ Examples from practice

Purdue University
Purdue University Library in Australia worked with the developers of CAT-Hub, a VRE for researchers working with assistive technologies, to develop tags within the VRE to enable users to more easily find resources within the platform (Carlson and Yatcilla, 2010). Librarians used their knowledge of controlled vocabularies to contribute to the development of the environment, thus contributing in a practical way to the research itself.

University of Westminster
In response to a research exercise carried out with researchers, the University of Westminster in the UK developed a VRE in order to 'build a series of solutions' to the issues identified. The VRE contains comprehensive details of all members of the research community. It details all doctoral research projects and additionally contains useful documentation such as ethics forms. Researchers are able to upload their research outputs into the VRE, which then feeds the institutional repository. The University now has a much more accurate picture of research activity and is benefiting from timesaving and transparency (Enright, 2015).

⚠ To think about
In a closed, local VRE, you may need to be invited to become a member. Ensure you are able to demonstrate the value your presence will offer by detailing specific ways in which you might be involved. Be careful, once you are part of the community, to find your place and contribute appropriately, not too much but not too little either; the idea is not purely to lurk and listen but to actively engage and to show the value the library can add to the research process. The aim is for researchers not to think it's unusual to have a librarian in their space, but to assume this is normal.

References and further reading

Candela, L., Castelli, D. and Pagano, P. (2009) On-demand Virtual Research Environments and the Changing Roles of Librarians, *Library Hi Tech*, **27** (2), 239–51.

Carlson, J. and Yatcilla, J. K. (2010) The Intersection of Virtual organizations and the Library: a case study, *Journal of Academic Librarianship* **36** (3), 192–201.

Enright, S. (2015) Supporting Researchers with a Research Information Management Platform, *SCONUL Focus*, **63**, 24–33.

JiscInfoNet (2014) *Implementing a Virtual Research Environment*, www.jiscinfonet.ac.uk/infokits/vre. (Accessed 5.5.15)

Wusteman, J. (2008) Editorial: Virtual Research Environments: what is the librarian's role? *Journal of Librarianship and Information Science*, **40** (2), 67–70.

The Jisc website has examples of VREs linked to specific stages in Jisc's research lifecycle model and its VRE Knowledge base links to examples of VREs from around the world.

5.10   Provide for visiting scholars

IT IS INCREASINGLY common for researchers to collaborate with colleagues from around the world and researchers at your organization will frequently be hosting visiting scholars from elsewhere. In addition, if your library has a particularly valuable collection of resources, that in itself will attract researchers from far and wide. Many libraries have a well defined mechanism for enabling access to their specialized resources, even if it simply comprises access to the building and appropriate reading space. It is less common, however, to find well articulated policies aimed at those scholars visiting existing researchers within the institution, especially if they are visiting for a short period of time. Visiting scholars may feel isolated and access to the local library facilities is a familiar environment.

Developing such a policy, maybe even providing a welcome pack, is a relatively inexpensive way of demonstrating the library's value and can be very valuable in building relationships with the research community. Researchers want to be proud of their local library and being able to present their visiting colleagues with a friendly introduction to it is a welcome bonus. To be cynical, it can be seen purely as a marketing ploy, bringing together existing services and presenting them in such a way as to suggest a special service.

🖒 Best for:

- raising the library's profile in the research community
- demonstrating the library's value to the wider research community.

★ Examples from practice

American libraries

There are several examples of visiting scholar information in US libraries, relatively few from elsewhere. At Berkeley University and the University of Washington, for example, services are aimed at those with official, short-term status:

The Library provides borrowing privileges and other services to our community of visiting scholars and postdocs. Visiting scholars must receive official appointments with a UC Berkeley Department or Organized Research Unit, and register with the Visiting Scholars and Postdoc Affairs (VSPA) Program.

www.lib.berkeley.edu/information/visiting-scholars

To obtain borrowing privileges as a 'Visiting Scholar' individuals must be designated as such by a University of Washington academic department.

www.lib.washington.edu/services/borrow/vscholar

At Penn State the definition of a visiting scholar is more inclusive:

The Libraries defines 'visiting scholars' or 'visiting faculty' as faculty users who are not employed by Penn State, but are visiting from other academic institutions for the purpose of short-term instruction, research, and scholarship.

www.libraries.psu.edu/psul/lending/visitingscholars.html

SCONUL Access

In the UK and Ireland, the SCONUL Access Scheme allows reciprocal access and borrowing rights to staff and postgraduates from other universities which participate in the scheme:

SCONUL Access is a reciprocal scheme which allows many university library users to borrow or use books and journals at other libraries which belong to the scheme. The scheme covers most of the university libraries in the UK and Ireland.

If you are:

- a member of staff (both academic and support staff) on an open or fixed term contract
- a postgraduate research student registered for a PhD, MPhil or similar qualification
- a part-time, distance learning and placement student
- or a full-time postgraduate

and your university or college is a member of the scheme, you may be able to borrow from other college or university libraries.

www.sconul.ac.uk/sconul-access

A welcome pack

What to include in your visiting scholars' welcome pack – this can be an actual pack, a leaflet, a web page:

- a short welcoming statement
- specific information on library access and opening hours backed up by a practical policy, e.g. visitor passes specifically for visiting scholars
- specific information on borrowing rights, access to electronic resources
- details of library staff, such as subject specialists and liaison librarians
- information on how to get help
- brief details of specialist collections.

⚠ To think about

In universities, the term 'visiting scholar' may have a specific meaning within the institution, so any policy developed by the library must clearly define who is included in the description. Is the policy aimed at short-term visitors or do visitors need to have official status within the organization? Can you differentiate services to different users?

It's important to articulate very clearly what visiting scholars can and can't do in order to manage expectations. Of course, you won't be able to anticipate every request, but you can predict the most common, often relating to access to electronic resources, downloading and copyright!

SECTION 6

Library staff roles

6.1 Assess and develop staff skills and expertise

AS TECHNOLOGY HAS developed and also as libraries have changed focus over recent years, so the traditional role of the librarian has changed. A librarian in a modern research library needs to be outgoing, multi-talented and agile, able to adapt and continually learning and developing new skills. Even long-standing activities such as collection development require new approaches in monitoring and managing stock, whilst developments in open access, bibliometrics and research data demand a wide range of new tactics.

As Parker (2012) puts it, 'we are moving from a cosy library to a scary library', where our role is less about being custodians of knowledge and more about 'assisting to increase the productivity of research and scholarship'. This can be intimidating for staff; Hansson and Johannesson (2013) talk about librarians feeling insecure in approaching researchers, so it's essential to have a well considered, focused staff development programme available.

Initially, it may help to do an audit. Identify the different aspects of the library provision to researchers; what do you do now and what else do you want to achieve? What skills will be needed to meet your aspirations? How might these be developed? Can existing staff help their colleagues? Do new roles demand new staff with different skills? What are the priorities? What is the timescale? What will happen if you don't deliver the relevant training?

Once you have a definitive (for now) list of skills, you can start to look at how you might address their development. Is there material available online, are there trainers who can run courses for staff, do staff need to be sent on training courses? Some excellent OER (open educational resource) materials are becoming available, though they may need repurposing for your own situation.

Loughborough University Library worked with the Digital Curation Centre to develop training sessions on research data management for their staff. It was felt important to take the time to build up staff confidence as 'people haven't always enjoyed learning' (Helen Young, Loughborough University).

👍 Best for:

- getting a clear picture of the skills you and your colleagues have and need to operate in the research environment
- ensuring you are well prepared for any new responsibilities
- building staff confidence.

★ Examples from practice

Audit of staff skills

In one UK university library, the subject liaison team informally assessed their own skills and confidence, concluding that their highest confidence was in knowledge of resources and literature searching, awareness of research interests and trends and the Research Excellence Framework, whereas the greatest training needs were around how to advise on data management and curation and their ability to contribute to research bids. Following on from this, a more detailed identification of research areas and library staff skills was undertaken, using the following headings:

- research discovery
  - conceptualizing new research
  - finding information
  - keeping up to date
  - critical thinking
  - evaluation of sources
  - our own awareness of research interests
- research behaviour
  - develop a personal profile
  - integrity, IP and copyright
  - commercialization
  - collaborate and network
  - physical space
- research organization
  - funding, bid writing, identifying sources
  - literature reviews
  - referencing, bibliographic software
  - data management and curation
  - research workflows
  - tools for smarter working
- research dissemination
  - publication: where and how
  - open access: awareness, compliance, practicalities

— e-theses
— research impact
— Research Excellence Framework.

For each of these, notes were made about

- which library staff need this
- online training resources
- external providers
- in-house training potential
- events to attend
- mailing lists/blogs
- relevant literature
- target date for action
- lead person to action.

RDMRose Project, Sheffield, UK

The Jisc-funded RDMRose project was a collaboration between the libraries of the University of Leeds, Sheffield and York with the Information School at Sheffield to provide an open educational resource for information professionals on research data management (RDM). Although existing staff were competent it was felt that there were some gaps in knowledge and people were unclear about the direction of development. As well as raising awareness of key theories the project aimed to help librarians understand the viewpoint of researchers towards research data management. The learning outcomes of the programme include learners having the ability to explain and apply the key concepts of RDM and data curation to real situations. The materials are available at http://rdmrose.group.shef.ac.uk/?page_id=10#session-23-the-rdm-agenda for re-use by other educators and have also been designed for self-supported CPD. Designed as eight half-day modules, they cover:

- introductions, RDM, and the role of LIS
- the nature of research and the need for RDM
- the digital curation lifecycle
- key institutions and projects in RDM
- what is data?
- managing data
- case studies of research projects
- institutional case study and conclusions.

⚠ To think about

What level of expertise do staff need? This may depend on whether they have a main responsibility for the topic or whether it is undertaken in addition to another role. What funds are available to realize the development programme? How will it be managed?

References and further reading

Brewerton, A. (2013) *RLUK: Redefining the research library model: workforce survey findings*, www.rluk.ac.uk/strategicactivity/strategic-strands/redefining-research-library-model/. (Accessed 4.1.16)

Corrall, S. (2010) Educating the Academic Librarian as a Blended Professional: a review and case study, *Library Management*, **31** (8/9), 567–93.

Corrall, S., Kennan, M. A. and Salo, D. (2013) Research Know-How for Research Support Services: preparing information specialists for emerging roles, *Proceedings of the American Society for Information Science and Technology*, **50** (1), 1–4.

Cox, A., Verbaan, E. and Sen., B. (2012) Upskilling Liaison Librarians for Research Data Management, *Ariadne*, **70**, www.ariadne.ac.uk/issue70/cox-et-al. (Accessed 27.5.15)

Cox, A., Verbaan, E. and Sen, B. (2014) A Spider, an Octopus, or an Animal Just Coming into Existence? Designing a curriculum for librarians to support research data management, *Journal of eScience Librarianship*, **3** (1). Available at doi:10.7191/jeslib.2014.1055. (Accessed 21.10.15)

Hansson, J. and Johannesson, K. (2013) Librarians' Views of Academic Library Support for Scholarly Publishing: an every-day perspective, *Journal of Academic Librarianship*, **39** (3), 232–40.

Parker, R. (2012) What the Library Did Next: strengthening our visibility in research support, *VALA 2012*, Melbourne, Australia, www.vala.org.au/direct-download/vala2012-proceedings/435-vala2012-session-1-parker-paper/file.

6.2 Become an author yourself

RELATIVELY FEW PRACTISING librarians are also published authors. This is probably because we have enough to do in our day job and have a personal life to lead outside. Writing is a time-consuming process, involving commitment and dedication as well as a fair serving of selfishness. Certainly, writing this book has been both a challenge and sometimes an irritation, at a time when I had other activities and interests to distract me. Whitchurch (2009) labels librarians as 'blended professionals', who are expected to take a more active role in the publication output of the university by publishing their own work.

Frequently, colleagues have told me they have nothing to say and so don't feel they can write, but I find that hard to believe! We all have experience and opinions, we undertake research as a matter of course in order to do our jobs. I'm sure you've run surveys amongst users, talked to research groups, made plans with other colleagues in meetings, but taking time out to *write* about it is something we rarely think of doing. Many librarians don't see this as part of their role or they may simply lack the confidence to get started. And yet, one of the best ways to connect with another person is to be able to empathize with them, to demonstrate that you've shared similar frustrations and encountered the same kinds of issues. If we want to engage with researchers, therefore, being able to talk about our own experiences as authors can be very valuable, explaining that we understand the process and identify with their fears and uncertainties. Of course, not everyone has either the time or inclination to produce lots of scholarly articles, but writing a small piece for your professional journal, writing a regular blog or writing a book review (see Tip 6.3) can give you some experience to talk about and may feel less intimidating.

Mercer (2011) believes that if librarians want to encourage open access publishing they can lead by example and publish in open access journals themselves. This is a good way to get started. Publications such as the *Journal of Information Literacy* and others are high-quality, peer-reviewed open access titles which can be used to demonstrate how the process works.

👍 Best for:

■ understanding the writing process and engaging with researchers
■ empathizing with the difficulties researchers encounter with writing
■ using your own personal experiences to give your advice real meaning.

★ Examples from practice

Writing a blog

A blog is just an online diary, a way of recording your thoughts and ideas on a (semi) regular basis. At whatever stage you are in your career, a blog can be a useful reflective tool, helping you to put your experiences into context. As well as giving you practice in writing for an audience, a blog related to your work serves the dual purpose of raising your profile within the community, hence becoming a useful addition to your CV too. Of course, you don't have to blog about work. If you have a hobby or interest which absorbs you, try blogging about that. You'll still learn a lot about writing and about considering your audience (who is reading my work, why?). You may also gain experience of dealing with feedback and criticism, all useful to draw upon when considering the writing process for researchers.

Helen Fallon from the University of Ireland Maynooth has run courses on writing for librarians for many years. She also maintains a very useful blog (Fallon, 2010a) which includes top tips from journal editors and top tips from published authors.

⚠ To think about

Getting started with writing is the hardest part. What can you write about? Think about the issues which are exercising you at present: can you find an aspect which keeps you awake at night that you want to explore? Conversely, what is it (about work) that makes you get up in the morning?

A good way to get started in writing is to find a colleague or friend to write with. Knowing that someone else is relying on you can be a great motivator and writing together is good for confidence boosting, too.

A few key dos and don'ts to getting started with writing for publication:

Do:

- ensure content is relevant, practical, interesting for your readers, tailored to your audience
- ensure it's understandable and clearly presented, using plain language
- try to convey something new or tackle an issue from a new perspective
- include any relevant data
- write about something you care about
- write at the right time – some topics are time-limited
- cite accurately and consistently – librarians have to get this right!
- keep copies of all versions of your work.

Don't:

- include unnecessary detail
- take too narrow a view or miss out key information from published works
- deal with something already well written about
- make unsubstantiated conclusions
- use jargon, acronyms, country-centric terms
- lose heart if your work is criticized; understand this is inevitable, take on board any comments and make it better
- rely on your memory, make notes about any decisions you make.

References and further reading

Fallon, H. (2010) And So It Is Written: supporting librarians on the path to publication, *Journal of Library Innovation*, **1** (1), 35–41.

Fallon, H. (2010a) *Academic Writing Librarians* blog. Available at: http://academicwritinglibrarian.blogspot.co.uk/. (Accessed 21.10.15)

Gordon, R. S. (2004) *The Librarian's Guide to Writing for Publication*, Lanham, MD, Scarecrow Press.

Mercer, H. (2011) Almost Halfway There: an analysis of the open access behaviors of academic librarians, *College & Research Libraries News*, September, 443–53.

Smallwood, C. (2009) Librarians as Writers, *American Libraries*, **40** (6/7), 54–7.

Smallwood, C. (2010) *Writing and Publishing: the librarian's handbook* (ALA Guides for the Busy Librarian), Chicago, American Library Association.

Whitchurch, C. (2009) The Rise of the Blended Professional in Higher Education: a comparison between the United Kingdom, Australia and the United States, *Higher Education*, **58** (3), 407–18.

Acknowledgements

Dos and don'ts repurposed from Gannon-Leary, P. and Bent, M. (2009), *Writing for Publication – Hints and Tips*, Newcastle University (internal document); Lucy Keating, Newcastle University

6.3 Write book reviews

WRITING FOR PUBLICATION can seem very daunting for people for whom it is a new experience. However, it's possible to build confidence and gain writing experience by starting with smaller, less ambitious pieces of writing, such as book reviews, which are normally quite short (500–750 words). One university library encourages all staff to volunteer to review books within the information sciences domain and to share their review with the rest of the team. This can be done on an informal basis, without ever contacting publishers and subsequently publishing the review. As well as enabling staff to develop their writing skills in a safe environment, this approach has the benefit of providing a current awareness service for the team, who are sharing knowledge about new book content in their field.

'I've learned a lot from reviewing books but it's not easy. For a start, you have to read the whole book, which can take ages, and then you have to somehow condense the whole thing into just a few paragraphs. It's great to see your name in print, though, and I was very pleased with the feedback I got from the editor.' (Librarian, UK university)

If staff become proficient in writing reviews they can then volunteer for more formal reviewing for journals or publishers. Book reviews can get you known to editors, as well as giving you a feel for writing in the discipline and on behalf of particular journals. At the very least, reviewers are usually given a free copy of the book, thus potentially creating a staff room collection of useful books.

Some journals and publishers send out calls for reviewers on a regular basis; you need to respond to these very quickly. Another approach is to contact the reviews editor of key journals and ask to be added to their list of reviewers. Book publishers may also be interested in soliciting reviews directly.

⫶ Best for:

- gaining an understanding of the process of writing for publication
- being able to speak from a position of knowledge
- keeping up to date with new developments in the profession
- getting your name known to editors.

★ Examples from practice

Some guidelines for writing book reviews

- set the book in context and show its significance in its field
- summarize the main theme, the stance taken by the author and their conclusions
- balance strengths and weaknesses of the book, drawing on examples to illustrate these.
- when making a negative point, make sure you can back it up and include a constructive comment on how it could be improved
- highlight any outstanding attributes of the book
- write clearly and factually and to capture the readers' interest
- avoid a chapter-by-chapter account of the themes and try a more integrated approach to the review
- indicate the likely readership
- treat the author of the book as you would wish to be treated yourself.

Book reviewing template
Use the following headings to structure your review:

- book title
- author(s) – affiliations/expertise
- place, publisher, edition, date

- first impressions – your initial reaction, presentation, organization
- intended audience – who is it for, relevance
- context and theme – scope and aims of the book (cover notes, introduction, contents list)
- sources – original research, references
- key strengths – include any outstanding attributes (including page numbers)
- weaknesses – include suggestions on improvements
- score – how would you rate the book.

⚠ To think about

Writing a book review commits you to reading the whole book, forming an opinion and putting that into writing. It is a serious time commitment, so ensure you have the support of your line manager before you commit to the process.

References and further reading

The University of Toledo has a short libguide on writing reviews:
Duhon, L. (2015) *How to Write a Book Review (for Librarians)*, http://libguides.utoledo.edu/write_a_review. (Accessed 21/7/15)

6.4 Become a researcher yourself

PRACTITIONER RESEARCH IS still rare (Schloegl and Stock, 2008; McCluskey, 2013) but it has value in several ways. As well as informing the practitioner community, the experience of being a researcher and writer is invaluable when engaging with other researchers. Evidence-based practice is common in many professions, but less so in library and information science. Being a researcher helps to empathize with other researchers; librarians are able to share common experiences and talking about personal, but recognizable, concerns can change the perceptions researchers have of librarians. Rather than seeing the library staff as separate, a 'support' or a service, they are more likely to be accepted as an equal. This can contribute to re-evaluating the identity assigned to librarians by themselves and others. In this situation it can be much easier to engage with the research population on the same level; having a personal research profile yourself can give one a more authoritative voice.

> *'If you have experience of the research process, you can assist research queries from the position of an "insider", whether it's about formatting a bibliography, publishing an article, sourcing a difficult document, or something as simple as arranging a visit to the British Library.' (Karen McAulay, Royal Conservatoire of Scotland)*

Not all practising librarians may feel able to conduct their own research. It's rare for library staff to have specific research time built into their work, although in fact many of us are undertaking routine research when we are investigating how best to meet user needs. This very practical research helps the library to develop but is rarely formally documented. Aligning your research with your work practice, identifying your library's priorities and strengths, can be a good way to get started.

It's important not to feel intimidated by the idea of becoming a researcher, but you don't need to produce a full-scale doctoral thesis as your first attempt. Start with a small piece of work. I have found that working with collaborators can be very supportive too, sharing and discussing ideas and approaches as well as making the workload more manageable.

Carol Tenopir, Chancellor's Professor at the School of Information Sciences, University of Tennessee, Knoxville, USA, has written a handy little booklet (Tenopir, 2015) which, as well as summarizing the issues faced by librarians engaged in their own research, includes a useful bibliography.

👍 Best for:

- empathizing with researchers about the research process
- demonstrating that you have experiences in common, so that you can speak with a more authoritative voice
- learning about the publication process from an author's perspective.

★ Examples from practice

My National Teaching Fellowship research

When planning my own research project for my National Teaching Fellowship, I initially felt very isolated. Although it was to constitute a major piece of work, it didn't fall within any formal structure so I had no natural supervisor, mentor or other advisers to call upon. My first task, therefore, was to identify some key experts with whom I could discuss my ideas and who could advise me on the suitability of my research question. Fortunately, the library community is very generous and I was able to solicit help from some of the leading authors in the field. In general, if you're researching in an area which also excites other researchers, it shouldn't be too difficult to identify one or more people prepared to act informally in this capacity and it's an extremely valuable validation of your work.

In addition, I lacked the practical knowledge and skills in research methodology to enable me to undertake quality research. As I work in a university I was fortunate to be able to go along to the training and development programme for our PhD students and I completed the whole of the research methods course alongside them. As well as providing me with the requisite skills to undertake my research, studying alongside other researchers helped me to situate myself within their community and to build relationships. At the same time, coincidentally, I was able to offer help and advice to my peers in terms of what else the library could offer.

Practitioner researcher

> *'I find I am often asked to talk about the research process, doing literature searches, etc. I'm able to draw upon my own experience here, but I think I also have a broader overview of supporting researchers as a result of being actively involved in research communities both within and, even more, beyond the institution. I keep an eye open for useful weblinks and archive them on Diigo, also updating our performing arts blog, http://Whittakerlive.blogspot.com on a daily basis, and e-mailing either the links directly or blogposts citing them, to our research community.' (Karen McAulay, Royal Conservatoire of Scotland)*

⚠ To think about

Not everyone feels able to, or is in a position to, contemplate joining the research community as a fully fledged researcher. Start small, look for ways in which your everyday activities relate to research. Research is about answering a research question, so in order to get started, think about what it is that excites you. What questions do you want to answer? Who can help you? Consider how you are going to build in communication and dissemination of your work right from the start. If you find this difficult or problematic, the chances are that other researchers will encounter the same issues and you can talk together about how to resolve them.

References and further reading

McBain, I., Culshaw, H. and Walkley Hall, L. (2013) Establishing a Culture of Research Practice in an Academic Library: an Australian case study, *Library Management*, **34** (6/7), 448–61.

McCluskey, C. (2013) Being an Embedded Research Librarian: supporting research by being a researcher, *Journal of Information Literacy*, **7** (2), 4–14.

Schloegl, C. and Stock, W. G. (2008) Practitioners and Academics as Authors and Readers: the case of LIS journals, *Journal of Documentation*, **64** (5), 643–66.

Tenopir, C. (2015) *Librarians Do Research Too*, Elsevier, http://libraryconnect. elsevier.com/sites/default/files/LC_Tenopir_Librarians_Do_Research_ Too.pdf.

Acknowledgements

Karen McAulay, Royal Conservatoire of Scotland.

SECTION 7

Collections

7.1 Develop modern research collections

ARE THE DAYS of the large research library, conscientiously collecting all resources just in case, a thing of the past? Will libraries of the future consist solely of virtual resources in some format given physical form by archives, or is there a place for more modern, actively acquired collections? If so, what does this mean and how might it be realized?

It is much less common these days for university libraries to identify a gap in the market, so to speak, and start to actively purchase and develop materials to develop modern research collections reflecting current research activity. However, if funds permit and especially if you can identify potential future specialisms focused on key research activity, there are opportunities for libraries to work with researchers to grow their own research collection in a more systematic and potentially marketable way. Not all modern resources are digital and even those which are may still be produced in formats which are unsustainable in the future. Building a collection on a specific research area is also an activity with which researchers themselves can engage, so it can have unanticipated benefits. However, making a case for funding for this kind of speculative acquisition is not easy; perhaps kick-starting with some external funding or taking a proposal to a university research committee might be a way of initiating such a project.

⚑ Best for:

- developing collections based on research interests
- enthusing and engaging researchers
- making your collections unique
- contributing to future research and knowledge
- enhancing the library's reputation both within and outside the organization.

★ Examples from practice

Liverpool University Library
Liverpool University Library's Special Collections include the Science Fiction Collections, which comprise Europe's largest catalogued collection of SF material, including the Science Fiction Foundation Collection and a wealth of literary archives.

European Library
One librarian from Europe describes her plans to develop a modern collection:

> 'Our university is very strong in researching into alternative energy and we in the library get a lot of queries about resources. It's a fast-moving field and there's such a lot of grey literature around – things like reports from the EC, conference papers, internal working documents, as well as the more mainstream books and scholarly articles. We decided that this would be a good opportunity to try to have our library recognized as a centre of excellence on these kinds of energy, so a few years ago we started to consciously start to search for and collect as much ephemeral material and grey literature as we could. It's still a work in progress, I think, so we haven't really marketed it properly yet, which is why I'd prefer to be anonymous for now. We are working on the best way to keep the collection fresh as well as build it up as a more historic collection of how alternative energy is changing. You only need to look at fracking and attitudes to that to see what I mean. But it's really interesting and some of the researchers have become quite excited about what we are trying to do and are starting to bring us their own material, maybe the kinds of things they'd have just kept in their offices in the past. I think they feel quite proud to be able to say to colleagues elsewhere that we have such a comprehensive collection . . . and it's made quite a difference to our relationship with them as a group too. We are friends and colleagues and we have a common interest to talk about. It's not all been easy, though; to begin with I had to convince other library staff it was a good idea and then we had to bid for some extra budget – we were lucky that a fund was available and gave us a small grant. So, yes, it's been good and I do feel proud of what we've achieved so far.'
> (European librarian)

Historic Computing Collection
Computing science is a relatively young discipline but in the last 70 years computers have transformed our lives. Newcastle University is fortunate to host one of the pre-eminent scholars from the early days of the subject and, recognizing this, library staff have been working with him to catalogue his papers, which include fascinating insights into the development of the first computers and computing companies. The collection comprises personal papers, letters, notes, meeting reports and print-outs of e-mails, along with some unique reports of legal decisions from the early days of computing history and

first editions of early texts. Alongside this, based on his advice and expertise, a collection of historical computing books is being developed. It includes early programming textbooks that would normally have been withdrawn from stock, as well as modern books on the history of the subject. Although not widely used at present, it has the potential to be a valuable and unique future special collection.

⚠ To think about

What are the high-profile research activities within your organization? Are there specialisms which could be exploited so that you can start to initiate the development of a modern special collection? Make sure they are long-term research activities.

Before embarking on such a project, think about how it will be funded and maintained.

Liaising with the research community to get them on board with such a project right from the start will help, too.

7.2 Promote special collections as a unique selling point

MANY UNIVERSITY LIBRARIES maintain archives and special collections, often developed organically, dependent on philanthropic donation from local families and businesses, the library seen as a secure location to preserve historic documents. Such collections can be the mainstay of arts and humanities departments, providing a rich source of original research material and attracting scholars from far and wide. As digital resources have become more ubiquitous, the uniqueness of a library's special collections can help to differentiate research libraries. Not every library can rival the Bodleian Library in Oxford for the range and value of its archives, but there is much that can be done to raise the profile of such material and to use it as a distinctive identifier for the library.

Most special collections teams are skilled at mounting exhibitions to promote key aspects of the collection. In order to attract interest from the university community and the wider public such displays need to be linked to current events (the centenary of World War 1 is a good example) or to current research interests in the organization. Although it is, of course, valuable to promote any newly acquired material, marketing and potential funding bids are much easier if the relevance to researchers can be clearly demonstrated. Librarians who engage with researchers regularly need to build up their awareness of the resources in the archives, so that they are able to make linkages between the current research and the older material.

Although libraries will, and should, continue to build up their archive collections opportunistically, there is also a case to be made for identifying potential future special collections and actively acquiring resources whilst they are still relatively new. The emergence of new disciplines and recognition of current key scholars and public figures are examples of this kind of opening. Rather than wait for the material to be donated as part of an estate, working with potential living donors can provide a much richer collection. Special collections do not need to be old, they just need to be distinctive.

👍 Best for:

■ engaging researchers with archives
■ developing and exploiting unique collections
■ raising awareness of potential sources for new research projects.

★ Examples from practice

Linking old and new material

Looking for ways to promote archive material to their research community, one university library is highlighting relevant historic material alongside modern resources within their subject library guides. Tailoring links in this way breaks down an amorphous collection into pertinent, easily digestible chunks and has generated interest from unexpected quarters.

> 'One of the engineers saw that we have some photos of when their building was first built, with some of the original equipment, and now they've decided to use them along with some properly produced boards on the history of engineering here as part of the design of their new building. In fact, they've even asked if we will work with them on some kind of interactive digital display in their reception area, which is really exciting for us. It's such a great way to raise our profile with the students, too.' (UK university librarian)

Durham University Library

The library at Durham University in the UK contains a wealth of treasures from the past. In recent years the library has hosted some exciting exhibitions, showcasing some of the rare materials from the archives. In 2015, 'Magna Carta and the changing face of revolt', an exhibition to mark the 800th anniversary of the charter, was extremely popular with scholars and the general public. The unique charter, on loan from the collections of Durham Cathedral, was shown alongside objects from the library's collections and loans from other regional and national museums and libraries. The University ran a programme of activities and events alongside the exhibition, from public lectures and family activities, to hands-on workshops and re-enactment events. Such an event relies heavily on the expertise of researchers and scholars to bring the material to life and is an excellent example of library staff working in collaboration with the research community to publicize resources.

⚠ To think about

How much do your researchers know about the material currently held in your special collections? In fact, if you don't work in that section of the library yourself, how much do you know? In particular, if you work with scientists and engineers, how might you raise their awareness of these resources?

Even though historical material may not be relevant to current research projects, many researchers are interested in the history of their discipline – how many biologists, for example, would not be excited to touch a first edition of Darwin's *On the Origin of Species*?

Look for anniversaries coming along which might generate interest amongst your scholars and try to identify relevant materials to link to these. Make sure you are aware of any conferences, public lectures and other activities with which researchers might be engaged and think of ways to become involved. For example, how about providing some digital images of special collections resources to create a set of welcome slides whilst the audience settles down for a keynote?

Acknowledgements
Newcastle University Library.

7.3 Explore alternative document delivery models

THE ACCEPTED MODEL of a large research library in the past has usually been to develop a deep, comprehensive collection of resources, originally in printed form, to meet the majority of the needs of their researchers. However, due to the sheer amount of information as well as the diversification of format, this model is breaking down in all but a few libraries, to be replaced by a more pragmatic approach. Librarians today rarely have sufficient funding to second-guess demand and to purchase resources just in case. Instead, an effective just-in-time document delivery process needs to be available. In the current higher education climate, we need to demonstrate that our service is designed to meet user needs.

National libraries, such as the British Library, underpin interlibrary loan (ILL) services, lending monographs and providing digital copies of articles. Although not free, this service is much more cost effective for libraries with limited budgets. Some costs can also be passed to researchers to mitigate the effect on the budget.

An alternative approach to providing books, which is growing in popularity, is the Patron Driven Acquisition (PDA) model. This kind of books-on-demand service actively encourages individual library users to suggest books for purchase and for many books can be comparable in costs to paying for an external ILL service.

In a similar vein, the PDA model can be extended to journal articles and grey literature by setting up a fund to enable researchers to purchase article downloads direct from publishers. To be cost effective, it is likely that such a service will need mediation from library staff, as researchers are often unsuccessful at discovering their local library holdings and may inadvertently order resources that the library already owns. This can happen when researchers are away from the organization and 'just Google for information' or, increasingly commonly, because they expect everything to be electronic and miss print holdings. However, properly managed, this kind of download on demand can be invaluable, especially for researchers working in niche or newly emerging fields.

👍 Best for:

- maximizing access to research resources
- using limited budgets effectively.

★ Examples from practice

PDA for e-books at Newcastle University

Newcastle University Library in the UK implemented a patron-led e-book acquisition service in February 2010, working with the company EBL. Initially a pilot in response to undergraduate demand for more textbooks, it is now an accepted service with an annual spend of over £150,000. The service is available to all library users, not just researchers, and enables either short-term access to an e-book (a loan) or permanent purchase. Details of all available e-books have been loaded into the library system, and so are discoverable by users, and data can be obtained on both resources and users. In 2012, the system processed approximately 11,000 loans and 500 purchases, predominantly for undergraduate and masters students, although it is increasingly being used by researchers too.

'All of these loans that have been provided have been really useful for me, it should be something done more often!' (Research student)

Books on Time at Newcastle University, UK

Following on from the success of the EBL project, Newcastle University Library extended the PDA model to printed book recommendations in 2011/12. Funded from overdue charges, this on-demand service encourages both staff and students to suggest print materials, although e-books not available via EBL are also put forward through the system. In its first year, 700 titles were purchased.

⚠ To think about

Funding a PDA service adequately is essential to its success. If you don't have a large budget, think of ways in which expectations can be managed. Can recommendations be restricted to the research community? If so, it can be marketed as being provided specifically for researchers.

References and further reading

Blummer, B. and Kenton, J. (2012) Best Practices for Integrating E-books in Academic Libraries: a literature review from 2005 to present, *Collection Management*, **37** (2), 65–97.
Taylor-Roe, J. (2014) *Introducing PDA into an Academic Library: natural evolution or reckless abandon?*, PowerPoint, http://library.bcu.ac.uk/squaring/taylorroe.pdf. (Accessed 5.5.15)

Acknowledgements

Newcastle University Library.

7.4 Involve researchers in enhancing research monograph collections

AS BUDGETS FOR library resources have become tighter and the emphasis on the student experience and national league tables increases, many libraries have inevitably had to focus attention on undergraduate reading lists and high-demand items, often to the detriment of the more holistic research collections of the past. High-quality interlibrary loan services, shared access schemes and the development of e-book collections serve to bridge the gap for many researchers and can be sufficient for the majority. Perhaps the research library of the past, with its rich, deep and varied print collections, is no longer necessary. Certainly, fewer librarians now spend time developing their print collections by buying material just in case.

However, it's clear when talking to researchers that they do still value having access to a substantial print collection, not least because it is visible evidence of a library of which they can be proud. Not everything is available electronically, especially in the arts and humanities disciplines, and the serendipitous aspect of browsing through a collection of print books or indeed through an individual printed book is difficult to replicate virtually.

If we want to maintain, or indeed continue to develop, our research collections, we need to find imaginative ways to do so, balancing print and electronic and harnessing the expertise of researchers to ensure that money is invested wisely. Involving researchers in developing the research monograph collection has the dual benefit of engaging them actively with the library and ensuring that the collection reflects current research interests. Being aware of new research staff and their interests is a simple way to do this. You might invite new researchers to comment on the section of library stock that is relevant to their research, solicit their advice on out-of-date material and actively encourage recommendations to enhance the collection. If you attend research meetings, remember to mention collection development and management, with the expectation that scholars will have a vested interest in assisting you to strengthen the library's offering in their discipline. In some universities, library 'champions' within the research community have been identified, with a remit to advise library staff on relevant materials.

⭕ Best for:

- developing research monograph collections
- actively engaging researchers with the library
- ensuring that your research collections mirror the research interests of the organization.

★ Examples from practice

Read for Research

The library at the City University London, UK, operates a scheme called Read for Research. Essentially a patron-driven acquisition scheme, it encourages research and post-doctoral students and staff to recommend titles for purchase via a web form. What makes this scheme different from other PDA schemes is that books requested via the Read for Research scheme are tagged on the library catalogue and the library has created a 'reading list' of titles ordered so far. It is felt that by targeting this at researchers, the resulting list demonstrates the breadth and diversity of research taking place across the university. The scheme has been very popular with researchers, costing approx. £20,000 in its first year of operation (2013).

'The popularity has meant that we have been able to continue the scheme since with the support of our Library Leadership Team. I have found it a great way to engage with researchers and have an insight into their research topics. I also think it makes researchers feel valued and feel that their research is important to the University. One of our research students has created her own #readforresearch reading list on her blog and one of our academic colleagues has created a Read for Research Community on Mendeley. It has also helped Library Services to support the University strategy and focus on building up research collections. We also engage with students on social media #readforresearch and students mention the titles they have recommended.' (Diane Bell, City University London)

Researchers reviewing the collection

One university library in Australia has developed a strategy for targeting high-profile research groups and inviting them to actively work with the library to develop the research collection in their subject area.

'We started by simply providing a print-out of the books within a small shelfmark range and taking it along to a research group meeting. It generated immediate discussion amongst the group as they commented on the value of some of the older materials and started to identify gaps. From that, a couple of them volunteered to come into the library to look at the books more closely and to start to look for material to enhance the collection. Now they've taken on a role of actively suggesting new titles when they see them.' (Australian librarian)

⚠ To think about

Before embarking on a campaign to engage researchers with developing collections, funding to support such an initiative must be in place, so that you can manage expectations sensibly.

'Once they got going, the researchers got very enthusiastic about suggesting new titles and we realized we should have set a specific budget to work within. Now we say we have x dollars to invest in developing this part of the collection and that helps them to not go too crazy.' (Australian librarian)

References and further reading

Bell, D. (2015) Read for Research blogpost, *Citylibresearchers blog*, https://citylibresearchers.wordpress.com/2015/04/24/read-for-research-campaign-at-city-university-london-library. (Accessed 25.4.15)

Acknowledgements
Diane Bell, City University London.

7.5 Exploit the modern collection

LARGE RESEARCH LIBRARIES often rely on researchers using their catalogue or discovery system to find the resources they need. However, as researchers become accustomed to new resources being available digitally, they may be less inclined to burrow into printed materials, even though these are very visible reminders of what libraries are about. Unless we can devise creative ways of raising the profile of our printed materials, some libraries may run the risk of jeopardizing the depth of their research collections in favour of undergraduate texts supplemented by e-books. This may be inevitable eventually, but libraries are still a treasure trove of undiscovered delights for researchers and it is the librarian's responsibility to maximize their use.

There are some imaginative ways of exploiting the collection and ensuring that it is better used. Hansson and Johannesson (2013) suggest cataloguing book chapters in library catalogues to raise their visibility, perhaps working with publishers to extract the relevant metadata to enable this to happen. Modern discovery systems also allow increased functionality in searching the collections.

It is much easier nowadays to digitize out-of-copyright material and libraries around the world are taking advantage of this. As well as large-scale national projects, individual libraries are working hard to identify the unique materials in their collections and to make them available.

A simpler approach is to focus on exhibitions and displays, both physical and virtual. An exhibition might be linked to a research activity in a university, to a special event in the region or a notable anniversary. At Newcastle University Library, UK, for example, exhibitions have been mounted to mark the anniversary of the Titanic, Alan Turing's anniversary (and film) and Darwin's anniversary, as well as the local iVamos festival.

Regarding the institutional repository as part of the library collection and marketing it as such can also be beneficial in raising awareness of the range of formats in which material is available.

🖒 Best for:
- raising the profile of library resources
- maximizing the use of the library collections.

★ Examples from practice

Brunel Library Book Stop

Staff at Brunel University Library, UK, recognized that high use of undergraduate texts was masking hidden collections on the shelves that are rarely used, but still might hold an appeal for other readers. Borrowing ideas from retail, the Book Stop was born. In essence, the Book Stop is simply a display of little-used books from the collection, relying on topical issues to theme displays and presenting them in an attractive and light-hearted way.

> The aim of the Book Stop was therefore to promote such texts to a wider audience, such as students from other courses, staff and other borrowers. This also supported our ongoing development of the role of the library on campus, reaching out to staff and students and changing the tone of our relationship with them. The Book Stop has provided a different way of connecting with this audience, presenting collections in a more light-hearted way, using a topical approach that fits with engagement on social media.'
>
> McPhie and Wannerton, 2014, 40

Spotlight pages

At University College Dublin, Ireland, LibGuides have been used to create Spotlight pages on different topics, enabling relevant library resources to be highlighted to the research community. An example is shown in Figure 7.1. UCD Library Spotlight Guides are available at http://libguides.ucd.ie/spotlight.

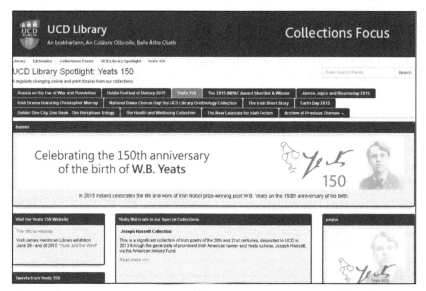

Figure 7.1 *Example of University College Dublin Spotlight pages (reproduced with permission)*

⚠ To think about

If the aim of mounting displays of hidden, current stock is to encourage use, then it needs to be accessible and able to be borrowed. The exhibition must therefore be planned to change and update regularly, to keep it fresh and interesting. This can be challenging, as it's much less easy to manage a changing display than a static one.

References and further reading

Hansson, J. and Johannesson, K. (2013) Librarians' Views of Academic Library Support for Scholarly Publishing: an every-day perspective, *Journal of Academic Librarianship*, **39** (3), 232–40.
McPhie, J. and Wannerton, R. (2014) Marketing Our Collections, *SCONUL Focus*, **61**, 39–41, www.sconul.ac.uk/page/focus-61. (Accessed 8.5.15)

7.6 Explore access to shared research collections

A S BUDGETS IN many university libraries are reduced in size, and demands for study space to accommodate rising undergraduate numbers escalate, the inevitable outcome is a reduction in the size of the physical library collection. In the science disciplines this is a relatively minor concern, as researchers rely in the main on journal literature, much of which is available in digital form. In arts and humanities, however, scholars still demand access to printed material, both journals and research monographs, and can perceive the emphasis on information or learning commons as a negative development. Librarians need to balance the needs of their large undergraduate customer base with those of their researchers by ensuring quick and easy access to research resources.

Wealthy institutions can expand library space or develop off-site stores to house less well used material and these solutions work well in several university libraries, such as Oxford, Manchester and Newcastle in the UK and Harvard and Florida State in the USA. It's important to ensure that there is a rapid retrieval service in place if off-site storage is to be successful.

An alternative to individual off-site storage is to collaborate with nearby libraries to share a storage facility. Care must be taken to agree percentages of space, retrieval mechanisms and procedures for the participating libraries to have equal access to the shared stock.

🖒 Best for:

- ▪ maximizing access to research collections
- ▪ making the most of limited storage space
- ▪ protecting less well used material from withdrawal.

★ Examples from practice

The UK Research Reserve (UKRR)
The UK Research Reserve is a shared service initiative between the British Library and UK higher education libraries, aiming to ensure that printed copies of journals are preserved indefinitely, but at the same time minimizing duplication and so freeing up space in many libraries. At least three copies of journal titles are held in collections around the UK, the primary copy at the British Library with two back-up copies at member libraries. Other libraries can dispose of duplicate copies, secure in the knowledge that they have quick access to the centrally held material via the interlibrary loan service maintained by the BL.

SCONUL Access Scheme, UK
An alternative to document delivery via interlibrary loan is to allow researchers access to all the major research collections in the country and this is what the SCONUL Access Scheme achieves. SCONUL Access is a reciprocal scheme which allows researchers to borrow or use books and journals at other libraries which belong to the scheme. The scheme covers most of the university libraries in the UK and Ireland.

CAVAL
In Australia, CAVAL is a consortium of academic libraries, based in Melbourne, which operate the CARM Centre, demonstrating that 'variant models for storage configurations and collection ownership can co-exist and meet the differing needs of member libraries within one facility' (Jilovsky and Genoni, 2014). The need for off-site storage and the terms and conditions under which member libraries are willing to accept it differ widely, but the scheme has been successful.

⚠ To think about
If there are no formal national or local collaboration schemes in place near you, it is still possible to collaborate with colleagues at neighbouring institutions on an informal basis. Joint development of research collections, consulting over purchase of printed materials so that collections complement rather than duplicate each other, can be very successful, especially for smaller libraries.

   If you plan to share a storage facility be very clear whether the sharing relates purely to the space or whether it will also be possible to share the stock.

References and further reading
Harvard Depository. Available at: http://hul.harvard.edu/hd. (Accessed 21.10.15)

Jilovsky, C. and Genoni, P. (2014) Shared Collections to Shared Storage: the CARM1 and CARM2 print repositories, *Library Management*, **35** (1/2), 2–14.

SCONUL Access. Available at: www.sconul.ac.uk/page/about-sconul-access-0.(Accessed 18.10.15)

SECTION 8

Specific interventions in the research process or lifecycle

8.1 Identifying opportunities in research workflows (see also Tip 3.6)

TO ENGAGE EFFECTIVELY with researchers we need to understand who they are and what they do and, particularly, *when* they are doing it and what their issues and concerns are. By getting involved at all stages of the research workflow and looking for opportunities to participate, we will be better able to demonstrate value.

In *A Slice of Research Life* Kroll and Forsman (2010) surveyed researchers in four universities in the USA and concluded that there are eight topics with associated tasks which would benefit from the use of information within the research lifecycle:

1 Learning about grant funding opportunities. The library may have a role in co-ordinating information from different sources and publicizing it to researchers.
2 Issues surrounding intellectual property and exploiting commercial value. This need varies between disciplines but a role for the library might be identified with respect to copyright, licensing and referral.
3 Finding potential collaborators, whether multi- or cross-disciplinary or even cross-organization. It's certainly true that in the sciences there are fewer individual researchers and many more working in teams.
4 Management and storage of documents and datasets. The rapid developments in technology make it more difficult to retrieve older material, with researchers expressing concern for the safety of work recorded on already outdated media or using obsolete software. Cloud services can help but this still requires the development of metadata to organize the materials.
5 Analysing text and datasets.
6 Improving information retrieval and management skills. This is often low on a researcher's priorities. Researchers live by 'satisficing' and will

often use tools and services which are fast and easy if not optimal.

7   Citing references, using bibliographical management tools.

8   Choosing where to publish, understanding the difference between pre- and post-prints in making work open access.

These topics and tasks can be a useful starting point to better understand research workflow processes and hence when to devise lifecycle interventions.

👍 Best for:

- planning interventions in the research lifecycle
- demonstrating value through timely interventions
- identifying opportunities to participate.

★ Examples from practice

University of Westminster

Consultants working for the University of Westminster in the UK identified a set of 'information and data management pain points' spread throughout the research lifecycle:

- Research administration and governance
- Collaboration
- Marketing and profile raising
- Research outputs management

Enright, 2015

This project resulted in the design of a virtual research environment structured around these key pain points.

Research workflows meetings

Library staff at Newcastle University in the UK were chatting to researchers after a library workshop and listening to them sharing ideas on some of the tools they used in their research. It was clear that all those participating in the discussion were gaining a lot from the sharing of experiences and the idea of the Research Workflows Community of Practice was born. The concept is a mixture of face-to-face meetings and a virtual space in which to share additional information. Two researchers agreed to initiate the first meeting and library staff help with the administration (booking rooms, sending invitations, marketing) to provide some consistency and permanence. The library also provides refreshments, but the meeting itself is planned and led by the researchers themselves. After the first meeting staff from the IT service also offered help to set up the virtual part of the community.

Entitled 'Research Workflows: tools, tasks and techniques', the first meeting was advertised like this:

> Do you ever wonder if you're accomplishing research tasks in the most effective way? Are other researchers using tools you don't know about, or have you discovered an amazing new app you'd like to share? What techniques and platforms are out there which might help you in your research life? We invite you to join an informal community of practice for researchers from all disciplines and at all different stages of the research lifecycle to get together to share experiences and ideas on tools and techniques that will help in our workflow.

> It's an experiment which we hope will work and will provide a useful forum to share tips and ideas, summarize discussions from face to face meetings and add links to information and resources which others might find useful. All members of the community can contribute, so, although staff from the Library and ISS will help keep it fresh, it's really up to you!

The first meeting was very successful, with researchers encouraged to contribute five-minute informal talks about some tool or technique they found useful and to suggest topics for future meetings. The topics suggested are wide-ranging, including, for example: document collaboration, project management, note taking, using tags, reference management, research tools, cloud services, task management, mind maps, statistical techniques and much more. To date, only two meetings have taken place, but more are planned.

⚠ To think about

Asking researchers what they think are key issues and barriers within their daily workflows can be a good starting point, but it can be helpful to set this in a wider context than the library. Many researchers have a fairly limited perception of the potential opportunities for engaging with librarians – asking what they want from the library will elicit common themes around access to resources and spaces but they may not be aware of what else might be possible. Starting a broader, more open conversation without a specific library focus can tease out less obvious openings for engagement.

References and further reading

Enright, S. (2015) Supporting Researchers with a Research Information Management Platform, *SCONUL Focus*, **63**, 24–33.

Kroll, S. and Forsman, R. (2010) *A Slice of Research Life: information support for research in the United States*, www.oclc.org/content/dam/research/publications/library/2010/2010-15.pdf. (Accessed 4.1.16)

8.2 Make early contact with the research community

UNLESS YOU KNOW and understand the research community with which you are working, it's unlikely that you will have a very effective relationship. However, the community may be large and diverse and, certainly initially, it can be daunting to find ways in which to connect. Liaising is time-consuming. You need to make time to listen, to talk, to record what you learn and to think about how to respond.

Making the first contact is crucial. Perhaps you can obtain a regular listing of newly appointed research staff from your HR department and send a tailored welcome package to each new member of research staff, inviting them for a personalized introduction to the library.

If numbers seem overwhelming, how about setting up a regular monthly introductory meeting for all new research staff. Maybe the organization has a central welcome for new staff where the library can have a presence. The important thing is to be proactive in seeking out new research staff, regularly and consistently.

If you yourself are new to the role, try to identify key researchers, perhaps chairs of research groups or principal investigators and propose a meeting. Ensure that you attend the meeting with a clear purpose – what will the outcome be for you both? – and with something to offer. It's not sufficient to have a woolly aim such as 'I'm hoping to find out what you need from the library'; try to be more specific – 'I want to discuss your research to help me plan what new journals we might need' or 'Can we talk about your research group's recent publications and how we might improve the number of open access papers?'.

Research administrators can also be invaluable allies. Invite them to the library and show them around. Explain how they can use the library for personal use and chat about your plans for engaging with the researchers in their section. Ask their advice – which researchers are most likely to be receptive to you, what methods of communication will work best? Suggest they add you onto relevant mailing lists and invite you to research meetings in the department; ask if they can send papers of meetings even if you can't attend in person.

We recognize that building relationships with researchers is critical and we try to ensure that we are involved in their world.

Hall, 2015

👍 Best for:

- increasing knowledge of the research community
- building relationships
- promoting the library effectively.

★ Examples from practice

An example of a welcome letter/e-mail

Dear Dr xxx

As you're a new member of staff here at xxx University, I'd like to welcome you to the University Library on behalf of the Library Liaison team. My name is xxx and I'm the Liaison Librarian for your School; xxx is the Liaison Library Assistant for the School. If you have time, we'd be delighted to arrange a time to meet with you and explain in more detail how the Library works and what we can do to facilitate your teaching and research. Just e-mail me at xxx with some times which are convenient for you and we can set up a meeting.

In the meantime, you may wish to explore the Library's web pages:

The Information for Academic Staff section has some general information as well as going into more detail about support for teaching and research. [URL]

The Subject Guides are a tailored set of web pages bringing together key information resources for your subject. [URL]

The Research pages link to information on different aspects of the research process

I hope you find these helpful and I look forward to meeting you. [URL]

Tours for research administrators

One UK university library recently organized some library tours for administrative, clerical and technical staff in the university. The tours were advertised on the library web pages and by e-mail to all departments and were run every week during the summer vacation. A booklet was printed to accompany the visits, with details of borrowing rights and also highlighting resources such as newspapers, maps, films, literature, IT skills books and even some genealogy resources which all staff might find interesting. The tours included a general look around the library, with explanations of how it works for both staff and students.

'I found the tours a great way to build relationships with the staff, many of whom had never been in the library because they thought it wasn't for them. Now it's much easier to get help from some of them and one lady in particular now makes sure I'm included in everything the researchers in her area do. It's made a real difference and we will definitely be doing it again.' (UK librarian)

Contacting postgraduate (PGR) students

One UK university library makes a point of e-mailing every new postgraduate student directly:

'Although we always run workshops as part of the training programmes for the postgraduate students, we know they don't all come and we were worried that it was the people who didn't come who might need the most help. We decided to e-mail every postgraduate student directly, rather than passing messages through the graduate school office, to see if that would help. We were able to get lists of all the new PGRs in each Faculty so we tailored the messages by Faculty and sent them out a few weeks after the start of term, when we thought most of the students would have arrived. We did the same thing for the intakes in January and May. The e-mail just welcomes them to the library and briefly explains what we can do, what the workshops will do for them and how to get in touch. We've definitely had more folks sign up this year and we've also seen an increase in individual contacts, so we think that a more personal touch has helped.' (UK librarian)

Cake for questions

We can be very dismissive of the traditional approach of hanging around the coffee bar in the hope of engaging with researchers, but in practice this simple approach can be very effective:

'I used the simple but effective ruse of offering a piece of cake in exchange for sharing with me any tips (or problems) the research team had on a particular topic that I was putting together a short training session about (in this case, information management/keeping organized during a literature review). This really worked – lots of people were forthcoming and it helped tailor my session. A lot of the research team seem to be motivated by cake! Also I think I was acknowledging that they had more experience in conducting literature reviews than I had (although I've done a lot more searching) and they understood that I genuinely wanted to learn from their experiences, good and bad.' (Melanie Gee, Sheffield Hallam University)

⚠ To think about

Having something specific to engage interest always helps when building relationships. Make sure you do some research beforehand to find out about the people you will be meeting. Check out their area of research and look to see how well it is resourced in the library. If they are new staff, ask where they have come from and whether there were particular aspects of their previous library experiences they are hoping to find here. This gives you the opportunity to highlight what you can offer and to explain how you hope the relationship will develop. You may not be able to replicate their previous experiences, or even provide the same resources, but having an open discussion from the start will help identify strengths and weaknesses and may enable you to better manage their expectations.

References and further reading

Hall, B. (2015) Getting to Know our Researchers and Understanding their Needs, *SCONUL Focus*, **63**, 45–7.

8.3 Attend research group meetings (see also Tips 4.1 and 5.7)

WHEREVER POSSIBLE, it helps if library staff are perceived by researchers as part of the project rather than outside it. This can be difficult to achieve. Researchers may not see the need to have a librarian as part of the team; librarians may feel they have little to offer. However, even if you feel that you will be playing a minor role in the whole project, if you can afford the time, it can be well worth attending a research group meeting, especially where they will be discussing the initial approaches, planning the project and thinking about the systematic review. In order to do this, it is necessary to monitor research activity very closely, attending any regular meetings to discuss new research plans, chatting informally to individuals about their current and future work and not being diffident about asking questions. Most researchers are passionate about their work and will be happy to tell you more. Perhaps you can offer to meet the lead researcher to discuss the project. You might ask if someone could explain the research area to you in layman's terms, as this often forces the research group to clarify their research question. The better you understand the research area and the group the easier it will be to work with them.

'I try to go to research meetings whenever I can, it's about being opportunistic, that personal contact often means you can give a quick response. I also try to take the initiative and look for every chance I can to explain what it is I do.' (Helen Young, Loughborough University)

'Get yourself onto the research committees and provide a regular update about services and any upcoming training sessions.' (Nicola Foxlee, University of Queensland, Australia)

In a large organization, one librarian may be liaising with many research groups across a wide range of discipline areas and it simply isn't practical to expect to be involved in every one to the same degree. In such situations maybe the best you can aim for is a phone conversation or perhaps an e-mail exchange. What is important, however, is to try to keep a record of such interactions, so that, however slim they might be, you can build on them to gradually develop a clearer picture of the research and to identify opportunities to engage with it.

👍 Best for:

- understanding what researchers are doing
- building relationships with researchers
- making sure researchers are aware of new developments in the library.

★ Examples from practice

Database of researchers

One library team keeps a joint database to record interactions with researchers, detailing the names of the staff and their roles, the broad research topic and any details of the research, as well as logging contacts between the researchers and library staff.

If you have the luxury of time and the opportunity for more interaction you can also note, for example, what publication output they are aiming for, their timescale, what they know about this subject area already, whether they have done any previous work on this topic and whether they have already identified some key publications that should be included in the final output. This kind of detail will help to jog your memory next time you attend a meeting and is also invaluable when passing information to other colleagues in the library.

Sheffield Hallam University, UK

Melanie Gee's experience of being embedded into the research community has given her easy access to research meetings, but her ideas can be easily adapted to different situations:

'I secured a regular slot in the research centre staff meetings and sub-centre ('theme') meetings, and made sure I had something to say at each one. Examples of how I used this 10-15 minutes slot included:

- *explaining how to get to the JCR impact factor data (and what it meant)*
- *using our institutional open access repository (SHURA) and what stats can be pulled from it*

- *explaining the different types of intellectual property rights and how they were relevant to the researchers (I gained this knowledge from a previous job)*
- *asking for what they were interested in receiving training on, and (later) pitching the lunchtime training sessions I had developed*
- *recent changes in database interfaces, RefWorks, etc.*
- *providing an overview of the sort of work (information enquiries, literature searching, 1:1 training) I had performed to date since joining the research centre.*

Similarly, I would send regular e-mails to the centre researchers and the wider research community in the faculty, passing on important updates to databases, pertinent information about Journal Impact Factors, tips for using RefWorks, etc., and circulating any training materials that I had produced. As I was establishing myself in the research centre, I would try to find a reason (or excuse!) to e-mail every few weeks – just to remind the staff that I was around, and there to help.' (Melanie Gee, Sheffield Hallam University)

⚠ To think about

Whilst this approach can work well in a small organization, it is much more difficult to achieve in a large university setting, where sheer numbers of researchers and variety of research areas preclude such a detailed level of knowledge. Nevertheless, it is an extremely valuable approach, so rather than dismissing it out of hand, consider if there are aspects of the tactic which will apply in your own circumstances.

'Having a regular slot on the agenda of staff meetings has helped to establish me as one of the "team" rather than "just" a service. Also I found that each time I sent out an e-mail it would prompt one or two people to "remember" that I was there and they would get in touch, often asking for help about something completely unrelated (but still in my remit) or even for input to a bigger project.' (Melanie Gee, Sheffield Hallam University)

Be wary of raising expectations that you may not be able to meet.

Acknowledgements

Helen Young, Loughborough University; Melanie Gee, Sheffield Hallam University.

8.4 Communicate your message effectively

COMMUNICATION IS A two way process. Once you understand the research community with which you want to engage, the next step is to think about the messages you want to convey and how you might accomplish this. Whole books have been written about marketing and publicizing libraries. Ned Potter's excellent book (2012) addresses issues such as the library brand, marketing with social media and new technologies and marketing special collections, amongst many other key issues. Ned describes seven key concepts to bear in mind:

1   *Everyone is trying to get from A to B – we have to show them how we'll help them to get there quickly and more successfully.* This applies most particularly to researchers, who may not visit the library regularly.
2   *Market the service, not the product, market the benefits not the features.* Think about the services and benefits you wish to promote to the research community.
3   *Market what they (our users) value but continue to do what we (as providers) value.* Think about how you might apply this idea to the messages you wish to convey.
4   *Market personality.* You and your colleagues are the features that make your library unique for your researchers, think about how you will project your own personality into interactions with researchers. The personal touch is important.
5   *Never, ever market something you can't deliver.* Don't make promises you can't keep. In very practical terms, an example of this might be trialling a resource which you know you can't afford to buy – is this good practice, making sure you know what is important for the research community, or does it just raise expectations you can't meet?
6   *Create and market different value propositions for different groups.* In essence, by focusing our attention on the research community, this concept may already have been met. However, even within the research community there are differences – remember the seven ages model in Tip 3.2. Consider how you might differentiate messages to make them more attractive for different groups of researchers.
7   *Understand the cost curve and how it applies to libraries.* Researchers need to understand that our services have a worth and that the value they get out of using them exceeds the effort they have to put in to use them. (Potter, 2012)

The first consideration is to identify the audience and to decide if one size fits all or if different groups of researchers will benefit from differentiated messages. Groups may be distinguished by level and experience/seniority or by discipline. Next, attention needs to be given to the mode of delivery and this may be dependent on the message you wish to convey, as well as the group it is aimed at. Blanket e-mails are rarely as effective as more targeted approaches but the more tailored you make the message, the more time-consuming it will be to deliver. Mailmerge e-mail letters can offer a compromise if you have a small and fairly stable audience, as they will allow some personalization. Alternatively, enlisting the help of research administrators and programme leaders can assist in reaching specific cohorts of postgraduate students. More libraries now use social media tools such as Facebook and Twitter to connect with users and a blog for researchers can be a useful strategy. Posters and leaflets to distribute around the organization shouldn't be dismissed and probably most effective of all is delivering your message face to face.

👍 Best for:

- ensuring your approach is tailored and relevant to your audience
- getting the message about the library to researchers.

★ Examples from practice

University of Northampton, UK

The University of Northampton Library, in collaboration with the Graduate School and the Research and Strategic Bidding Office, have created a Research Support Hub. This is a blog, which is promoted as a one-stop shop for all news, events and information relevant to Northampton researchers.

> 'It gives us somewhere to put out latest news as well as tips on information and resources.'
> (Miggie Pickton, University of Northampton)

⚠ To think about

What methods do you currently use to communicate with users? Are these the most effective approaches for liaising with researchers? Are there other sections of the organization with whom you can collaborate to offer a more coherent approach?

References and further reading

Pickton, M. (2015) Research Support Hub,
    http://Researchsupporthub.northampton.ac.uk. (Accessed 25.5.15)
Potter, N. (2012) *The Library Marketing Toolkit*, London, Facet Publishing.
Potter, N. (2015) The Library Marketing Toolkit,
    www.librarymarketingtoolkit.com. (Accessed 25.5.15)

Acknowledgements

Miggie Pickton, University of Northampton.

8.5 Contribute to research proposals

FREQUENTLY, **LIBRARY STAFF** only become aware of research projects once funding has been received and researchers may not consider that librarians can contribute at the proposal stage. However there are ways in which LIS staff can add value to research proposals and this trend is growing.

At an early stage of the application, researchers may need to explore opportunities for collaboration, as being able to demonstrate cross-disciplinary, cross-organizational and international partnerships can strengthen the bid. Librarians are well placed to advise on this, perhaps simply by exploring the literature to find like-minded authors, or by making researchers aware of the many networking and collaborative tools such as ResearchGate and Academia, which are available to them.

The proposal will need to demonstrate how the new research will add value to existing knowledge, so some form of literature review is essential to explain the context of the bid. Whether librarians, as part of the team, perform the search for the group (discussed in more detail in Tips 8.7–8.9) or whether they assist researchers to do it themselves, this is an obvious intervention.

In addition, each of the researchers involved in the bid needs to validate their credentials by showing what their track record of research has been to date and what impact their past research has had. Directly supplying bibliometrics or working with researchers to show how to find and, more usefully, interpret them can also be a key role for librarians.

All research proposals will need to include a data management plan to explain to their funder how they will collect, preserve and manage the data generated by the research – this is another area where librarians can contribute (see Tip 8.11).

🖒 Best for:

- keeping up to date with research activity
- demonstrating the value of library services
- ensuring that researchers are aware of what resources are, and are not, available before they start their research.

★ Examples from practice

Queensland

In a survey in Queensland, Australia, Richardson discovered that of the libraries contacted:

> . . . all provide, or are in the process of planning for the provision of, advice and reports that will assist researchers in demonstrating their research impact in grant applicants to major funding bodies. . . . This advice and/or reporting are based on the use of traditional bibliometric indicators (citations, h-index). Training in bibliometric analysis for grant writing as well as support for compiling literature reviews for grant writing is provided by some libraries. 62% (8) of libraries provide assistance in the form of bibliometric reports, literature reviews and workshops for grant applicants. 23% (3) provide one-on-one and ad hoc assistance to individual researchers. 15% (2) are looking at options for future (formal) involvement.
>
> Richardson et al., 2012

⚠ To think about

Supplying data for research proposals can soon become an accepted role for the library and may take up a considerable amount of time. Before venturing down this route, consider whether you have sufficient resource to continue if the idea takes root. Treating the contribution as a pilot or experiment will ensure that you are able to draw back or even investigate if a percentage of the subsequent grant might devolve to the library in recognition of the work.

References and further reading

Richardson, J., Nolan-Brown, T., Loria, P. and Bradbury, S. (2012) Library Research Support in Queensland: a survey, *Australian Academic & Research Libraries*, **43** (4), 258–77.

8.6 Charge for literature searches

A LITERATURE SEARCH is a key component of any research proposal or bid for funding. For many years, as part of both formal and informal information literacy interactions, librarians have encouraged researchers to develop search strategies, learn effective search techniques and perform their own literature searches. It makes sense, the thinking goes, that the person who is most knowledgeable about the topic is the person best placed to perform the search. However, although we can't be polymath subject experts, librarians undeniably have expertise in searching for information and, as well as teaching others how to do it, perhaps there is a role for us still to perform this task, most effectively in conjunction with a subject expert.

In small, specialist libraries with relatively few researchers a tailored, personal literature service may be possible, often coupled with a personal current awareness service.

'If it means nannying them, then we do.' (Karen McCaulay, Royal Conservatoire of Scotland)

However, in large research organizations this level of personal service is no longer possible, which is why librarians have focused instead on developing the searching abilities of researchers. Charging for such a service seems an alien concept to librarians and researchers are used to all library services being centrally and freely provided, so the idea of paying for a literature search may seem unacceptable. However, it seems entirely reasonable to pay for expert consultancy and if the library can demonstrate expertise and added value then introducing a premium option may be possible. In fact, it is often the case that specific services are valued more highly if they have a cost attached.

👍 Best for:

■ demonstrating the value librarians can bring to the research process
■ generating income.

★ Examples from practice

Northumbria University Library
Northumbria University Library, UK, has been piloting a charged literature search service for researchers who are preparing funding bids. The work is done in consultation with the researcher, using flowcharts to help estimate costings which are based on the librarian's hourly salary rate. Results are shared with the researcher, who is responsible for refining and evaluating the material, using online bibliographical management software.

This approach recognizes that researchers work to tight deadlines when submitting research bids, and so the expertise of library staff feeding into the process is much appreciated.

'Having a pilot was very good, as it enabled us to develop good practice, develop procedures and ensure the practice is supportive to researchers.' (Suzie Kitchen, Northumbria University)

Delft University Library

Delft University Library in the Netherlands also offers a charged literature search service, as well as an exploratory search for patent applications.

> We execute a custom literature search according to your wishes. In an introductory interview you discuss the literature search with one of our information specialists and you reach an agreement on the most appropriate search terms. The search is tailored to your budget. The result is a bibliography of relevant references. The search explores the context of the research area, placing it within a broader framework. The cost of the custom search starts at €500.
>
> www.library.tudelft.nl/en/support/researchers/literature-search

References and further reading

For more details see Northumbria University Library's consultancy service: http://library.northumbria.ac.uk/info-researchers/consultancy. (Accessed 2.1.15)

Acknowledgements

Northumbria University Library.

8.7 Systematic reviews – get involved in the planning process

ORIGINALLY THE PURVIEW of medical sciences, the practice of systematic reviews is becoming increasingly popular in social sciences, as well as in some science and engineering disciplines, and they are beginning to replace traditional narrative reviews as a way of summarizing research evidence. A systematic review aims to identify all relevant information, both published and unpublished, evaluate the quality of the sources and synthesize the outcomes in an objective manner. A good systematic review is based on a rigorous methodology, with a protocol which is often peer reviewed so that it can be replicated in future. All these approaches are familiar to LIS staff – they are, in essence, fundamental to the development of information literate researchers – so it seems logical and right that librarians should have a central role in any systematic review. However, this may be less simple than it first appears. Some librarians may feel intimidated by the research topic – 'I'm not a chemist/dentist/geographer, how can I possibly be involved at this level?' Researchers often don't recognize the contribution we can make and so there may not be the opportunity to get involved. Conversely, the will and demand may exist, but librarians may not have the time within an already busy working week to enable them to engage to the depth required; a systematic review can be a very time-consuming and meticulous process. As with other areas of the research process therefore, we can choose different options:

- Teach researchers a robust approach to developing a search strategy; make them aware of all the sources they will need to consult and provide general advice and guidance.
- Provide high-quality resources about the systematic review process to aid researchers.
- Become part of the research team and actively manage all or selected parts of the review.

The first two options are dealt with elsewhere in the book; the following tips relate to active involvement in systematic reviews.

👍 Best for:

- demonstrating skills and expertise
- adding value to the research process.

★ Examples from practice

Bangor University
Beth Hall from Bangor University in the UK talks about her experiences of assisting with systematic reviews:

'It helps to get involved right from the start so that you can be involved in the planning stages. Once you have a properly defined (and costed) description of your role in the systematic review process you can encourage research groups to write your time into the grant, so that a small proportion of your time is bought out or contracted to the group. This will enable you to shape the methodology and help to scope the review process.

'Even if you are playing a more minor role I would still recommend asking the research group whether they would be interested in having a brief meeting to discuss the methodology. In my experience, the information retrieval gets least thought about in the planning process, perhaps reflecting how interested the researchers are in this process. Ask questions about the inclusion and exclusion criteria and challenge decisions, e.g. retrieve publications in all languages: have you got some way of translating non-English language publications? You are asking the research group to look again at the method, talk about any limitations of resources at the institution, e.g. searching Embase: we don't have a subscription here, but it is available via the NHS – are you going to use NHS access? Talk to the researchers about their experiences with using the platforms and databases and if *possible offer additional training if required, e.g. they may never have combined search strings on Web of Science before. Ask the research group to look again at how long they have budgeted for information retrieval, deduplication and recording. Could you do some quick scoping to see how much literature is out there and do some back-of-the envelope calculations as to how long this would take to export into RefWorks, and record?' (Beth Hall, Bangor University)*

⚠ To think about

What skills might you and your colleagues need to develop in order to fully engage with systematic reviews? Can you find any short courses (such as those delivered by the Centre for Research and Dissemination at York University, for example) which might help?

Will the payback from getting involved at this level justify the investment of time and training costs?

Having the confidence to question what researchers say they want and using your own professional judgement to tailor the search can be difficult, especially if people are very senior or experienced in their field.

'I have learned not to take at face value what it is the researchers say they want you to search for, when you are undertaking a literature search on their behalf. I have learned to get around this by looking at the research proposal to unpick what literature they actually need and then discussing possible strategies with them. Talk about search terms, run pilot searches, look at the results together, modify the searches and try to help them understand the recall/precision trade-off that the searches will inevitably entail. Offer choices with a gentle steer towards the choices that seem the most sensible to you.' (Melanie Gee, Sheffield Hallam University)

References and further reading

Andrew Booth's wiki on realist reviews, http://realistsearch.pbworks.com/w/page/88622804/FrontPage.

Centre for Research and Dissemination, www.york.ac.uk/inst/crd/services.html.

Harris, M. R. (2005) The Librarian's Roles in the Systematic Review Process: a case study, *Journal of the Medical Library Association*, **93** (1), 81–7.

McGowan, J. and Sampson, M. (2005) Systematic Reviews Need Systematic Searchers, *Journal of the Medical Library Association*, **93** (1), 74–80.

Newcastle University's systematic reviews guide, http://libguides.ncl.ac.uk/c.php?g=130239&p=850624.

Acknowledgements

Beth Hall, Bangor University; Melanie Gee, Sheffield Hallam University.

8.8 Systematic reviews – advise on resources

THE PREVIOUS TIP looked at the rationale behind LIS staff involvement in systematic reviews, especially our role in the planning process, which is arguably the key part of the whole exercise. Following on from that, however, librarians still have a key contribution to make in monitoring and advising on the process itself. Once a clear methodology has been agreed, with researchers encouraged to articulate keywords and phrases, inclusion and exclusion criteria, scale and scope, the next stage is to advise on the resources themselves. What other resources ought to be considered; are researchers aware of all the different databases available to them?

Researchers may be familiar with a few large databases, but how well do they understand how to run a complex search strategy through them? Librarians can assist in translating the search for a different database that may have different search parameters or offer practical tips to the research team about the peculiarities and strengths of individual databases. How comparable are the results from different sources? How might that affect the integrity of the systematic review? These are all questions which an information professional is well equipped to answer and which a busy researcher may not have considered.

As a paid part of the team, the librarian's role might be to actually apply the search strategy to the resources or to read the search strategy and suggest edits and improvements. Librarians can suggest search filters and limits and run an initial search to check that the strategy is working as expected.

In addition, there may be key sources and resources to which researchers don't have local access and, if so, the library may be able to facilitate access. As more and more information is available electronically, the fact that some material is still only available in print can be a surprise and irritation to a young researcher.

Systematic reviews follow a fairly structured pattern, so although they may be a new, not to be repeated, process for a researcher or research group, there are many aspects from one review that can be carried across to another. As a neutral contributor a librarian can devise a generic approach that can be individually tailored to each review, saving time and ensuring that no part of the process is omitted. This can be as simple as a checklist for the librarian or the researchers (e.g. Are you sure you have searched all relevant databases? Yes/no), or a more detailed list of recommended resources.

'Understand what the researchers need from the databases platforms. For example, if you know that they are going to need to run long search strings you could pass on any tips you

know about how effective the databases and platforms are at managing this. Pass on any local knowledge, e.g. we have found some databases are slower in the afternoon when USA wakes up.' (Beth Hall, Bangor University)

👍 Best for:

- demonstrating skills and expertise
- adding value to the research process.

★ Examples from practice

Simple review summary sheet

Figure 8.1 illustrates a simple summary sheet for a systematic review.

Review title	
Review scope Time period Country/location Exclusions	
Keywords, proper names . . . *Note here any spelling variations, truncation, etc.*	
Search strategy Search term combinations	
Databases to search	This can be prepopulated with most popular resources
Reference works (print and online) *(Encyclopedia, etc)*	
Other specialist sources *(e.g. audiovisual resources, reviews, theses, image collections)*	
Primary sources *(e.g. archives, letters, special collections)*	
Resources elsewhere	
Useful websites	
People and events	
Monitoring for new materials	
Any other things to consider? *(e.g., foreign language material, items which may be hard to obtain)*	

Figure 8.1 *Simple review summary sheet*

⚠ To think about

What level of contribution are you able/willing to make at this stage of the process?

What options are there for access to resources outside your own library? Rather than reacting when the need arises, can you prepare ahead of time by finding out what alternatives there are?

Acknowledgements

Beth Hall, Bangor University; Lucy Keating, Newcastle University.

8.9 Systematic reviews – help with writing up

YOU MAY WELL feel that after advising on planning and resources for a systematic review that your main contribution is over. The researcher is responsible for managing the information they find, for analysing it, drawing out themes and writing up the final review itself. However, a key part of a systematic review is to record the methodology and here again library staff can participate, perhaps even writing that section of the final report.

> 'Some researchers have forgotten what they did by the time they write the final publication, they are often not interested in the detail that I would spot, such as the deduplication, the platform used. Ask if you can see the final publication and the methods section about information retrieval, especially if you will be acknowledged in the article, because this is your contribution.' (Beth Hall, Bangor University)

If the researcher or librarian has been diligent in recording the process, perhaps using structured forms as in the previous examples for planning and executing the search, then writing up the methodology can be straight-forward. In fact, yet again, the librarian could develop a fairly generic text which can be tailored to the specific review and writing style of the discipline.

It is difficult, if not impossible, to perform a systematic review without using some form of reference management software to organize and manage the information and this should have been addressed long before the writing up stage. However, specific knowledge of the software is also pertinent in the final stages, for using citation features, adapting to journal styles and ensuring correct and accurate referencing. Here again, library staff can make an important contribution, perhaps taking over management of the database of references on behalf of the team, checking for consistency and accuracy of metadata and advising on appropriate output styles.

👍 Best for:

- demonstrating skills and expertise
- adding value to the research process.

★ Examples from practice

Some librarians have built up a small collection of examples of good practice in how to write the methods section of a systematic review, which they can share with researchers.

Bibliographic software packages often have sophisticated tools that can be helpful when managing large datasets: for example, the use of controlled vocabularies. Take some time to investigate which tools will be of most benefit, even if you can't be an expert yourself it helps to be aware of options which researchers can choose.

Using a mind-mapping tool, such as MindView, can also be helpful in structuring the sections of a systematic review. MindView was used to organize the tips for this book, as the structure can be designed as a visual map and then exported directly into Word to create the structure for the subsequent document.

⚠ To think about

What other benefits might accrue from your involvement with systematic reviews? Might these less tangible outcomes, such as closer acceptance by the research community, balance the not insubstantial time and effort involved?

> 'I have learnt so much by being directly involved with systematic reviews, and developed my understanding that I can pass on as guidance to others looking for my support. In addition, I have been given the opportunity to have my name on publications, which is good for my own research profile.' (Beth Hall, Bangor University)

However, it is equally important not to over-commit and to promise more than you will be able to deliver. It's easy to feel excited or flattered to be included in a research project in this way and to devote time to it to the exclusion of the 'day job'.

> 'Personally I know that I get sucked in and spend too long on work for the review that I can really allocate, also the research group ask more of me if they know I can help. It is important early on in the process to explain the boundaries of what support you can offer, e.g. are you able to attend regular team meetings or stakeholders meetings or not. I have found that if you show the research group some useful ways to use RefWorks, for example, then they will ask if you could manage all the references and marking up/annotation after every sift.' (Beth Hall, Bangor University)

References and further reading

Kramer, B. (2013) *Using Refworks for Systematic Reviews*, www.slideshare.net/bmkramer/using-refworks-for-systematic-reviews-sept-2013. (Accessed 24/3/15)

Acknowledgements

Beth Hall, Bangor University.

8.10 Engage with research data

THERE ARE MANY definitions of research data. The Australian National Data Service (2015), collating statements from several universities, concludes that it is 'all data which is created by researchers in the course of their work, and for which the institution has a curatorial responsibility'. In the UK, the Engineering and Physical Sciences Research Council (2015) states that research data is 'recorded factual material commonly retained by and accepted in the scientific community as necessary to validate research findings; although the majority of such data is created in digital format, all research data is included irrespective of the format in which it is created'. Going into specific detail, the University of Melbourne (2005) describes data as:

> . . . facts, observations or experiences on which an argument, theory or test is based. Data may be numerical, descriptive or visual. Data may be raw or analyzed, experimental or observational. Data includes: laboratory notebooks; field notebooks; primary research data (including research data in hardcopy or in computer readable form); questionnaires; audiotapes; videotapes; models; photographs; films; test responses. Research collections may include slides; artefacts; specimens; samples. Provenance information about the data might also be included: the how, when, where it was collected and with what (for example, instrument). The software code used to generate, annotate or analyze the data may also be included.
>
> University of Melbourne, 2005

The rise in importance of 'digital affordances' (Kenney, 2014), such as repositories, data management and bibliographical software, brought about by advances in technology, has influenced scholarly practice in relation to the handling and management of data, with a variety of different terms evolving, such as e-scholarship, e-research and e-science. Although initially found mainly in science subjects, recognition is increasing in social sciences, arts and humanities. Data is increasingly viewed as a valued product of research in its own right, distinct from the traditional academic output of papers, books and reports; it can take many forms: text, numbers, audio and images, to name just a few.

As well as defining data itself, terminology around the production, use and management of data is confusing. In the UK, e-science refers to the large-scale science that will increasingly be carried out through distributed global collaborations enabled by the internet (National E-Science Centre, 2012), whereas the preferred term in Australia is e-research. In the USA, cyberinfrastructure refers to research environments that support 'advanced data acquisition, data storage, data management, data integration, data mining, data visualization and other computing and information processing services over the internet' (Gold, 2007). In library and information science, data literacy is yet another aspect of information literacy.

Against the national infrastructures, mandates by funding bodies such as the UK Research Councils and Wellcome Trust, the Australian Research Council and similar bodies in other countries now require researchers to consider how they organize, manage and share their research data and this has provided opportunities and challenges for librarians. Lewis states the situation neatly:

> Perhaps the starting point for any discussion about libraries and research data is to ask whether managing data is actually a job for university libraries. The answer to this question is a straightforward yes and no. Yes, in the sense that data from academic research projects represents an integral part of the global research knowledge base, and so managing it should be a natural extension of the university library's current role in providing access to the published part of that knowledge base. No, because the scale of the challenge in terms of infrastructure, skills and culture change requires concerted action by a range of stakeholders, and not just university libraries.
>
> Lewis, 2010, 145

Be that as it may, many libraries have taken up the challenge and are upskilling existing staff or developing entirely new roles to address this latest challenge.

In addition to the large-scale data management debates, concerns are also being raised about supplementary data in journal papers and how this is being handled. In the USA, NISO, the National Information Standards Organization, has developed recommended practice for publisher inclusion, display and handling of such materials (National Information Standards Organization, 2013), but this is relatively uncommon in other countries.

👍 Best for:

- getting involved with research data.

★ Examples from practice

Research Data Management pyramid

In the Research Data Management pyramid for libraries (Figure 8.2), Lewis (2010) identifies different ways in which libraries can engage with research data.

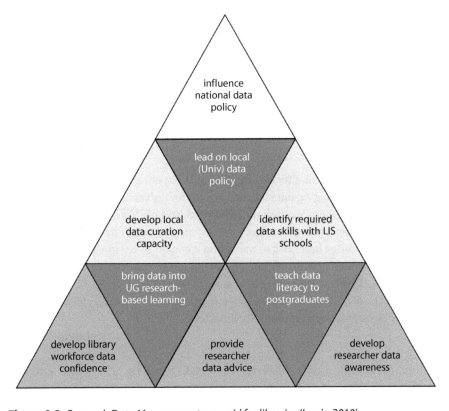

Figure 8.2 *Research Data Management pyramid for libraries (Lewis, 2010)*

These revolve around data literacy – raising awareness of issues relating to research data such as ethics, access, skills to find and interpret the data, and data curation – how to manage, store and develop the data. For librarians seeking to engage with data, therefore, we can include it in information/digital/data literacy development, treat data as a collection and curate and manage it and manage the accompanying metadata.

Australian libraries

Richardson (Richardson et al., 2012) describes how libraries in Australia have developed proficiency in the curation and management of data. For example, existing staff at the University of New South Wales have developed their skills relating to research metadata and e-research infrastructure. New data librarian posts have also been created. At the University of Western Australia 'a unit has been created that sits at the intersection of the library and the IT support models. The anticipated benefits include cross-fertilization of knowledge and services based on the synergies between research analytics, data management, research outputs and eresearch systems.' (Richardson et al., 2012).

⚠ **To think about**

Data management is technically challenging and extends the scope of the library's traditional activities. Some existing staff may feel intimidated by the challenge, which demands a whole new set of skills. Even if new, appropriately skilled staff are appointed, decisions need to be made about staff training for existing staff if they are not to feel excluded and 'left behind' by the new direction.

Just being aware of the challenges researchers face in dealing with their data can be beneficial. Many researchers are unaware of the benefits of early recording and management of their data and will leave any curation until the end of their project. Library staff can encourage researchers to start thinking about data management right from the start. Even if you aren't an expert yourself, do you know other people in the organization to whom you can send researchers, or from whom you can learn yourself?

References and further reading

Australian National Data Service (2015) *What is Research Data?*, http://ands.org.au/guides/what-is-research-data.html. (Accessed 4.8.15)

Brown, S., Bruce, R. and Kernohan, D. (2015) *Directions for Research Data Management in UK Universities*, https://www.fosteropenscience.eu/sites/default/files/pdf/1240.pdf. (Accessed 4.1.16)

Christensen-Dalsgaard, B. (2012) *Ten Recommendations for Libraries to Get Started with Research Data Management*, The Hague, Liber Working Group on E-Science/Research Data Management, http://libereurope.eu/wp-content/uploads/The%20research%20data%20group%202012%20v7%20final.pdf. (Accessed 24.5.15)

CILIP (2014) *Research Data Management Briefing Paper*, www.cilip.org.uk/sites/default/files/documents/Research%20data%20management%20briefing%20July%202014_0.pdf. (Accessed 27.5.15)

Cox, A., Verbaan, E. and Sen, B. (2014) A Spider, an Octopus, or an Animal Just Coming into Existence? Designing a curriculum for librarians to support research data management, *Journal of eScience Librarianship*, **3** (1), 15–30.

Engineering and Physical Sciences Research Council (2015) *Research Data: scope and benefits.* Available at: https://www.epsrc.ac.uk/about/standards/researchdata/scope/. (Accessed 21.10.15)

Gold, A. (2007) Cyberinfrastructure, Data and Libraries, Part 1, *D-Lib Magazine*, **13** (9/10), 1–12, www.dlib.org/dlib/september07/gold/09gold-pt1.html.

Kenney, A. (2014) *Leveraging the Liaison Model: from defining 21st century research libraries to implementing 21st century research universities,* www.sr.ithaka.org/blog-individual/leveraging-liaison-model-defining-21st-century-research-libraries-implementing-21st. (Accessed 25.5.15)

Lewis, M. (2010) Libraries and the Management of Research Data. In McKnight, S. (ed.), *Envisioning Future Academic Library Services: initiatives, ideas and challenges,* London, Facet Publishing, 145–68.

National E-Science Centre (2012) *Defining e-Science,* www.nesc.ac.uk/nesc/define.html. (Accessed 2.5.15)

National Information Standards Organization (2013) *NISO RP-15-2013: Recommended Practices for Online Supplemental Journal Article Materials: a recommended practice of the National Information Standards Organization and the National Federation of Advanced Information Services,* Baltimore, MD, NISO, www.niso.org/apps/group_public/download.php/10055/RP-15-2013_Supplemental_Materials.pdf. (Accessed 17.7.15)

Richardson, J., Nolan-Brown, T., Loria, P. and Bradbury, S. (2012) Library Research Support in Queensland: a survey, *Australian Academic & Research Libraries*, **43** (4), 258–77.

SCONUL (2015) *Research Data Management: briefing for library directors,* www.sconul.ac.uk/sites/default/files/documents/SCONUL%20RDM%20briefing.pdf. (Accessed 23.4.15)

University of Melbourne (2005) Policy on the Management of Research Data and Records. Available at: www.unimelb.edu.au/records/pdf/research.pdf. (Accessed 21.10.15)

8.11 Advise on data management plans

AS RESEARCH DATA has increasingly been recognized as having value in its own right, so in order to comply with funder mandates, researchers are increasingly expected to provide a data management plan as part of any bid for funding. A data management plan (DMP) describes what researchers expect to do with the data they collect, both during and after their research. The DMP commonly articulates what kinds of data will be created, explains the standards and metadata which will be used with the data, how the data will be accessed and shared, policies and provisions for the re-use of the data and plans for the long-term archiving of the data.

With their skills in managing information and metadata, librarians are often well placed to contribute to data management planning. As a minimum, we can point researchers to external high-quality information sources and training resources to help them develop their skills. Expert workshops can be hosted by the library, bringing key speakers from elsewhere, for example from the Digital Curation Centre in the UK. With more resources, internal training programmes can be developed, along with detailed, location-specific guidelines for researchers on how to deal with their data. Ultimately, such a programme will need to be supported by a fully fledged internal data repository. In order to accomplish this, however, it is likely that specialist staff will need to be employed, or existing staff will need to develop their own data management skills. In the meantime, small steps to encourage good practice in data management planning can still be taken by LIS staff.

👍 Best for:

■ getting involved with research proposals right from the start
■ demonstrating skills and expertise.

★ Examples from practice

Examples of resources relating to data management planning are easy to find, so just one or two are highlighted here.

The Digital Curation Centre

In the UK, the Digital Curation Centre (www.dcc.ac.uk) provides a wide range of information and resources to assist researchers in their curation of data. They describe a digital curation lifecycle, which is a useful structure on which to base a DMP.

The DCC digital curation lifecycle comprises the following steps:

Conceptualise: conceive and plan the creation of digital objects, including data capture methods and storage options.

Create: produce digital objects and assign administrative, descriptive, structural and technical archival metadata.

Access and use: ensure that designated users can easily access digital objects on a day-to-day basis. Some digital objects may be publicly available, whilst others may be password protected.

Appraise and select: evaluate digital objects and select those requiring long-term curation and preservation. Adhere to documented guidance, policies and legal requirements.

Dispose: rid systems of digital objects not selected for long-term curation and preservation. Documented guidance, policies and legal requirements may require the secure destruction of these objects.

Ingest: transfer digital objects to an archive, trusted digital repository, data centre or similar, again adhering to documented guidance, policies and legal requirements.

Preservation action: undertake actions to ensure the long-term preservation and retention of the authoritative nature of digital objects.

Reappraise: return digital objects that fail validation procedures for further appraisal and reselection.

Store: keep the data in a secure manner as outlined by relevant standards.

Access and reuse: ensure that data are accessible to designated users for first time use and reuse. Some material may be publicly available, whilst other data may be password protected.

Transform: create new digital objects from the original, for example, by migration into a different form.

Digital Curation Centre, 2015

In addition, the DCC provides a series of useful checklists relating to data management plans and the curation of data, www.dcc.ac.uk/resources/how-guides. All are free to download and use.

University of Western Australia

The University of Western Australia also provides a Data Management Toolkit with links to the university's guidelines for writing a DMP.

The Research Data Management Plan helps researchers to document and establish:

- Metadata standards which will be used for data formats.
- Storage and backup procedures and provisions.
- Future access to the research data for sharing and/or reuse.
- Retention and disposal procedures and provisions.
- Ownership and protection of intellectual property.
- Documentation describing all of the above.

www.library.uwa.edu.au/research/research-data-management-toolkit

University College Dublin

UCD Library in Dublin provides a very useful four-page data management plan checklist for researchers, shown here as Figure 8.3.

PROJECT DESCRIPTION
☑ Project title   ☑The aim/ purpose of the research   ☑ Project duration

CONTEXT: Administrative and contact information
☑ Principal investigator (PI)   ☑ Researchers/other project members   ☑ Main contact details
☑ Collaborators/Partner Institutions   ☑ Funding source(s) and requirements

DATA TYPES
Provide a description of the data your project will capture, create or use. It is important to record this detail to help you and subsequent users understand why and how the data was created.
☑ How will data be created (captured)? e.g. interview data, questionnaires, imaging, experimental measurements etc.
☑ What data formats will be used? e.g. File formats such as excel, word, open source etc.
☑ Will the data be reproducible? What would happen if it got lost or became unusable later?
☑ How much data will there be and what will its growth rate be? How often will it change?
☑ Will existing data be used? If so, from where, and what is the relationship to the existing data?
☑ Are there special tools or software needed to create/process/visualise the data?
☑ How will metadata be captured, created and managed?

DATA ORGANISATION, DOCUMENTATION AND METADATA
Organising, documenting and describing data is important in order to assure quality control and reproducibility of data
☑ What metadata standards will be used?
☑ How will metadata be captured, created and managed? Is there a discipline-specific standard?
☑ How will folders and files be structured and named?
☑ How will different file versions be managed?
☑ What data identifiers will be assigned?
☑ What other documentation and contextual information will be available in order to help others understand the data? E.g. data dictionaries, codebooks, questionnaires

DATA STORAGE AND SECURITY
☑ Storage: – Where and what media? Short-term, longer-term?– Who will be responsible?
☑ Back-up: – How will it be done and how often will it be done?– Who will be responsible?
☑ Security: – How will data security be guaranteed e.g. data encryption, password etc.
☑ How will the data be shared during the project?

LONG-TERM PRESERVATION
☑ What data will be kept or destroyed after the end of the project?
☑ How long will data be kept? e.g. 3-5 years, 10-20 years, permanently?
☑ Where will the data be stored? e.g. archive, data repository, network etc.
☑ What file formats will be used? Are they long-lived?
☑ Who will manage the long term data?
☑ What is needed to prepare the data for preservation or data sharing?
☑ What related information will be deposited with the data?

ETHICS AND INTELLECTUAL PROPERTY
☑ Are there any ethical and privacy issues that may prohibit sharing of some or all of the data? If so, how will these be resolved?
☑ Do your data contain confidential or sensitive information? If so have you discussed data sharing with the respondents from whom you collected the data?
☑ Who owns the data arising from your research, and the intellectual property rights relating to them?

Figure 8.3 *UCD Library data management plan checklist (taken from http://libguides.ucd.ie/ data/checklist_plans, with permission) (Continued on next page)*

DATA SHARING AND RE-USE
- ☑ In addition to the owners of the data you generate, who else has a right to see or use this data? And who else should reasonably have access? Who will be the audience for your data?
- ☑ Are there any limits to data sharing required?
- ☑ Are there any sharing requirements? E.g. funder data sharing policy
- ☑ How will the data be discovered and shared?
- ☑ What tools/software will be needed to work with the data?
- ☑ Will there be embargo periods?

IMPLEMENTING YOUR PLAN
- ☑ Who will be responsible for ensuring your plan is followed?
- ☑ How often will your plan be reviewed and updated?

Figure 8.3 *Continued*

⚠ To think about

Some librarians express concerns about their abilities to engage with DMPs, seeing them as the domain of specialists, needing extra skills and knowledge which we may have neither the time nor the inclination to develop. However, they are growing in importance and can also offer a great opportunity to embed the library more firmly within the research process. The situation can be confusing for both library staff and researchers, especially if a few library staff are more skilled than others. Think carefully about the level of engagement you can offer, make sure this is clearly stated and that all library staff understand the position and where to get help, even if they are not directly involved. If there are high-quality resources freely available elsewhere you can make use of them to build a seemingly tailored guide without a great expenditure of either time or money.

References and further reading

Digital Curation Centre (2015) *What is Digital Curation?*, www.dcc.ac.uk/digital-curation/what-digital-curation. (Accessed 29.3.15)

Acknowledgements

Joy Davidson, Digital Curation Centre; Julia Barrett, University College Dublin.

8.12 Facilitate the writing process

THERE ARE MANY motivations for writing. It may be an expectation of the job, or a condition of the funding, resulting in a feeling of obligation and a need to keep up with the peer community. Many researchers relish the intellectual challenge of writing about something they are passionate about and feel a need to contribute to the body of knowledge on their subject. Others may be driven by more pragmatic incentives such as enhancing their CV, furthering their career or generating income. Writing can be used to clarify thinking and to develop skills, it can be very enjoyable and give a sense of achievement, but it can also be very frustrating and the cause of much stress and anxiety. It is certainly extremely time-consuming!

It is not only new or inexperienced researchers who can struggle with the writing process. Senior staff may feel they are too busy or have too many conflicting demands to take time away to write and writing successfully does demand both mental and physical space. Confidence is a huge issue for aspiring writers, who may fear rejection or open criticism of their work. Helping to manage these fears in a constructive way can be as simple as making clear how frequently even senior researchers have work returned and discussing how criticism can be turned into debate.

Although initially writing may be viewed as only the preserve of the researcher there are opportunities for librarians to contribute. Writing and the subsequent publication process are time-consuming and take time away from research itself, so many researchers welcome advice. There are many facets to the writing process apart from the actual writing itself: aspects of peer review, editing, proofreading, finding out about journal requirements and correct citation are all intermingled and all need to be dealt with by both aspiring and experienced writers.

Although few librarians will feel qualified to advise on some of these activities directly, drawing together information about them can be immensely helpful to busy researchers. Librarians are used to being the 'go-to' people for answering queries, whatever they may be about, so this is a natural step. A web page that acts as hub to highlight all the different activities and experts across the organization is a useful place to start. For aspiring writers, practical hints and tips to think about may also be welcome.

🖒 Best for:

- enabling researchers to improve writing skills
- providing a go-to place for researchers seeking help with their writing.

★ Examples from practice

'One thing'

'As part of the writing for publication workshop we asked different people to tell us 'one thing' – one piece of advice they would pass on or wanted to ask. We've been able to turn

this into a set of tips that researchers seem to find very helpful. They like the idea that these suggestions come from real people:

Journal editors – what is the one thing you would say to aspiring authors?
- *Make sure it's relevant to the readership. Check the aims and scope of the journal.*
- *Answer the so what question. Stress why it matters, what is original and new.*
- *Take time to check grammar and spelling. If it's not well written it's hard to read.*
- *Make sure all sources are acknowledged – you can be sure peer reviewers will recognize some of them.*
- *Ask a colleague to read it through before you submit it.*

Experienced writers – what is the one thing you wish you'd known when you started writing?
- *Start the manuscript with the preparation of figures, then the results, conclusion and discussion.*
- *Learn to say no – don't publish in poor journals.*
- *How to be strategic about being named as first author.*

New writers – what is the one thing you want to know before you start writing?
- *How to identify the right places to aim for to reach the widest audience.*
- *To what extent do papers get altered in editing?*
- *What's a good length for a paper?*

Librarians – what is the one thing you can offer to help writers?
- *Give background on status of journals.*
- *Make sure they have access to relevant resources.*
- *Help with citation and referencing.*

Publishers – what is the one thing you say to authors submitting to your journal?
- *Read the instructions to authors, observe deadlines, unpack acronyms.*
- *Be aware of the turnaround time for a response from us.*

Using this approach enables researchers to focus on some of the key issues relating to writing for publication.' (Librarian, UK university)

Writing for publication hints and tips
Figure 8.4 is taken from a booklet on writing for publication (Gannon-Leary and Bent, 2009). The booklet was devised as part of a Writing for Publication workshop. The checklist can be used with researchers during workshops, or made available to them independently.

Do . . .	Don't . . .
Ensure content is relevant, practical, interesting, applicable to the readership	Submit an article on a topic outside the remit of the target journal/conference
Ensure information is understandable, clearly presented	Include unnecessary detail
Ensure you address the major issues of the topic or cite other sources that do	Take too narrow a viewpoint which fails to discuss or take account of other issues or fails to draw on the published body of knowledge
Ensure the information conveys something new or tackles an old issue from a new perspective	Deal with a subject already extensively covered in the target journal or at previous year's target conference
Ensure you include the data that led to your conclusions	Make conclusions that are not substantiated by your article/paper
Use plain language where possible and bear in mind you are writing for an international audience	Use jargon, acronyms, Anglocentric terms
Write about something about which you are passionate	Write about the 'b****ing' obvious!
Clarify your motivation for wanting to write, what is in it for you	Be pressurised into writing by others
Write at the right time: some topics are time-limited	Write about something now superseded
Find a mentor or co-author with experience – if the former, identify who is contributing what	Allow a peer on board as co-author only to lend their name but not contribute
Tailor your writing to your intended target readership	Be self-indulgent, writing for yourself without regard for the needs/requirements of the target readership
Eliminate unnecessary words that do not add to the meaning	Be afraid to cut – most pieces are improved by some judicious editing
Explain how and why you chose what to include (and this may be indicative of what you chose to exclude/cut)	Cut to the extent that you render the text unintelligible, reading like notes rather than continuous prose
Be confident in, and on top of, your subject	Be frightened to go for it!
Ensure you can handle criticism and the peer review process	Lose heart. Even the best authors have faced rejection at some stage
Get a colleague to act as informal proofreader-come-peer reviewer	Rely on your own proofreading
Decide on the form of your name you wish to publish under and stick with it – this will maximise citations and make your writing career easy to follow (useful when applying for jobs)	Use variant forms of your name – sometimes forename, sometimes initials

Figure 8.4 *Dos and don'ts of writing for publication (Continued on next page)*

Do ...	Don't ...
Be punctilious about citing others (do as you would be done by). Keep a record of all your references	Lose the references you have cited
As your piece of work develops, keep copies of all versions, clearly labelled and backed up	Get sloppy about saving versions of your writing as you add and amend
Keep a chart recording where you sent articles, when, rejections and resubmissions with dates, contact names, etc., so that you can keep track	Rely on your memory as to what articles/papers are where and with whom!
Keep a prepublication, post-refereed copy of all your writing as both a print and an e-copy	Rely on your memory as to where your various articles/papers are located

Figure 8.4 *Continued*

⚠ To think about

Are there experts within your organization with whom you can work to offer a more coherent approach to helping with the writing process? Even if you can't offer the service yourself, the library can act as a central hub to bring people together, perhaps by devising and hosting a series of talks given by others.

References and further reading

Elsevier (2015) Publishing Campus, https://www.publishingcampus.elsevier.com. (Accessed 8.5.15) The Elsevier Publishing Campus is an online platform offering free lectures, interactive training and professional advice.

Gannon-Leary, P. and Bent, M. (2009) *Writing for Publication – Hints and Tips*, Newcastle University, internal document.

Gannon-Leary, P. and Bent, M. (2010) Writing for Publication and the Role of the Library: 'Do have a cow, man!' ('Don't have a cow, man' – Bart Simpson), *New Review of Academic Librarianship*, **16** (1), 26–44.

8.13 Make researchers aware of what editors and publishers want

J̲OURNAL WEBSITES INCLUDE practical information about layout, referencing and the submission process for authors wishing to publish with them. However, aspiring authors also need to know about the selection process for inclusion and why editors and publishers respond in the ways they do. The best way to discover this is to hear from those involved in the process. The library can facilitate this by hosting seminars; perhaps there are journal editors within your organization who would be prepared to contribute their experience and expertise. Ascertain who they are by checking internal web pages, asking key publishers to give you a list of their editors based at your institution or just by sending an e-mail and asking. If you have published yourself, talking about your own experiences can add an extra dimension to such an event.

Publishers themselves will often be willing to send representatives to talk about their selection and publishing process. In some disciplines, publication is limited to a few main publishers, so hearing directly from them will be very beneficial for new authors. Avoid accusations of favouritism and bias by inviting a range of publishers. Badging them as a special series of events is a good way of advertising them.

🖒 Best for:

- ■ enabling new authors to understand publisher requirements
- ■ creating a shared understanding by bringing publishers and authors together.

★ Examples from practice

What publishers want
One librarian describes his experience:

> 'For the last few years we've run a series of lunchtime workshops at which publishers come along and talk about things like their peer review process, their selection criteria, things that really irritate them and that kind of thing. We do it over lunch because then we can usually persuade the publisher to fund some food. Sometimes they attract a wide audience, others times, when they're focused on a particular area, we get fewer folks, but actually they usually ask more questions because it's very subject-specific. I always like to start the session off by providing some local context and I always stay to pick up on local questions but otherwise they are very easy sessions and get us a lot of street cred.' (UK librarian)

⚠ To think about

Before asking for contributions from local editors, have a clear agenda and explain exactly what you expect from them.

> 'I found the first tIme that some editors were inclined to hustle for their own journal or to focus on just how their journal works rather than generalizing. Some of that was fine, as we did want a personal perspective, but it also turned some of the audience off. The next

time we ran it, I wrote a short brief, like a framework really: explain who you are/which journal you edit, explain rejection rates, peer review process, describe selection criteria, common mistakes, give general advice.' (Librarian, UK university)

Publishers will come with their own agenda and so it's helpful to discuss beforehand exactly what they plan to offer. However, publishers may also be prepared to offer refreshments or other incentives to encourage attendance.

8.14 Develop awareness of fraudulent publishing practices (see also Tip 10.11)

IT IS BECOMING increasingly common for new researchers to be approached by publishers, often after receiving an award for a higher degree. They may be encouraged to publish their thesis with the publisher or to pay a fee – common practice in the open access environment, so not in itself suspect – to have their work published. However, not all such approaches are authentic; a dishonest publisher will not provide the editorial and publishing expertise of a legitimate journal and publishing in a less credible journal can harm the reputation of a less well established researcher. Sometimes referred to as 'predatory' or 'vanity', some publishers can be aggressive and persuasive and their journal titles often mimic more established, reputable titles, and so it can be difficult to identify them initially. Library staff can raise awareness of such activity in workshops with researchers (see Tip 10.11) and by providing clear advice on their websites.

In some cases, senior staff in your organization may, without their permission or even without their knowledge, be listed as editors of such publications. This can be very embarrassing and annoying, as it can damage their reputation amongst their peers as well as lead to misunderstandings with aspiring authors. It can be very difficult to have names removed from such spoof editorial boards. In order to mitigate the damage, researchers in this position may wish to add a clear statement to their personal website and social media profiles to the effect that they do not endorse the publication.

Conversely, of course, authors may deliberately enter into less honest arrangements with publishers in order to build up a fake reputation in the scholarly world, to deceive their employers and colleagues and to manipulate their citation counts. This kind of scholarly malpractice is much easier to do when journal titles are so similar and are likely to be overlooked, for example, in a list of publications on a CV, leading to the possibility of the employment of less well qualified researchers.

👍 Best for:

■ ensuring authors are aware of publishing pitfalls.

★ Examples from practice

Beall's list

Beall's list, created by Jeffrey Beall from the University of Colorado, claims to list potential predatory open access (OA) publishers and journals, although there is some controversy about the reasons for listing some publishers, so it should be used with care. The website also includes suggested criteria to assist in identifying potential predatory OA publishers. An alternative to this 'blacklist' is the *Directory of Open Access Journals* (DOAJ) and, to some extent, large indexing databases that assess the quality of journals before including them, commonly referred to as a 'whitelist'. By their nature, whitelists are not comprehensive, so whilst inclusion on a whitelist may confer respectability, omission from such a list does not necessarily imply malpractice or poor quality. However, using both types of list together can help distinguish, but not definitively confirm, fraudulent or reputable operations.

Checklist for authors on predatory or vanity publishers

Some questions to pose to researchers aspiring to publish:

■ Have you heard of the journal before? Perhaps the title is very similar to a well known journal – check the details.
■ Has the publisher approached you directly, do they seem to be very persistent and/or aggressive?
■ Have they suggested that your article will be published very quickly?
■ Is there a clear process which explains costs before you submit your work?
■ What evidence is there of a peer-review process?
■ Check the editorial board credentials. Do the editors really exist? Do they have a publication profile?
■ Look at the journal website. How is it designed? What other titles are connected to this one? Where is the publisher located?
■ What is the quality of existing articles in the journal?
■ If they are quoting an impact factor, can you verify this in the Journal Citation Reports database?

'Think, Check, Submit'

Think, Check, Submit (http://thinkchecksubmit.org) is a campaign initiated by organizations such as the Association of Learned and Professional Society

Publishers and directories such as the *Directory of Open Access Journals*. It aims to help researchers identify trusted journals for their research. It is a simple checklist researchers can use to assess the credentials of a journal or publisher.

⚠ To think about

New predatory journals appear on a regular basis, so you can't assume that if a journal isn't listed on Beall's list that it is a genuine journal. As well as using the checklist for authors above, you can check *Ulrichsweb* (Proquest, 2015) and other reputable journals directories to see if the title is listed.

References and further reading

Beall, J. (2015) *Criteria for Identifying Predatory Publishers*, https://scholarlyoa. files.wordpress.com/2015/01/criteria-2015.pdf. (Accessed 8.1.15)
Beall's list, http://scholarlyoa.com/publishers.
Directory of Open Access Journals, http://doaj.org.
Proquest (2015) *Ulrichsweb: Global Serials Directory*. Available at: www.ulrichsweb.com/. (Accessed 21.10.15)

8.15 Facilitate a Community of Writers

WRITING, ESPECIALLY WRITING for publication, can be a daunting process and researchers at all levels and from all disciplines can sometimes struggle with feelings of isolation or inadequacy. Assumptions can be made that because they have obtained a research position that they will automatically be able to produce good written work. However, there are many different forms of writing for publication; researchers may be familiar with writing an academic paper, but can they translate their findings into a technical report or into a form suitable for a non-specialist audience? How might they cope with using social media tools, such as blogs, as a means of communicating research outcomes?

One way to address these issues is to discuss them with other researchers and to learn from a shared experience. The library is ideally positioned to facilitate this kind of activity by initiating a Community of Writers.

The Community of Writers concept (Gannon-Leary and Bent, 2010) is a community of practice integrated with a community of learners. A community of practice refers to the process of social learning that occurs, and shared sociocultural practices that emerge and evolve, when people who have common goals interact as they strive towards those goals (Wenger, 1998). A community of learners/learning community, on the other hand, refers to a community whose first purpose is not practice but rather the advancement of learners (Wubbels, 2007).

A Community of Writers is both a community of practice and a community of learners – a safe place for people to practise their academic writing and also to learn about academic writing – it could be conceived as either a physical or a virtual 'writing retreat' but rather than being a short-term experience it is a more long-term solution.

A Community of Writers aims to help people write, research and teach more confidently and creatively. It might be organized to include exercises and activities to enhance confidence, stimulate creativity and develop writing skills but crucially it depends on the willingness of participants to share their own experiences and knowledge of writing. It should be framed by research concerns and be situated within the broader context of the organization.

Some of the benefits which might accrue from a Community of Writers include:

- helping to develop, integrate, and enculture new research students/staff
- providing a speedy response from a peer audience
- affording an opportunity for collaborative critique that may inform manuscript revision prior to submission for publication
- giving greater understanding of the writing style and format expected for publication
- ensuring regular accountability
- establishing friendships/networks
- identifying potential research and/or writing projects
- affording opportunities to engage in collaborative writing ventures
- renewing or sparking of an interest in writing for publication
- overcoming barriers to publication
- aiding the completion of unfinished work/reviewed work for submission
- matching journals appropriate to the group members' work
- providing resource materials such as instructions for authors for various journals and writing support literature
- decreasing manuscript development time
- increasing quality of work
- influencing productivity
- giving a feeling of being supported as opposed to being pressured
- giving a sense of forging a scholarly identity
- fostering collegiality.

🖒 Best for:

■ engaging researchers with the writing process.

★ Examples from practice

Writing retreat, University of Huddersfield

The 'Developing a culture of publication' project at the University of Huddersfield in the UK began in 2013 with the aim of encouraging collaborative writing between students and their supervisors. The project was funded internally and was linked to the University's strategic goals to increase the volume and quality of outputs and student employability. The overall outcome of the project was to increase research and scholarship capacity whilst establishing a community of scholarly practice. The first year included two Schools, Human and Health Sciences and Art, Design and Architecture and was run over nine months, with four mandatory days' attendance; a preparatory pre-workshop event, a two-day writing retreat and a dissemination event. Students attended in pairs with their supervisors. The retreat itself was held in a rural off-campus location and comprised a combination of writing time, scheduled panels, such as a journal editor's panel, and social activities. Now in its third year, the writing retreat is funded by the School of Human and Health Sciences and is facilitated by the Department of Nursing and Health Studies and Computing and Library Services. Library staff were closely involved in the planning and running of the retreat.

> 'My role was to assist with open access enquiries, help with selection of appropriate journals and contribute as an experienced writer, peer reviewer and journal editorial board member. I also mentored a number of the pairs.' (Graham Stone, University of Huddersfield)

Student feedback indicated that students had felt valued and had increased in confidence in their writing, with seven published papers and three conference papers as tangible evidence of success. However, some issues were encountered with initial engagement, especially as postgraduate research students had other workload pressures and in subsequent years the focus has been on MRes students.

> 'The whole experience has been one of the most rewarding things I have done. There is a wealth of excellent research undertaken at masters level, which deserves to be published. It is also very rewarding to see the pride and importance of publishing when the student's articles are accepted.' (Graham Stone, University of Huddersfield)

⚠ To think about

What might your role be in facilitating a Community of Writers? Does it need to be physical and/or virtual?

Can you participate as a writer/developing writer yourself? What difference might that make to your relationship with other researchers?

References and further reading

Gannon-Leary, P. and Bent, M. (2010) Writing for Publication and the Role of the Library: 'Do have a cow, man!' ('Don't have a cow, man' – Bart Simpson), *New Review of Academic Librarianship*, **16** (1), 26–44.

Garside, J., Bailey, R., Tyas, M., Ormrod, G., Stone, G., Topping, A. and Gillibrand, W. P. (2015) Developing a Culture of Publication: a joint enterprise writing retreat, *Journal of Applied Research in Higher Education*, **7** (2), 429–42.

Wenger, E. (1998) *Communities of Practice: learning, meaning and identity*, Cambridge, CUP.

Wubbels, T. (2007) Do We Know a Community of Practice When We See One?, *Technology, Pedagogy and Education*, **16** (2), 225–33.

Acknowledgements

Graham Stone, University of Huddersfield.

8.16 Assist with open access advocacy

ALTHOUGH MARKETING AS a concept is much more prevalent in libraries these days, it can still be difficult to strike the right tone when thinking about how to publicize specific messages. Open access (OA) is a good example. For several years librarians have been preaching the OA doctrine, explaining the financial imperatives for library budgets alongside the more philanthropic contexts of publicly funded research being available to all and access to cutting-edge research in developing countries. More recently in the UK, mandates from research funding bodies, along with direction from central government with respect to the next Research Excellence Framework exercise, have provided a stick rather than a carrot approach to encouraging researchers to engage with open access. Not unsurprisingly, this can cause resentment and misunderstandings and can muddy the existing, and still valid, messages we are trying to convey. Senior management in the university may or may not align themselves with the whole OA message, but they will certainly understand the financial imperatives incumbent on them to comply with the practical aspects of the debate. For library staff, whilst this central support must be welcome, it can have the effect of skewing the OA message we are trying to convey.

👍 Best for:

■ communicating the open access message.

★ Examples from practice

University of Leicester

The University of Leicester has used a wide range of communication techniques to spread the word about open access, including:

Figure 8.5
The Open Access Owl, University of Leicester (reproduced with permission)

■ an OA Owl mascot to front the campaign (Figure 8.5)
■ a letter from their Pro Vice-Chancellor for research
■ flags and banners around the campus
■ leaflets sent to all research staff
■ drop-in sessions
■ departmental briefings
■ library outreach stall around the campus
■ Twitter campaign
■ videos on practical aspects of how to submit articles to the institutional repository
■ a dedicated website pulling all the information together.

'The multipronged approach seems to have helped reinforce the message.' (Selina Lock, University of Leicester)

⚠ To think about

Consider what messages you want to convey about open access and how these relate to the current approaches in your organization. How can you harness the current interest in OA amongst the research community to best advantage?

Think about your audience and tailor the message appropriately. It's important that new research staff and research students are aware of open access and the implications for them now and in the future. More senior researchers, who may have to comply with mandates and directives more immediately, may need to hear a slightly different message.

Consider the wording you use in your messages – terminology with which librarians are familiar may not have immediate resonance with researchers.

'We found that talking about depositing a manuscript instead of a paper seemed to help make the message clearer.' (Selina Lock, University of Leicester)

A pragmatic, rather than idealistic, approach may have short-term benefits which will nevertheless contribute to a better overall understanding of open access. The *Advocating Open Access* toolkit for librarians and research support staff includes a seven-step checklist:

1 Gather essential information for accuracy and consistency.
2 Understand your audiences and find the best ways to reach them.
3 Build a profile of open access stakeholders and their attitudes.
4 Create compelling messages that appeal to stakeholders' interests.
5 Plan and develop your communication and advocacy campaign.
6 Begin communicating and do so regularly, honestly and consistently.
7 Monitor, measure and evaluate the impact of how you communicate.

References and further reading

Advocating Open Access – a toolkit for librarians and research support staff, produced by University College London, University of Nottingham and Newcastle University as part of a Jisc-funded project, http://find.jorum.ac.uk/resources/10949/20121.
University of Leicester (2015) *Make your Publications Open Access.* Available at: http://www2.le.ac.uk/library/for/researchers/publish/open-access. (Accessed 21.10.15)

Acknowledgements
Library Research Team, University of Leicester.

8.17 Do some research into open access issues yourself

IN ORDER TO better understand how researchers are responding to the imperatives of open access publishing, it helps to know more about the decisions they make in terms of when, how and where to communicate their research. As librarians, we can make assumptions about this and presume we know what the main concerns are and, although this can lead to some high-quality initiatives, we also run the risk of being viewed as patronizing or 'not understanding what it's really like to be a researcher' (UK researcher). If we are researchers ourselves, then we may have experienced some issues personally, but there may well be stumbling blocks of which we are unaware or which are perceived differently by different researchers. Knowing more about these areas can help tailor OA advocacy to address them with a clear researcher-centred approach. Before embarking on any OA advocacy campaign, therefore, it is wise to conduct some research of your own in this area.

If appropriate and manageable, you can conduct your own investigations with researchers with whom you work, perhaps simply by informal conversations or by asking questions within meetings. A more structured approach could consist of focus groups with selected researchers, online or paper surveys or semi-structured interviews.

An alternative might be to build on the work of others, ensuring that you have read recent reports (see below for examples) and are aware of any ongoing projects.

⚑ Best for:

- planning OA advocacy by getting to know your research community better.

★ Examples from practice

MIAO and CIAO
A current (2015) Jisc Pathfinder project 'Making Sense of Researcher Funder Mandates' seeks to explore researcher behaviours and the 'pain points' surrounding the publication process. It has produced several outputs:

- MIAO – My Individual Assessment of Open Access – 'is a self-assessment tool for researchers to assess how prepared they think they, and their institution, are for Open Access (OA) compliance.' It can be downloaded from http://bit.ly/ 1DCmIW9.
- CIAO – Collaborative Institutional Assessment of Open access – 'is a benchmarking tool for assessing institutional readiness for Open Access (OA) compliance'. The tool is based on CARDIO: Collaborative Assessment of Research Data Infrastructure and Objectives, http://cardio.dcc.ac.uk is available at http://bit.ly/1ElNIKY and is licensed under CC BY. You can download it and there are also instructions on how to use it.

Intervention mapping guides for understanding researcher behaviour
This process was developed by Julie Bayley at Coventry University as part of a Jisc-funded project. Intervention mapping is a process whereby you can think through:

- what the problems are
- what a better situation would look like (goal)

■ what (and whose) knowledge, attitudes and processes would help achieve the goals

■ what activities/approaches will most effectively produce the changes.

The process involves the use of a grid to identify the problems, goals to address the problem and the actions resulting from the goal. A facilitator's guide and blank mapping grid are available from http://find.jorum.ac.uk/resources/20119.

⚠ To think about

Think of ways in which you can learn more about the open access debate. Look for workshops to attend, follow blogs such as *The Scholarly Kitchen* (http://scholarlykitchen.sspnet.org/) to see what other people are saying. Don't just lurk, join in the debates.

References and further reading

Crossick, G. (2015) *Monographs and Open Access: a report to HEFCE,* www.hefce.ac.uk/media/hefce/content/pubs/indirreports/2015/Monographs,and,open,access/2014_monographs.pdf. (Accessed 28.7.15)

European Universities Association (2015) *EUA'S Open Access Checklist For Universities: a practical guide on implementation,* www.eua.be/Libraries/Publications_homepage_list/Open_access_report_v3.sflb.ashx.

Jisc (2015) Open access website, www.jisc.ac.uk/open-access.

Acknowledgements

Rowena Rowse, Oxford Brookes University; Julie Bayley, Coventry University.

8.18 Create open access and publication process flowcharts

INCREASINGLY, AUTHORS ARE becoming aware of the need to publish their work in an open access journal, but many struggle with understanding the process and with identifying the most appropriate options. It can be helpful to create a simple open access flowchart or checklist that could be used by authors, or perhaps by administrators, to help them to work through the different stages of the submission process.

If publication has already been accepted in a printed journal the situation is even more complex. Anyone with experience of writing for publication will know that once your work has been accepted by a publisher the focus is all on the future. Earlier versions of the work are often deleted, or at least not saved in any systematic way; filing and organization are rarely a key component of the creative process of writing. In practical terms, this approach creates a real barrier to open access deposit in the institutional repository as, already moving on to new areas, a researcher may be reluctant to spend time going back to sort out material that they feel is completed.

In addition, authors may simply be unaware of the limitations placed on them by their contract with the publisher or in many cases they feel it's safe to ignore the small print. A common attitude is that 'it's my work, surely I can do what I want with it'. Librarians working with researchers to encourage deposit in an institutional repository are frequently presented with inappropriate versions of the work; rarely is a publisher's PDF acceptable. Providing a flowchart for the writing-up process can help researchers to develop a more systematic publication workflow.

👍 Best for:

■ developing a publication workflow to encourage researchers to make their work available via open access routes.

★ Examples from practice

Australian OA Support Group
The Australian Open Access Support Group provides a useful OA journal options flowchart (Figure 8.6), available on a CC BY licence.

OA Checklists
Some universities provide a checklist of reminders to researchers when writing up their work, for example:

■ Lancaster University, UK, www.lancaster.ac.uk/media/lancaster-university/content-assets/documents/library/open-access/OpenAccessCheckl ist.pdf.
■ York University, UK, www.york.ac.uk/library/info-for-researchers/open-access/guide.

> 'I don't use the checklist in any kind of formal way, but just knowing about it reminds me that I have to think about saving different versions as I'm writing – I think it's probably saved me time in adding stuff to the repository.' (UK researcher)

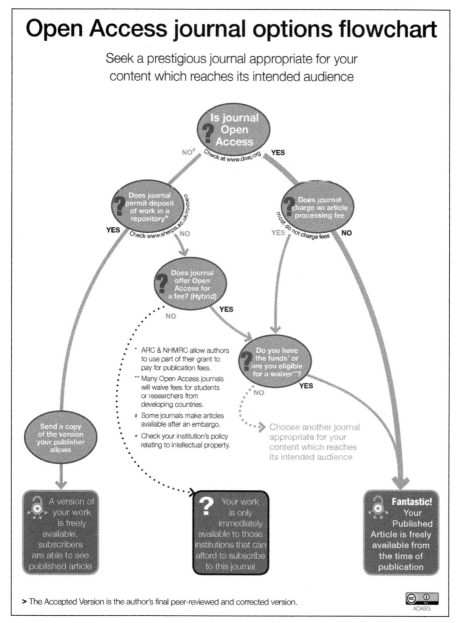

Figure 8.6 *Open access flowchart (Australian Open Access Support Group, CC BY)*

⚠ To think about

Before creating a flowchart, it may be helpful to talk to researchers from different disciplines about their research workflows to ensure that you take all eventualities into account.

References and further reading

Australian Open Access Support Group,
    http://aoasg.org.au/welcome-to-the-aoasg/about.

Acknowledgements

Steve Boneham, Newcastle University.

8.19 Promote your institutional repository

MANY ORGANIZATIONS try to collect their published output in an institutional repository but it can be difficult to encourage researchers to deposit their work. One of the issues is lack of awareness of the repository, coupled with a belief that only traditional publishing methods (i.e. academic journals) have any real influence over future impact. Researchers may feel that the process involved in depositing materials is opaque and don't understand what the benefits can be. Advocacy, raising awareness of the existence of the repository, as well as the benefits that may accrue, is a key way in which information staff can help. Advocacy can take many forms; you can try:

- talking to individuals and groups
- giving formal presentations
- providing background information on web pages
- providing real-time information on downloads.

Devising a way to demonstrate the impact of your institutional repository can seem a difficult task, but with a little creativity you can draw out some key data and present it in a tailored way to key researchers.

👍 Best for:

- engaging researchers with the institutional repository
- ensuring researchers are aware of the benefits of their institutional repository.

★ Examples from practice

Open University, UK

Staff at the Open University produce faculty-specific infographics (see an example in Figure 8.7) each year demonstrating deposits, downloads, the percentage of open access deposits, top authors, top items and five-year trends. This visualization of the repository data is delivered to senior faculty staff during meetings with the

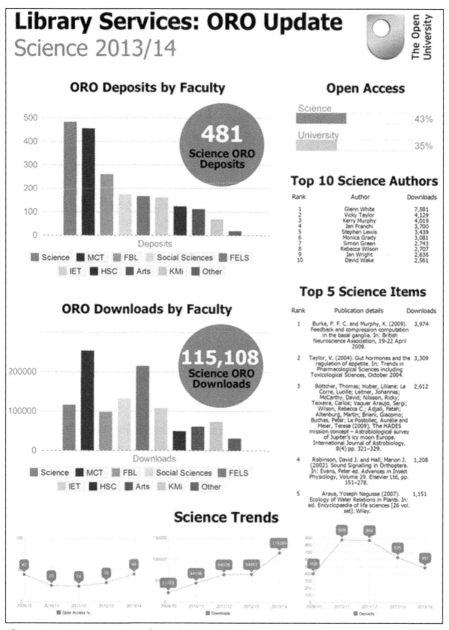

Figure 8.7 *An open access infographic, Open University (reproduced with permission)*

Faculty Associate Deans for research and provides them with key statistics in a visually striking way. Trends over time can be identified, as can comparisons with other faculties. The graphics evolve over time as priorities change: for example, percentage of open access materials is increasingly important.

'This has had the result of getting me invited to the next Science Research and Enterprise Committee next week to discuss it in more detail. The Associate Dean has just rung me and asked for more figures.' (C. Biggs, Open University)

Trinity College Dublin, Ireland

At Trinity College Dublin, the Research Support Librarian regularly contacts all 158 researchers in her discipline area by e-mail, soliciting recent author manuscripts. These are checked for copyright and versioning and deposited on behalf of the researcher into the institutional repository.

'This integrates me into the work flow of the researcher and fulfils the library's need to be in a strategic position.' (Jessica Eustace-Cook, Trinity College Dublin)

⚠ To think about

Do some research beforehand to determine what repository data is important to your organization. (see Tip 4.5)

Don't assume you know all the reasons that are inhibiting deposit. Individuals may have different priorities, skills and approaches that influence their behaviour.

Take time to talk to researchers and listen to their responses, factoring them into the solution where feasible.

'Make sure you know the research environment around OA and the different models. In Ireland we only support Green OA so the UK Gold model causes some confusion.' (Jessica Eustace-Cook, Trinity College Dublin)

Acknowledgements

C. Biggs, N. Dowson, Open University; Jessica Eustace-Cook, Trinity College Dublin.

8.20 Create unique researcher identifiers

ALTHOUGH SEVERAL SYSTEMS exist to allocate unique registration numbers to authors, for example ResearcherID from Thomson Reuters, the current most commonly used system is ORCID (Open Researcher and Contributor ID). ORCID is an international, interdisciplinary, open and not-for-profit organization created to solve the researcher name ambiguity problem and aims to become the universally accepted unique identifier for researchers. The ORCID system provides a unique, persistent digital identifier for every researcher. This is helpful, as it avoids issues of attribution that may arise if a researcher has a common name or if they have used different forms of their name when publishing work. Perhaps they have changed institution, used different combinations of initial or changed their name completely. It's important that researchers receive credit for all their published work, as this information can affect applications for jobs and future career prospects, as well as enhancing their standing in the academic community. ORCID is also increasingly being used to support automated linkages between researchers and online platforms and databases so that publications are correctly assigned and details automatically uploaded. Library staff can create their own ORCID identifier (this obviously works best if you have publications to link to it, but you can still create one for demonstration purposes) and can also encourage all researchers to register. ORCID identifiers can be added to author records in the institutional repository and link to other online platforms, such as ResearcherID.

Individual registration for an ORCID identifier is free, but premium organization-level membership, for a fee, provides additional benefits. As well as connecting systems to ORCID, to enable synchronization with local repositories for example, member organizations can receive alerts from ORCID on the activities of their researchers with respect to ORCID and published works. This can feed into institutional reporting systems to help create a picture of the research output of the organization.

In the UK at the time of writing there are 13 HEI ORCID members and Jisc has just concluded a successful consultation on membership of a consortium to reduce membership costs. In addition, a wider group of national funding bodies, such as the Higher Education Funding Council and Research Councils UK, along with library bodies such as SCONUL and RLUK, have signed a joint statement supporting the ORCID initiative (Jisc,2015).

🖒 Best for:

- encouraging researchers to register a unique author identifier.

★ Examples from practice

Texas A&M University, USA

At Texas A&M University the library started work in 2013 on integrating ORCIDs into the work of all researchers, focusing initially on early career researchers and graduate students. By integrating ORCIDs into their management systems, all theses and dissertations from 2014 onward are automatically associated with the author's ORCID. This approach ensures that 'our newest scholars can benefit

from a carefully-curated and unique scholarly identity over a lifetime career'
(Texas A&M University Libraries, 2015). As masters and doctoral students
enrolled for their courses in 2014, the Libraries assigned over 10,000 ORCID
identifiers to them. Anyone who received an ORCID from the University Libraries
in February 2014 has a record in the Libraries' ORCID master file and the campus
directory. Other researchers can request an ORCID be created for them or, if they
already have one, can have their details added to the master file.

Imperial College, UK

In 2014 Imperial College London became a member of ORCID. A cross-College project
was set up to issue all academic and research staff with ORCID IDs, under the
framework of the College's Open Access Project. The ORCID project identified 764
existing IDs linked to College staff and created 3,226 new ones. Within seven weeks
from ORCID creation, 1,155 academics had logged into their ORCID accounts and
linked them to Symplectic Elements, the College's publication management system.

Reimer, 2015

University of Northumbria, UK

At Northumbria, the University Library has been proactively promoting and
supporting ORCID, both as an identifier in the institutional repository Northumbria
Research Link (NRL) and as part of a well established research skills programme. Our
approach to the pilot project was to establish a partnership with stakeholders from
around the University to explore the broader implementation of ORCID at different
stages of the research lifecycle and researchers' career paths.

Cole, 2015

⚠ To think about

It helps if senior figures in your organization are supportive. You might contact
your Vice Chancellor or whoever is the head of your institution and offer to help
them sign up to ORCID.

Identify the key researchers in your organization and contact them directly to
offer to help them sign up to ORCID.

*'I found that starting at the top and getting our VC to register meant that it was much
easier to encourage others to do it.' (Librarian, UK university)*

Check to see which researchers have registered for ORCID recently and tweet,
blog or create a short news item about them regularly. Pass this information on
to your research office or faculty research contacts if you are in a university.

Make sure that, if you have published yourself, that you practise what you preach and have an ORCID yourself.

References and further reading

Cole, E. (2015) *Embedding ORCID Across Researcher Career Paths: final project summary*, https://orcidnorthumbria.wordpress.com. (Accessed 17.7.15)

Jisc (2015) Open access website, www.jisc.ac.uk/open-access.

Reimer, T. (2015) *Imperial College London ORCID Project*, https://repository.jisc.ac.uk/5876/1/Imperial_College_ORCID_project.pdf. (Accessed 30.4.15)

Texas A&M University Libraries (2015) *ORCID and Other Researcher Identifiers: ORCID integration*, http://guides.library.tamu.edu/content. php?pid=553864&sid=4564757. (Accessed 16.4.15)

8.21 Bibliometrics

IN RECENT YEARS, the use of quantitative indicators of quality and impact of research has grown in popularity, despite their being 'usually well intentioned, not always well informed, often ill applied' (Hicks et al., 2015). Some universities are using specific metrics, such as the h-index, to inform promotion and appointment decisions, whilst others insist that researchers only publish in journals which are ranked in the top quartile in journal impact ranking tables, using this as a measure to allocate funding. This can be particularly frustrating if data is used to compare research across disciplinary boundaries, as arts and humanities subjects are not as well represented as sciences. Metrics are also used in league tables to evaluate university quality, so it's understandable that managers become obsessed by them and sometimes apply them indiscriminately without a clear understanding of their meaning.

Librarians have been working with bibliometrics for years and so are well placed to offer advice and impartial information about their value. The use of such data, however, is relatively new territory for many researchers and research administrators, so this offers an excellent opportunity for librarians to add value to the research lifecycle.

Some libraries have developed new bibliometrician posts, in others existing staff are developing and extending their skills; what is clear, however, is that this is an area with which libraries have to engage.

There are many ways in which you can engage with the bibliometrics agenda with individual researchers, research groups or at a strategic level. Here are a few suggestions, drawn from different university libraries:

- Add bibliometrics data to entries in the institutional repository.
- Provide clear guidelines on how to calculate different metrics, with information on their strengths and shortcomings.
- Run workshops for researchers and research administrators to explain the different metrics available.
- Provide data on the organizations' most cited papers and researchers.
- Provide data on behalf of individuals or research groups.
- Contribute research impact metrics for grant applications and research proposals.
- Collect data to feed into benchmarking exercises.

As well as the more traditional metrics, which rely mainly on manipulation of citations in peer-reviewed journals, alternative metrics (altmetrics) are harvesting data from a wide variety of less formal sources. Researchers and many others may discuss the outcomes of research projects on social media platforms such as Facebook and Twitter and share information using tools such as Mendeley and CiteULike, or gateways such as ResearchGate and Academia. Altmetrics, therefore, might indicate how frequently a paper has been viewed or downloaded, can record discussions in journals, blogs and social media and highlight when items have been bookmarked, linking this data to citations in the literature. Although perhaps not a reliable tool for indicating the academic rigour and longevity of a paper, these metrics are nevertheless a useful indicator of initial impact. As the sources from which the data are derived are so publicly accessible, however, altmetrics can be manipulated even more easily than other metrics by authors who self-cite or use gaming techniques to create a false impression of their impact. Even so, several established publishers are collaborating with the Altmetrics organization to provide this additional data alongside their journal articles, giving instant, regularly updated snapshots of the impact of each individual paper.

👍 Best for:

- giving structured advice to the university on bibliographic indicators and metrics
- adding value to the research process by clarifying how metrics can be used to measure the impact of research outcomes.

★ Examples from practice

Adding altmetrics data to the institutional repository

Leeds Beckett University Library adds an altmetrics button to each entry in their institutional repository, indicating whether the research has been picked up by

news outlets or blogged or tweeted about: http://eprints.leedsbeckett.ac.uk/183.
See Figure 8.8. for an example.

Figure 8.8 *Leeds Beckett University institutional repository (reproduced with permission)*

Research Impact Measurement Service at University of New South Wales, Australia

In 2005, University Library staff at UNSW created a Research Impact
Measurement Service (RIMS) that in 2009 produced over 30 reports every month
and employed 6–7 full-time-equivalent staff.

Most of the reports are used to support promotion, grants, and institutional
comparisons. This research support service also informs and improves the
performance of such traditional library activities as collection development. RIMS is
now integral to the measurement of research outputs at UNSW, and has significantly
raised the profile of the Library throughout the academic community.

Drummond and Wartho, 2009

Online bibliometrics guides

Bibliometrics are not for everyone, but it is becoming increasingly important that researchers appreciate how they may be used to measure effectiveness or to provide evidence of success. Many libraries produce online guides to assist researchers to better understand what they are and how they work. Newcastle University Library's *Research Impact Guide* has pages explaining different metrics and how to calculate them: http://libguides.ncl.ac.uk/impact (accessed 1.6.15). As well as the citation and journal measures and tools the University of Oxford's *Bibliometrics and Citation Tracking* guide explains university rankings and league tables: http://ox.libguides.com/bibliometrics (accessed 1.6.15). Yale University Library's *Research Impact* guide also encourages researchers to broaden their impact by explaining how to develop a digital identity: http://guides.library.yale.edu/impact/home (accessed 1.6.15).

⚠ To think about

Keeping up to date with advances in bibliometrics is challenging; however, it's important to be able to give well informed impartial advice, so look for ways to keep up with the literature in this area. Following a blog, such as *The Scholarly Kitchen*, http://scholarlykitchen.sspnet.org/about, ensures that you are aware of key issues.

Bear in mind that publications in different disciplines have different timescales in terms of citation patterns and their cited half-life, which can skew results.

None of the sources currently available to track bibliometrics data is comprehensive, reliant as they are on the underlying database, so getting a true quantitative picture of the impact of an individual is impossible. However, despite their shortcomings they do offer a quick and dirty snapshot of the relative position of a researcher within their community and as such, should not be dismissed out of hand.

Do not apply the same indicators in all circumstances; select those that correspond to the context in which they are to be applied. For example, think about when it is appropriate to look at altmetrics and when other measures might be more relevant.

References and further reading

Corrall, S., Kennan, M. A. and Afzal, W. (2013) Bibliometrics and Research Data Management Services: emerging trends in library support for research, *Library Trends*, **61** (3), 636–74.

Crotty, D. (2014) Altmetrics: mistaking the means for the end, *The Scholarly Kitchen*, http://scholarlykitchen.sspnet.org/2014/05/01/altmetrics-mistaking-the-means-for-the-end. (Accessed 1.5.14)

Drummond, R. and Wartho, R. (2009) RIMS: the Research Impact
    Measurement Service at the University of New South Wales, *Australian
    Academic & Research Libraries*, **40** (2), 76–87.
Gumpenberger, C., Wieland, M. and Gorraiz, J. (2012) Bibliometric Practices
    and Activities at the University of Vienna, *Library Management*, **33** (3),
    174–83.
Hicks, D., Wouters, P., Waltman, L., de Rijcke, S. and Rafols, I. (2015)
    Bibliometrics: The Leiden Manifesto for research metrics, *Nature*, **520**,
    7548, www.nature.com/news/bibliometrics-the-leiden-manifesto-for-
    research-metrics-1.17351.
MacColl, J. (2010) Library Roles in University Research Assessment, *LIBER
    Quarterly*, **20** (2), 152–68.
Warr, R. B. (1983) Bibliometrics: a model for judging quality, *Collection
    Building*, **5** (2), 29–34.

8.22 Assist in tracking citations

OF MORE PERSONAL and relevant interest to researchers than the bare statistics
delivered by many bibliometrics tools is information about how their
research has been cited and subsequently used. Most large individual
databases capture citation information for articles and authors within their
system and some (Web of Science and Scopus, for example) provide analytics
demonstrating source of citation by country, year, etc. There are also several
freely available web-based portals which assist in recording and tracking
citations. ResearchGate (www.researchgate.com) harvests citation information
and alerts authors to new papers, as does Google Scholar (www.scholargoogle.
com) and a myriad of similar systems. At the time of writing, Elsevier are
developing their Researcher Dashboard, pulling in citations from their own
journals and elsewhere.

However, none of these sources consistently records a comprehensive list
of a researcher's total output and subsequent recognition; gathering this kind
of information can quickly become difficult to manage. Whilst it is relatively
easy to set alerts for new citations to a publication, maintaining a
comprehensive record of citing articles in a systematic way is much less easy.
For example, although an author can add details of their own publications to
ResearchGate and Google Scholar, it isn't possible to submit details of
subsequent citations. The F1000 Beta seems to promise this kind of
sophisticated functionality, but is limited by discipline.

👍 **Best for:**

■ keeping a comprehensive list of citations.

★ Examples from practice

Calculate Your Academic Footprint

This example from the University of Waterloo in Canada is an excellent example of how one library has tackled the issue of recording citations. Kathy MacDonald and Peter Stirling at the University of Waterloo have developed a LibGuide called Calculate Your Academic Footprint (see Figure 8.9), which takes researchers through the process of using bibliographic software (RefWorks) to track and monitor citations to their publications. The software is used to record an author's publications and a system devised to record and link citing articles to the cited paper within the software.

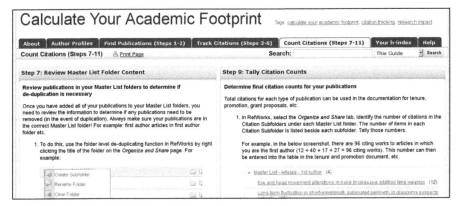

Figure 8.9 *Calculate Your Academic Footprint web page, University of Waterloo (with permission from Shannon Gordon)*

⚠ To think about

What can you offer to help researchers record citation information? This deceptively simple task is less easy in practice and, if you are able to offer a solution, this can provide a useful way into the research community.

References and further reading

F1000 Beta web page, http://f1000.com/work.

University of Waterloo Library, Calculate Your Academic Footprint web page, http://subjectguides.uwaterloo.ca/content.php?pid=84805&sid=2787897. (Accessed 24.4.15)

8.23 Publicize research output

GIVEN THE ENERGY expended in undertaking research and producing outcomes, the effort devoted to publicizing and celebrating the production of new knowledge can be relatively limited. This is an opportunity for library staff to help raise the profile of researchers both within their organization and externally. If work is deposited in an institutional repository, look for ways to highlight papers, perhaps simply by tweeting about new additions regularly, or by tweeting about papers with the highest downloads each week. Similarly, by registering on platforms such as ResearchGate, librarians can follow research activity, congratulate their researchers and select researchers or themes to tweet about. If local or national events are taking place, material from the repository relevant to such events can also be emphasized.

Often one of the first places where researchers report new research results is at conferences, but apart from a few specialized repositories, such as f1000posters (http://f1000.com/posters), unless the presentations are written up as conference papers, this cutting-edge information is often lost. The library can provide both physical and virtual spaces to retain and publicize this kind of activity. At a simple level, posters which have been presented at conferences can be regularly displayed in the library after the conference. Once this becomes accepted practice, researchers often appreciate the recognition this affords them.

Such posters can also be hosted virtually, as can slides from presentations. Some researchers may be in the habit of uploading slide presentations to online platforms such as SlideShare, but this is likely to be inconsistent. In the same way that libraries manage institutional repositories, libraries can create and manage databases of conference presentations and posters. As well as providing a central resource for the organization to manage all research output and an easy source for publicizing work, such a facility is helpful in harvesting information about the impact of research, always of interest for any research assessment exercise.

🖒 Best for:

■ demonstrating how the library can help publicize new research
■ keeping up to date with new research in your organization
■ building relationships with researchers.

★ Examples from practice

Leeds Beckett University, UK

Leeds Beckett University Library produces information guides linked to specific events or weeks, such as national Dementia Awareness Week (Figure 8.10). As well as highlighting library resources on the topic, it pulls data from the

Figure 8.10 *Leeds Beckett University Dementia Awareness Week web page, http://libguides.leedsbeckett.ac.uk/daw2015 (reproduced with permission)*

institutional repository to demonstrate how relevant the university's research is to the wider community.

▲ To think about

It is more likely that slides presented at a conference will include material that is not copyright-cleared. As well as providing a central repository for the presentations, therefore, you may also have to factor in time to check for copyright and attribution.

As platforms for hosting slides are already freely available, rather than creating a separate resource, might the library offer to manage and tag material on a public platform on behalf of researchers?

8.24 Celebrate theses

IT IS COMMON practice for university libraries to hold the definitive copies of theses submitted for a higher degree, traditionally in print, but also now in electronic form, as part of the institutional repository. However, even though our postgraduate students spend a minimum of three years researching their thesis and may get to know library staff well during that process, it is rare that libraries do more than receive the completed work, catalogue it and assign it to safe storage, whether physical or virtual.

Is there a case for celebrating the completion of such a major piece of research and if so, how might the library contribute? In large institutions the volume may be too great to do more than create a weekly or monthly list of new theses received, which could be highlighted on the library's website, or at a more granular level on specific subject pages such as LibGuides. Perhaps supervisors might be encouraged to nominate a thesis which they feel merits more publicity for a 'thesis of the month' or 'key new research' feature on the web pages?

👍 Best for:

■ building relationships with researchers
■ engaging doctoral students
■ demonstrating how the library can be involved in the whole research process
■ widening awareness of research.

★ Examples from practice

Nailing the thesis

In Sweden, before the final submission, candidates for PhD are encouraged to nail their thesis in a public space to invite feedback. In many universities, the library is the accepted common space and some libraries have a recognized space incorporating a noticeboard, where the thesis will be nailed with due ceremony (see Figure 8.11).

At Umea University, for example, the ceremony takes place three weeks before the official defence of the thesis and the thesis is made available on the digital repository at the same time. Although the nailing isn't compulsory, many of the approximately 200 theses published at Umea each year are also nailed. The procedure is said to originate from 1517, when Martin Luther posted his 95

Figure 8.11 *Nailing the thesis at Umea University (© Anders Lennver, reproduced with permission)*

theses on the church door in Wittenberg. The small nailing ceremony is attended by the candidate, often some family members, colleagues and supervisors and a member of library staff.

⚠ To think about

It's unlikely that you'll want to replicate the Swedish nailing ceremony, but it serves as an example of the library's involvement in the completion of a major piece of research. Are there other ways in which this could happen? Can you set up an automatic feed from the library catalogue to help publicize newly received theses? Might this be an opportunity to work with the research office to publicize them jointly?

References and further reading

A slightly more unusual example of the nailing ceremony at SLU Arlap, involving a singing supervisor, can be viewed on YouTube at www.youtube.com/watch?v=ONuJ2_8z6PI&app=desktop. (Accessed 20.4.15)

Information about their nailing ceremony requirements can be found on the Karolinska Institute website, https://internwebben.ki.se/en/nailing-and-distribution. (Accessed 20.4.15)

Acknowledgements

Therese Erixon, Umea University, Sweden.

SECTION 9

Teaching approaches

9.1 Learn some teaching theory to enable you to plan for successful teaching

HAVING AN UNDERSTANDING of the theories of teaching and learning is essential for running successful workshops and other learning experiences with researchers. Although it may not be possible to follow a whole course on teaching, it is helpful to sign up for any opportunities which arise. Many universities run academic practice courses for new academic staff and will welcome participation by library staff too. As well as giving you the chance to learn, they are excellent opportunities to network and build relationships – connections made during a shared experience like this will put any future communications on a different footing, as you are much more likely to be perceived as an equal.

If such courses aren't available, there are many online opportunities. In recent years, several MOOCs (massive open online courses) relating to teaching skills have been produced and over the years initiatives such as EduLib (McNamara and Core, 1998) in the UK have also sought to encourage library staff to develop their teaching skills. There are also several excellent books on teaching skills for library staff – see, for example Allan (2013), Powis, Webb and Blanchett (2010) and Secker, Boden and Price (2007).

One of the outcomes from any practical course on learning to teach relates to planning for a teaching and learning event. Successful planning is essential to the success of any lecture or workshop. When planning, keep in mind at all times what you want your participants to learn. This will help you to keep the session focused; remember, it's not about you and what you are going to say and do, it's about the learners and what they will be doing and thinking. Using a planning tool can help you to consider all the aspects, such as content and messages, timing, environment, activities, resources and the participants themselves. Bear in mind, too, that however well you plan, the unexpected may happen and this often relates to the learners themselves, who may have come along with different expectations. Building in sufficient flexibility to enable you to tailor a session to individual needs will ensure that both you and your learners will have a more enjoyable experience.

👍 Best for:

■ ensuring that teaching sessions are appropriate for the audience
■ developing a structured approach to teaching.

★ Examples from practice

Using a planning grid
Figure 9.1 is an example of a simple planning grid for a teaching session.

Time	Topic	Key points Purpose Learning outcomes	Presenter mode	Learners' activity	Resources needed	Environment
10 mins	Introduction	To provide a session map for group, to engage group in session, to check for prior knowledge	Discussion	Responding, answering questions, completing self-assessment quiz	Slides Handout	PC cluster
15 mins	Resources	To make students aware of key subject resources	Lecture demo	Listening, asking questions	Slides	
15 mins	Hands-on	To reinforce information	Workshop facilitation	Exploring resources	Worksheet	

Figure 9.1 *A simple planning grid for a teaching session*

The Learning Designer
Part of the London Knowledge Lab, a collaboration between the Institute of Education and Birkbeck College, the Learning Designer tool describes pedagogical patterns or approaches that can be adapted to different topics – see Figure 9.2. It includes a designer tool to help teachers to 'describe their own teaching ideas'. This can be used as an online planning tool in a similar way to the planning grid in Figure 9.1, but it also offers much more functionality to share approaches and to record teaching activity.

⚠ To think about

Consider what you can do to build flexibility into your teaching so that any sessions you are responsible for are responsive to the needs of the researchers

Figure 9.2 *The Learning Designer (reproduced with permission)*

attending. Think about the content and ensure you have sufficient variety to take account of individual needs. Teaching researchers is not the same as teaching undergraduates; although you may feel you know what they need to know, they are much more likely to have their own agenda, to have previous experience of different tools, resources and systems and to have differing expectations of what you can deliver.

> 'Some researchers are wedded to reference management tools other than the one that is officially supported here – e.g. if they have come from a different organization. I've learned it's better to work with them than to waste energy trying to persuade them to change (they won't) and any reference management software is better than none! I guess this could be generalizable – don't try to impose too much control over how researchers work and what they work with, it's about them becoming confident and competent using tools and systems that work for them.' (Melanie Gee, Sheffield Hallam University)

References and further reading

Allan, B. (2013) *The No-Nonsense Guide to Training in Libraries*, London, Facet Publishing.

Bewick, L. and Corrall, S. (2010) Developing Librarians as Teachers: a study of their pedagogical knowledge, *Journal of Librarianship and Information Science* **42** (2), 97–110.

Coursera MOOCs are listed at www.mooc-list.com/course/foundations-teaching-learning-1-introduction-coursera?static=true.

Future Learn MOOCs are listed at:
www.futurelearn.com/courses/categories/teaching-and-studying.
Learning Designer, http://learningdesigner.org/index.php. (Accessed 7.9.15)
London Knowledge Lab,
www.lkl.ac.uk/cms/index.php?option=com_content&task=view&id=610
&Itemid=91. (Accessed 7.9.15)
McNamara, D. and Core, J. (1998) *Teaching for Learning in Libraries and Information Services: a series of educational workshops: the EduLib Project and its teaching materials*, Hull, EduLib Project.
Powis, C., Webb, J. and Blanchett, H. (2010) *A Guide to Teaching Information Literacy: 101 tips*, London, Facet Publishing.
Secker, J., Boden, D. and Price, G. (2007) *The Information Literacy Cookbook: ingredients, recipes and tips for success*, London, Chandos.

Acknowledgements

Karen Crinnion, Newcastle University.

9.2 Track activity to help identify points of need in the research lifecycle

INFORMATION LITERACY IS a concept well understood by most librarians but the terminology is not familiar to many researchers or research administrators. Finding a way, therefore, to integrate the key aspects of information literacy into the research lifecycle can be fraught with complexity. Some libraries identify points of need, for example the literature review or writing up, within the research process and target specific workshops to meet those needs. Providing clear, unambiguous learning outcomes (without using librarian-speak) for such workshops makes this approach more easily achievable, if potentially less satisfying to deliver. Such workshops are often not compulsory, relying on individual researchers to identify their requirements and to actively both sign up and attend, but they are relatively easy to organize and advertise and enable the library to visibly demonstrate a contribution to the research process. There are many excellent examples of the content of individual workshops in Section 10 of this book.

Much less easy to achieve is proper integration into workflows and programmes so that information literacy development is viewed less as a skills-based element and more as a natural threshold concept in a researcher's learning life (see Tips 3.1–3.3).

A useful approach to engaging with researchers is to identify bottlenecks in the research process by actively tracking activity. For masters students, for example, knowing when dissertation projects are due to be handed in can help in planning specific workshops relating to writing up and referencing. Similarly, for postgraduate research students, targeting teaching at certain stages of their research so that it is relevant and can be applied immediately makes it much more effective.

> 'We used to offer a full programme of workshops covering getting started right through to measuring impact, right at the start of the postgraduate programme. Then we realized how silly that was, because it was far too soon for most of them to be tracking their h-index, for example. Now we have a workshop which gets them thinking about developing a profile and explains why, without going into the nitty-gritty of the metrics too soon. It works much better for them and for us too.' (UK librarian)

It may also be possible to track the progress of higher-level research. In Wisconsin, library staff actively check the websites of different research groups for possible copyright infringements and offer advice at an early stage. The health science librarians track grant awards, work with recipients on compliance requirements, check to confirm submission and follow up with those who are having difficulties for whatever reason (Kenney, 2014).

By being aware of the stages of a research project it is possible to offer advice and help in a timely manner.

> 'I try to chat to researchers on a regular basis and ask how their research is going, have they presented at a conference about it, have they started to write any papers and stuff like that. Sometimes it works so I'm then able to suggest I run a workshop that just fits with what they are thinking about. It's much better than having a standard programme and expecting them to slot into that, but it involves quite a lot of effort from me and you have to be able to tailor your workshop to fit very quickly.' (UK librarian)

👍 Best for:

- targeting interventions at pain points in the research process
- ensuring you are aware of the whole research process and what researchers are doing
- identifying new opportunities to get involved with researchers.

★ Examples from practice

University of Eastern Finland
At the University of Eastern Finland, the library staff 'follow the whole learning process and research careers' (Tomi Rosti, University of Eastern Finland). In practice this means postgraduate students have a series of courses integrated

into their syllabus, including 'Information skills for postgraduates' and 'Basics of academic publishing and research assessment' as well as short courses on specific aspects of research. 'The library is part of the academic community and structure, not a separate organization within the university' (Tomi Rosti, University of Eastern Finland).

Researcher development programme

In the Science Faculty at Newcastle University, UK, the Postgraduate Researcher Development Programme comprises a series of workshops linked to Vitae's Researcher Development Framework (Vitae, 2010). Using the associated Informed Researcher booklet (Bent et al., 2012), library staff have mapped their contribution to the RDF so that researchers can clearly see the relevance of the individual workshops to their overall personal development.

> 'The Library workshops are relevant to many of the domains of the Researcher Development Framework and we have added the RDF subdomains to each workshop description. If you are using the RDF to plan your CPD, you can use this to record how the Library workshops have contributed to your development as a researcher:
>
> Workshop 1: A1, A2, A3
> Workshop 2 & 5: A1, A2, B2, C2
>
> Workshop 3 & 4: A1, B1, C1
> Workshop 6: A1, A2, B2, B3' (Newcastle University)

Lund University Library, Sweden

Lund University Library staff use a model of the research process to help identify intervention opportunities (Wiklund and Voog, 2013). The model has four steps: start a research group, collect material, process/analyse/write and communicate results/make data accessible. The model was useful for identifying obstacles researchers might face and hence for visualizing appropriate services.

Interestingly, rather than focus on the library, in their discussions with researchers they asked them to identify obstacles and difficulties they faced during their research and then analysed the answers to identify opportunities. In some cases, this led to the library being purely a signpost to other sections of the organization but the overall outcome is a perception amongst researchers that the first place to go when facing a difficulty is the library.

⚠ To think about

As with any tailored or targeted interventions, the main issues to consider are scalability and flexibility. Is it practical to monitor research activity in this way in your context? Will you be able to produce high-quality teaching at very short notice?

Think about the difference between providing a suite of 'show and tell' workshops or online activities and a more complex information literacy development programme which challenges researchers to think differently about their interactions with information.

References and further reading

Bent, M., Gannon-Leary, P., Goldstein, S. and Videler, T. (2012) *The Informed Researcher*, London, Vitae, www.vitae.ac.uk/researcherbooklets.

Kenney, A. (2014) *Leveraging the Liaison Model: from defining 21st century research libraries to implementing 21st century research universities*, www.sr.ithaka.org/blog-individual/leveraging-liaison-model-defining-21st-century-research-libraries-implementing-21st. (Accessed 25.5.15)

Vitae (2010) *Researcher Development Framework*, www.vitae.ac.uk/researchers-professional-development/about-the-vitae-researcher-development-framework. (Accessed 20.4.15)

Wiklund, G. and Voog, H. (2013) It Takes Two to Tango: making way for relevant research support services at Lund University Libraries, *Sciecom Info*, 1. [Online.] Available at: http://journals.lub.lu.se/index.php/sciecominfo/article/view/6125. (Accessed 21.10.15)

Acknowledgements

Tomi Rosti, University of Eastern Finland; Hanna Voog, Lund University.

9.3 Aim for just-in-time teaching

HOW OFTEN DO you attend a workshop or event, learn something useful and then forget it because you don't have time or opportunity to apply it immediately? Relevance and timeliness are vital in learning and so if we are able to target workshops for researchers to the most appropriate points of need in the research process they are much more likely to be effective. Points of need will vary between different groups of researchers, and so it may not be possible to identify an optimum time for a session; rather, it may be necessary to repeat sessions or to compromise on timings to best meet the requirements of the majority (see Tip 9.1).

Fitting workshops into a larger schedule of events may also lead to compromise, so it's important to keep the aim and the needs of the audience in clear sight; after all, running a workshop with very few attendees wastes everyone's time.

Just-in-time teaching is about tailoring timing and content but it needn't necessarily add a lot of additional preparation time to your teaching. Devising a generic framework for a series of workshops enables a team of staff to teach from the same resources, adding consistency in approach while allowing flexibility in detailed content.

👍 Best for:

■ maximizing the impact of your teaching
■ targeting workshops at the most appropriate times to maximize attendance.

★ Examples from practice

Loughborough University, UK

Loughborough University Library offers a set of 34 workshops for researchers, covering all aspects of the research process from the theory and practice of finding information to details of open access and publication strategies. Sessions are tagged as appropriate for different stages of the research lifecycle and also with different levels of difficulty. For academic and research staff, the emphasis is on timing, so sessions are offered specifically for staff during spring and summer vacations. These short, 30-minute events aim for small groups and have a focus on refreshing and updating existing skills and knowledge.

⚠ To think about

What times of year will be most convenient for researchers to attend workshops? Are different times of day more suitable? Are you able to offer evening and weekend events? Are you aware of key times to avoid, perhaps because of events going on elsewhere or for religious or other personal reasons?

Do different groups have different constraints? Masters students usually have dissertation deadlines at the end of the summer vacation in the UK, but when do they start their research?

Acknowledgements
Helen Young, Loughborough University.

9.4 Offer individual consultations

LIBRARIANS HAVE ALWAYS offered individual help to researchers, often informally, responding to requests as the need arises.

'We are often the first people that academics contact – I know you aren't the right person for this but . . .' (Helen Young, Loughborough University)

However, this approach relies on the researcher being aware of the role of the librarian and actively seeking their help. If your researchers come from different countries or cultures, they may have differing experiences and expectations of the role of the library in research. An alternative, therefore, is to actively promote a consultation service and encourage researchers to seek your advice. Consultations need not be face-to-face meetings – they can take place by phone, e-mail, online chat or via a service such as Skype; the difference is that they are planned ahead and booked, offering the opportunity for a more structured discussion.

You may choose to make such an initiative available to all comers – after all, how does one define a research query? – or you may wish to restrict it to 'real' researchers, by which I mean people in the organization with a recognized research role. This will enable you to set limits to the number of potential enquiries and can also help to manage expectations, as well as being promoted as a premium service for the research community.

👍 Best for:

- getting to know individual researchers and their research
- finding out what researchers are struggling with
- raising awareness and developing information literacy amongst the research community.

★ Examples from practice

PLUS (personal library update sessions) for senior researchers

'Several years ago, at a meeting of research staff where resources were being discussed, I became aware that one or two of the older researchers had stopped contributing to the conversation. Afterwards, one confessed to me privately that he had felt embarrassed in front of his younger colleagues, as he had been relying on resources he had always known and hadn't kept up to date with newer developments. He asked if we could arrange an individual meeting so that I could update him on the newer resources and the search techniques needed to exploit them. Thus PLUS, the Personal Library Update Session, was born. We advertised PLUS as individual consultations for established researchers, acknowledging up front that they are busy people who can't be expected to keep up to date with developments in resources and other digital approaches as well as being experts in their research area. That, after all, is our job. PLUS was an instant success, with senior research figures seemingly relieved to be able

to admit that they were struggling to stay abreast of developments. "I usually ask one of my postgrads to look for information for me because to be honest, I'm not sure where to start these days" was a common refrain.' (UK university librarian)

Book a Librarian

A recent innovation at many, usually but not exclusively academic, libraries is the Book a Librarian offering, where users are encouraged to book an individual consultation with an experienced librarian in order to solve a specific query. At Newcastle University Library in the UK, Book a Consultancy is part of the wider Library Help service. Triaged through the help team, users are directed to a subject specialist to arrange an individual appointment. Once the appointment is arranged, but before it takes place, the researcher is encouraged to explain his or her query in more detail, so that the librarian is able to prepare for the meeting ahead of time. A simple Literature Search Planner form, adaptable for individual circumstances, is used either before or more often during the session to help inform and record it. Each year, the service is actively promoted at specific times of year, often with a theme to draw attention. For example, Library Bootcamp (see Figure 9.3) promoted a 'personal trainer' (individual consultation), 'a virtual gym' (online materials) and 'circuits' (specialized presentations).

⚠ To think about

An individual consultancy service is very demanding of staff time and can generate very high expectations of the outcomes, so it's imperative to be clear

Figure 9.3 *Library Boot Camp advertising*

from the outset about what you are offering.

> 'We can only fit so many sessions into a week but people always seem to think that we'll be able to fit just one more in.' (Helen Webster, Newcastle University)

Inevitably, people will turn up late or forget to come altogether, which can be frustrating if you've turned people away.

> 'Perhaps you can offer a clinic or surgery approach, making specialist staff available at a regular time each week for people to drop in with queries. This has worked well for our support for EndNote: users know that if they come to the surgery, they may have to wait their turn but there will be someone who has time to work through their problem with them.' (UK librarian)

Expectations of personal consultancies may not only relate to times and bookings; they may also be about outcomes.

> 'I was recently asked by a research student to help him identify all the different traits of a species with many sub-categories. In fact, this was the main thrust of his research project and he seemed to think I would be an unpaid research assistant, digging out all the data and going through it for him. It took a while to convince him that I would show him how to do it, but that he had to do the work himself.' (Librarian, Australian university)

Acknowledgements
Newcastle University Library.

9.5 Gain prior knowledge of participants

ONE OF THE difficulties for librarians who run workshops is that we only interact with the participants on an irregular basis and we rarely have the opportunity to get to know them well. Either people self-select and sign up individually, hence can come from anywhere and be at any level, or, even if they are an established cohort, it's unlikely that LIS staff have been able to spend a substantial amount of time with them. This can make designing workshops which are both timely and appropriate a difficult task, with the consequence that it can be more difficult to engage and keep the interest of the individuals in the group.

If you have time and opportunity, you can address this issue by finding out more about the researchers before you meet them.

If there is a sign-up list (or for research students a supervisor or graduate school administrator) you can look up individuals on the organization's web pages to see if you can find out more about their research interests. For a relatively small group, make time to check their publication profiles to see if they have published and hence how experienced they are. Alternatively, if there are contact details, you can e-mail them before the seminar to ask for information, perhaps by sending out a 'research summary sheet', which you can refer back to in the session.

With this prior knowledge you can prepare for the workshop by ensuring that you can demonstrate how to find information relevant to at least one participant. Foreknowledge also means you are less likely to be faced with a question on a topic you don't know.

> 'I was so pleased I'd checked what the terms meant beforehand so that I didn't lose face during the session.' (Indian librarian)

If you don't have the luxury of preparation time, it's still worth spending a few minutes at the start of a workshop finding out a little bit about your audience. Although you may not have time to ask about everyone's research in detail, you can ask for a show of hands, or use 'ask the audience' clickers to ascertain levels of knowledge and experience. As well as helping you understand your audience so that you can make the content of your talk more relevant, this technique encourages participants to engage and to feel that this session will really be relevant for them. If there is a member of the group with some expertise, it can be helpful to draw on this during the workshop, too.

👍 Best for:
- ■ ensuring workshops are relevant to participants
- ■ keeping your audience engaged.

★ Examples from practice

Liverpool University, UK
Library staff at Liverpool University run a compulsory monthly seminar for new PhD and MPhil students:

> 'When I send out an e-mail asking them to register, I also ask them to give me some keywords to describe their research. In advance of the session I run some searches using their keywords and when they arrive for the session I do a demonstration search relevant to one of the students in the room.' (Carole Rhodes, Liverpool University)

Carole explains that she always prepares multiple searches so that she can demonstrate a search for someone who is attending.

> 'You don't want to be committed to demonstrating a particular search if that student doesn't show'.

This also means she is confident of being able to offer individual search tips during the practical part of the workshop.

> 'I find it's a really simple technique that helps me feel prepared in advance and it increases student engagement in the session.'

Bangor University, UK
Beth Hall from Bangor explains her approach:

> 'I aim to gather information about the staff or students who will be in the audience before I give training sessions. If this is not possible I include questions at the beginning of the session about how much they already know.

> For PGR students I am trying to find out things like what information sources they have used before, what stage of their studies they are in, where they did and in what subject they did their UG studies.

> For research staff I am trying to find out what their research interests are, where and what they have published before, how long they have been in their career, are they editors of journals, how many PhD students do they have, how much teaching do they do, etc. Most of this is desk research – looking up their profile on the Uni webpages, ResearchGate or anywhere like that.

> Whether you discover someone interesting in the audience before or right at the beginning of the session, use them in the session by bringing them into the discussion, e.g. "Journal editors will give you feedback if you contact them to propose an idea for an article in their journal, would you say this is true for the journal that you edit Dr XXX?" or e.g. "How many of you blog at the moment? OK only one of you, Nicola, everyone ask Nicola if they want more advice about blogging then, do you blog about your research or other things in your life?"

> I still prepare slides for a planned session that would take around the time allotted, often with extra slides, but then I allow myself the option to go off-piste and to dip in and out of topics, depending on the audience. If the audience don't participate then they get the standard presentation. If the audience participate too much then I risk not getting important points across so I try to think of the 2 or 3 important take-home messages and try to get those back into the session.

I hope the audience thinks I am talking to them personally rather than just giving a standard presentation – the same for everyone. It's time-consuming and I can't afford the time to do this well, but I know it helps.' (Beth Hall, Bangor University)

⚠ To think about

When asking for prior information, don't ask for information you don't need: the simpler it is to respond the more likely you are to receive replies.

Suggest that people explain their research in simple terms, keywords and phrases rather than writing you a short essay!

Acknowledgements

Carole Rhodes, Liverpool University; Beth Hall, Bangor University.

9.6 Involve researchers in teaching

HOWEVER EXPERIENCED AN information professional is, few of us have the same depth of experience of research as a full-time researcher. Similarly, few researchers have the time or inclination to really understand the information world. Working together, however, can produce a much richer learning experience, allowing abstract concepts to be illustrated by real practical experiences.

Like me, I'm sure many librarians look for local examples of high-profile researchers to demonstrate, for example, what an h-index is and how it works. How much more effective it will be to invite that researcher to come along and talk about their personal impact and what it means to them. Perhaps they are actively looking for ways to increase their h-index; how and why are they doing this? As well as providing real examples, this kind of team teaching can validate sessions which might otherwise be dismissed as less relevant by less experienced researchers and can have unexpected benefits for more senior staff, too.

'Thanks for inviting me along to your workshop. I thought I was doing pretty well with my personal impact but some of the questions the researchers asked did make me think I can try harder.' (Senior researcher, UK university)

👍 Best for:

- adding authority to your workshops
- bringing a session to life
- using researchers' experiences to explain key concepts
- providing a local context for the workshop.

★ Examples from practice

Senior research staff may not have time to contribute to every workshop you want to run, so why not try recording them and then using a 'talking head'? This will also give you the flexibility (with their permission) of including the recording in any online materials you produce, as well as breaking up face-to-face workshops with a different voice.

Publishing companies have used this technique effectively too. The American Chemical Society videos on getting published, using respected authors, are a good example: http://acsoncampus.acs.org/resources/video/episode-1.

⚠ To think about

Remember that most researchers are very focused on their own research and may wish to use this opportunity to talk about what they are doing. Make sure you clarify the aims of the workshop and what you expect them to contribute, without constraining them too much.

> 'I've found it takes a few tries to get the balance right and also to make sure the folks you've invited understand what you're trying to do. The first time, he (the researcher) went off on a bit of tangent and it was hard to get the session back on track. The next time, I allowed time for that kind of thing because actually it was quite useful and the session appeared to be much more informal but still got the key stuff in there. So I'd say it's key to give them a bit of a steer but don't pin it down too much.' (Librarian, Australian University)

9.7 Video personal stories

PERSONAL STORIES CAN bring teaching to life. It's much easier to accept and understand something if you can see how it relates to your own work. Involving more experienced researchers in developing resources for other researchers can enhance the content immeasurably.

For example, rather than spending a lot of time producing high-quality, possibly slightly dry videos explaining a particular topic, why not film some researchers talking about how it works for them? It's possible to do this by just using a tablet or mobile phone, capturing short, direct snippets of information. This approach can also be very effective to demonstrate support for a topic in which you may not feel you can present yourself as an expert. A senior researcher may not have time to come along to every workshop you run on finding an h-index, but they may be willing to be videoed talking about their own experiences. How valuable do they find it? How do they use it? Do they try to manipulate the metrics by self-citation?

Similarly, controversial topics can be addressed by videoing several researchers who have different viewpoints on the same issue and this can be a helpful way to initiate a discussion amongst a group. An illustration of this might be when discussing the use of Twitter for academic networking. Many researchers dismiss it as irrelevant, but hearing a passionate proponent explain how it works for them can be very effective in changing perspectives.

If you have done some research yourself, at whatever level, talking about your own experiences brings the session to life; personal stories are always more memorable than abstract examples. Explaining how excited you felt the first time you saw your name in print, how frustrated you became at a certain obstacle, how disappointed when something didn't go to plan, helps your audience empathize and brings them into the session. If you don't have personal experiences to share, ask a colleague if you can use them as an example.

> *'I try to add in some interesting content that is new research or currently in development in the information profession, they are researchers and therefore I make the assumption that they are interested in new/novel ideas. For example, I talk about the research on the peer-review process, the data on costs of subscriptions now available online on figshare, about applying SR techniques from medical fields to other science disciplines.' (Beth Hall, Bangor University)*

🖒 Best for:

- adding authority to your workshops
- bringing a session to life
- using researchers' experiences to explain key concepts
- providing a local context for the workshop.

★ Examples from practice

Twitter addicts

One UK librarian was keen to encourage research staff to engage with Twitter as a serious research tool but was finding that it was often dismissed as irrelevant for serious research.

> *'I spent some time searching for folks at the university who do use Twitter seriously – it took a while trawling through Twitter and their web pages and then I monitored them for a few weeks to see how they were using them. Then I went and chatted to three people about what they were doing and eventually I asked if I could video them. The first time I tried it didn't work so well because he kept going off the topic and getting sidetracked so I learned to start off with a few key questions and I gave them beforehand so they could think about what they wanted to say. I found people were flattered to be asked to talk about what they*

were doing and one was keen to come along to the workshops when he could too – that
was a bonus.' (UK librarian)

'I've never really understood Twitter or why people waste so much time on it. Hearing how
Phil uses it with his research group has made me think I need to look at it again.'
(Researcher, UK university)

Researchers on writing

Keep in mind the kind of stories you are looking for and be prepared to capture
them informally at short notice:

'I was looking for ways to brighten up the classes we give for new authors – they can get a
little dull if you're just going through the processes and I realized how much better it would
be if I could pepper the points I was making with examples from real researchers here.
Obviously, I couldn't have a string of researchers waiting in the wings, so to speak, just to
say their piece, so I started asking if I could record snippets, usually when I was chatting to
them about something else. People are used to seeing short interviews on TV and YouTube
and they like the informality, so we have tried to go for the same kind of approach, nothing
slick and fancy, just talking heads really. I just use my phone, sometimes for a video, but
sometimes just an audio recording if they are more comfortable with that. You do have to
use the recordings sparingly, though, otherwise the novelty soon wears off, and they need
to be really, really short.' (Librarian, UK university)

⚠ To think about

Personal stories mean so much more if listeners can relate to them directly, so
linking to researchers from a different organization talking about their
experiences isn't nearly as effective as filming your own researchers. They can
add local colour and context and may be well known to other researchers
already.

Try to add diversity to your collection of stories by including researchers from
different disciplines and with different backgrounds; it's surprising how different
people will respond to the same question.

Even though you want the snippets to sound informal, you still need to plan
ahead. Prepare some open questions and give the researchers time to think
about their answers before you start filming. If you have time, chat informally or
run through their answers with them to ensure there are no unexpected
revelations: the less you have to edit the more natural the result will be.

If you can record researchers in their own research environment rather than in
the library, that adds an extra element of interest to the video.

Acknowledgements
Beth Hall, Bangor University.

9.8 Teach the teachers

AS HAS BEEN discussed elsewhere in this book, researchers may not always understand what librarians can offer and may not place a high value on our expertise and knowledge. This is particularly true of researchers coming from different countries and cultures, where their expectations of the role of the library are coloured by their previous experiences. Rather than feeling slighted or trying to justify your own worth, sometimes it is better to be pragmatic, accept the situation and look for ways around it. One such method is to identify people whom the researchers do respect and ensure that they are equipped and willing to be your messenger. For postgraduate research students the obvious choice is the research supervisor. Supervisors are more experienced researchers but they are not always fully abreast of the latest developments in resources and so are often less information literate than their younger counterparts, though not always willing to recognize or admit this. Finding tactful ways to 'teach the teachers' and to encourage them to pass on accurate messages can be a very successful way of upskilling more junior researchers.

'I tend to get the message across to senior staff by explaining I'd like to share with them what I plan to teach their students – I pretend I want to ask their opinion on the content to see if they think it meets the students' needs. Sometimes we will actually have that kind of discussion but more often they look a bit embarrassed and say "Oh, I didn't know about that", or "so what happened to . . ." whatever their favourite database of 10 years ago was. Then I can very tactfully suggest we look at it in a bit more detail and actually, if they get engaged with it all it can lead to some really useful suggestions from them on the workshop which makes it better for all of us.' (UK librarian)

The Research Information Network report on information literacy for supervisors (Research Information Network, 2011) concluded that researchers consistently look to supervisors for guidance but that supervisors may not be up to date with information literacy skills and knowledge. The report recommends that it is helpful to make it clear what opportunities are available for research students and supervisors and should also encourage peer support between supervisors.

👍 Best for:

- finding champions to reinforce your message
- ensuring research supervisors are up to date.

★ Examples from practice

PLUS (see also Tip 9.4)

'The PLUS (Personal Library Update Sessions) grew out of a chance conversation with a senior academic who confessed privately that he was very unsure of the latest databases available and was concerned that he wasn't giving the best advice to his research students. He felt embarrassed to admit this in front of his colleagues and students and had managed the situation by telling his students to "go to the library and ask the staff there". Good advice, but ineffective, as he discovered his students seemed to be missing out on key articles by searching unsuccessfully. PLUS gave senior academics and research supervisors an opportunity to have a one-to-one consultation with library staff, admitting their lack of knowledge in private and learning about the latest resources and techniques to recommend to others.' (UK Librarian)

'Thank you for explaining what happened to BIDS and Athens, I felt very out of date and I'm ashamed I just coasted along for so long. Things seem much more straightforward now.' (UK academic)

Supervisor training

One UK librarian has been successful in embedding information literacy workshops into programmes which the university research office runs for research supervisors.

'The workshops are perceived by supervisors as a central part of the training, not just a library add-on, so I think they do appreciate what we offer. We can talk explicitly about what research students need and what our role should be so it works from both sides.' (UK librarian)

▲ To think about

Getting the message across to research students via their supervisor is an excellent tactic, but sometimes messages can lose something in the translation. One way to ensure consistency in delivery is to back up your message with online or printed materials to which supervisors can refer their students.

References and further reading

Research Information Network (2011) *The Role of Research Supervisors in Information Literacy*, London, RIN.

9.9 Deliver short focused sessions (see also Tip 9.3)

ACONTINUING CHALLENGE for LIS staff engaging with researchers is how to develop their information literacy skills without seeming patronizing, or disengaging them by offering long workshops on topics which they feel they already know. One solution is to offer short, specific sessions on discrete topics, available at times when researchers are likely to be free, perhaps over a lunchtime or early evening. The location of short sessions may be the deciding factor in determining attendance – is it worth walking across to the library for just a half-hour workshop? Might the sessions be better held in a location closer to key research groups, or can they move around to different locations? Catering can be a big attraction for such sessions. Whilst it may seem inconsequential and an unnecessary expense, knowing there will be a drink and/or snack available just might make the time investment more attractive to busy researchers. It's just multitasking, after all!

👍 Best for:

- engaging researchers with key topics
- focusing on snappy specific messages.

★ Examples from practice

Research Bites at Aston University, UK

Aston University Library has addressed this issue by running a weekly seminar series called 'Research Bites' during July and August for the last four years. The formal part of each seminar lasts for approximately 30 minutes, though participants may stay longer than this if they wish to follow up on specific issues. The seminars are deliberately timed during the long summer vacation, partly because library staff have more time to deliver them and partly so that academic staff and researchers have more time to attend. Participants are invited to bring their own 'brown bag' lunch and drinks are provided by the library. Each session is recorded using lecture capture software for those unable to attend. Topics are varied each year to encourage repeat attendance and include quite specific topics such as: choosing a journal, social networks, company research, get more citations, safeguarding research data, ORCID.

> 'Although attendance at the seminars hasn't been huge, the people who have come have been very enthusiastic and keep coming back. Some sessions have initiated cross-school discussions which they seem to find very helpful.' (Georgina Hardy, Aston University)

Research Elevenses at Leicester University, UK

The University of Leicester runs 'Research Elevenses' sessions, specifically targeted to fit into coffee break time. These 30-minute sessions focus on current topics of interest, currently encompassing OA publishing, impact factors and research data management. As with their more ambitious distance researcher webinars (see Tip 5.2), the Elevenses sessions are run as simultaneous webinars and face-to-face seminars, enabling distant researchers to participate alongside local people. These sessions are recorded and are freely available to view.

Elevenses at Loughborough University, UK

Loughborough University also run 'Elevenses' sessions, which last for 30 minutes with an option to stay on and practise.

> 'It's important to manage expectations – we found that even though we advertised the sessions as being only 30 minutes, we still got comments that they were too short. We try to be realistic and to make sure we choose topics which can easily be covered in half an hour, something like beginners' Twitter for example.' (Helen Young, Loughborough University)

Lunchtime seminars at Sheffield Hallam University, UK

> 'I developed a short series of lunchtime seminars (45 mins–1 hour) going a bit deeper into literature searching and reviews, in particular focusing on practical issues such as keeping organized/staying sane during a review; and also one on choosing your title, abstract, and keywords appropriately to try to get your paper read and cited. I circulated all the materials (including slides with extensive annotations) after each session, more widely than the actual audience. I found that these also tended to get passed on to other research/teaching colleagues and postgrad students – a happy side-effect being that this has enhanced my reputation within the department and generated spin-off queries and literature reviewing work.' (Melanie Gee, Sheffield Hallam University)

ScHARR Research Hacks

Not all short focused sessions need to be delivered face to face. A series of short focused videos can deliver the same outcome. The Library at the University of Sheffield's School of Health and Related Research (ScHARR) in the UK has developed a set of over 40 very short and snappy videos using an app called Voice from Adobe. Their aim is to explain a very simple idea or technology to researchers, not to show them how to use them but just to raise awareness of their potential for research. Topics covered include, for example, tips to deal with information overload, post-publication peer review, how to maximize impact and many more. The videos are usually just a minute long and rely on a simple audio presentation enhanced by simple images and music. They are all available on YouTube and iTunesU. For a full list and to listen to the recordings visit:

www.youtube.com/playlist?list=PL1mJ7lZ3qFxjR8HhL9HX-ETHUFJz639Bt.

⚠ To think about

> 'Publicity is key. We send a direct e-mail to everyone who has attended before and we change our e-mail signatures each week in the summer to highlight the latest bite.' (Georgina Hardy, Aston University)

If you can identify a champion who will encourage colleagues to attend or suggest new topics then that also helps. 'Don't be afraid to fail, but don't give up straightaway' is good advice from Helen Young of Loughborough University. Try out a few different formats and events, at different times of day and on different days of the week, experimenting with topics and continually checking to see how participants respond. Just because you don't get a full house immediately doesn't meant the pilot hasn't been a success; it takes time for people to hear about new initiatives and to adjust to new routines.

Rather than talking about something in abstract, drawing from your own experience and using examples from local researchers can be beneficial.

> 'I think using real examples and sharing good and bad experiences (and what I have learned along the way) helps to bring to life what can be a fairly dry topic!' (Helen Young, Loughborough University).

Even short workshops can involve a lot of time in preparation, so it's also important to consider all the benefits, tangible and more intangible, which might arise from running face-to-face workshops. Is the aim to get your face known as much as to inform the audience?

> 'It was, of course, quite time-consuming to put together a comprehensive package of slides/notes, supporting handouts and exercises where appropriate. Yet the audience size was disappointingly low, despite wide advertising – it is very hard to get a group of researchers/academics together in one room! I think I would consider next time whether it might be worth putting my efforts into developing something that is available online rather than into developing a training session as such. Think about whether your projected "live" audience is worth the time and effort of putting together a training presentation/seminar. Online resources might have more reach.' (Melanie Gee, Sheffield Hallam University)

References and further reading

Elevenses,
   http://gradschoolreadingroom.blogspot.co.uk/search/label/Elevenses.

Research Bites programme, http://libguides.aston.ac.uk/ResearchBites.
ScHARR Research Hacks, www.youtube.com/playlist?list=
  PL1mJ7IZ3qFxjR8HhL9HX-ETHUFJz639Bt.

Acknowledgements
Georgina Hardy, Aston University Library; Helen Steele, University of Leicester; Helen Young, Loughborough University.

9.10 Involve employers
WHILST THE FOCUS throughout the book relates to opportunities for engaging with researchers within the research lifecycle, for research students it is also worth considering whether the requirements of future employers are also being met. Rarely do librarians have the opportunity to meet prospective employers of students to find out what kinds of skills and capabilities they are looking for which we might contribute to. Are we missing an opportunity? Might we be able to use this knowledge to promote our work?

Collaborating with the careers service is a good way to start this kind of activity. Careers staff will have a clear idea of the common requirements of many employers and will also be able to alert you to events such as local jobs fairs for researchers. Making contact with employers has several benefits. As well as discovering at first hand how the kinds of activities you offer researchers will benefit them in the future, you may discern other, hitherto overlooked, ideas to feed into your teaching.

Bringing potential employers into workshops can also be a very powerful way of motivating participants, as it provides a real example of how what you are teaching can benefit them in future. As well as making the session more engaging, it also helps confirm that the sessions you are offering really do meet the needs of employment.

👍 Best for:
- giving real-world relevance to otherwise dry topics
- making links with other sections.

★ Examples from practice

Employer partners
One university library has been working with staff from local industry to demonstrate the relevance of some of the skills the library is teaching:

'Last year we got the chance to bring a couple of guys from two of the big local employers into the instruction classes we were offering to the research students in the faculty of engineering. At first it was a little uncomfortable as we weren't sure exactly what we should ask them to do and consequently they also weren't sure why they were there. The class was about copyright and IPR so eventually we started to deliver it as usual and then the company guys were nodding and agreeing with us and one of them interrupted with a story about a problem they had had with a patent application. All of a sudden all the theory we had been explaining had a real-life example and it became much more relevant. After that it became more of a question and answer class and the students had a lot of questions for the company guys. This year we'll do it in more of a planned way because we have a better feel for what the links might be.' (University librarian, USA)

⚠ To think about

Consider what kinds of contribution you want from local employers so that when you approach them you're able to explain exactly what you're trying to achieve.

Information literacy skills workshops and programmes

10.1 Holistic information literacy programmes for researchers

IN RECENT YEARS, many university libraries have developed comprehensive information literacy offerings for undergraduate students, traditionally focusing on the immediate skills needed to exploit the library's resources. Often such programmes can be replicated, albeit in a little more depth, at postgraduate level and it may be that this is all that is possible in some circumstances.

However, ideally for the research community, a much more in-depth approach is needed. Researchers should be aware of the resources available to them: in particular, that there is more to life than Google Scholar, however useful a tool that is! In addition, researchers need to develop a more holistic understanding of the information environment and of their roles and responsibilities within it. This will enable them to construct robust search strategies and to really understand how to interpret and manipulate the results. This kind of approach is essential for any form of systematic review, a research technique that is becoming increasingly popular in applied and social sciences and engineering as well as in medical sciences (see Tips 8.7–8.9).

Librarians, therefore have a key role to play in developing this awareness, helping researchers to cross a 'threshold of understanding' about their information environment (see Tip 3.5 on threshold concepts). Although teaching the skills (we might think of this as training) is still essential, at this level it does need to be reinforced with a less tangible discourse (which we might think of as education) about the information landscape. This is not an easy task; library staff without much experience of teaching may feel challenged by such an intangible learning outcome and researchers, focused on a just-in-time, need-to-know requirement, may not perceive the need to acquire it at all. It's easier to ignore it and focus on developing training programmes that, on the surface, meet everyone's needs.

Nevertheless, there are tools that can help library staff who wish to develop more comprehensive information literacy offerings for researchers. The ACRL

Framework (Association of College and Research Libraries, 2015) and the SCONUL Seven Pillars model (Bent and Stubbings, 2011) both provide a scaffold against which a more rounded programme can be set. In the UK, Vitae, an organization dedicated to researcher development has produced the Researcher Development Framework and associated Information Literacy Lens (Vitae, 2012). Vitae's booklet *The Informed Researcher* (Bent et al., 2012), which can be downloaded from the website, is a helpful tool to initiate discussion amongst researchers about the more intangible aspects of information retrieval.

If you are developing a programme from scratch, the InformAll criteria (InformAll, 2014) are a useful tool. The criteria 'are intended for academic librarians, and more broadly for all those who, within HEIs, are responsible for devising, running or managing courses, sessions and other digital/online resources aimed at developing the information-handling knowledge, skills and competencies of researchers, students and teaching staff.' The criteria help to describe and review training interventions as well as providing a simple means of evaluating courses and resources, the aim being to evaluate their suitability and usefulness as transferable resources.

🖒 Best for:

- developing information literate researchers
- providing a more enriched experience
- enabling researchers to set their learning within a broader context.

★ Examples from practice

Loughborough University Library, UK
Loughborough University Library has successfully developed a programme for research students which addresses both skills and understanding; Figure 10.1 shows the contents of two workshops in this programme.

'Kick start to academic life', Lund University, Sweden
'Kick start to academic life' is a collaboration between the Social Sciences Faculty Library at Lund University and faculty staff. The programme aims to provide PhD students with generic knowledge to help them to 'socialize into academia' (Hanna Voog, Lund University). The underlying premise is that this socialization process is often expected to happen spontaneously, whereas evidence shows that new PhD students can be very uncertain about their roles and face many barriers in settling in and commencing their research.

Workshop title: Finding resources for your literature review and beyond – Theory

Target audience: This session is designed for first year PGRs
Course outline: This session enables you to turn ideas into an effective search strategy and statement. It outlines the current information landscape and takes you through the stages involved in deciding upon and developing an appropriate search strategy, as well as enabling you to create a search statement that you can put into practice immediately after the session. Participants will develop their knowledge and intellectual abilities, so that you will be able to seek and find research material in an effective and efficient manner using the resources available to you at Loughborough University, but also in the future too.

Outcomes: Participants will be able to:
1. relate the information landscape to their own research
2. translate their research question into a search strategy
3. construct and adapt their search strategies to suit their information needs and circumstances
4. apply different search techniques, e.g. phrase searching, Boolean operators, truncation, wildcards
5. recognise the strengths and weaknesses of citations for evaluating information
6. write their own search statement for immediate use in an electronic resource
7. identify the range of options available to them for obtaining material, e.g. book loans, electronic journal articles, ILL, visiting other libraries
8. identify sources of help within the University for their information needs
9. meet and network with other PGR students from across campus

Additional information: This session is recommended for all new research postgraduates and relates to the Researcher Development Framework's Domain A – Knowledge and Intellectual Abilities.

This session is a **pre-requisite** for 'Finding resources for your literature review and beyond – Practice'.

Workshop title: Doing a systematic review – why and how?
Course outline: This session will outline the necessary steps to construct a systematic literature review. Particular areas of focus will be on the differences between systematic literature reviews and other types of review; constructing a search strategy; selecting appropriate databases; creating a methodology; recording, analysing and evaluating search results, as well as the structure of reviews.

Target audience: This course is designed for early-career PGRs and Research Staff, particularly those who are working in medical, biomedical, scientific and engineering fields

Outcomes: Participants will be able to:
1. appreciate the purpose of a systematic review
2. identify how a systematic review differs from a 'standard' literature review
3. understand the structure and stages of a systematic literature review
4. critically evaluate the literature
5. construct a methodology for creating a systematic review
6. meet and network with other PGR students from across campus

Other information:
This session relates to the Researcher Development Framework's Domain A – Knowledge and Intellectual Abilities.

Participants are requested to have completed Activity 2 prior to this workshop. It can be found on Learn at: http://learn.lboro.ac.uk/mod/resource/view.php?id=291425

Participants are **strongly advised** to have attended the workshop on Finding resources for your literature review and beyond prior to this workshop.

Figure 10.1 *Workshop contents in Loughborough University's literacy skills programme (reproduced with permission)*

'It's a co-operation between professors and librarians and it's based on the idea that if
these things are addressed early in their careers it can become a smoother transition into
academia for new PhD students. The co-operation in the management of the course
means that the different professions bring different experiences and know-hows to the
table and together we build a course that covers some of the angles of a PhD student's life
that often are not addressed. By doing so, combining theory and practice, we believe that
we start a process that will, in the end, reduce anxiety and save valuable research time.'
(Hanna Voog, Lund University)

The course itself, delivered via a variety of lectures, seminars and workshops,
includes practical information literacy skills sessions, for example in reference
management, linked to more theoretical ethical issues, for example around
citation, or a talk by a journal editor on article submission linked to practical
sessions on how to identify journals in which to publish.

'We believe that the key to success of this course lies in the co-operation between
professions (professors and librarians) and the unique mix of theory and practice.' (Hanna
Voog, Lund University)

Northumbria University Researcher Development Week
The Researcher Development Week at Northumbria University, UK, is a focused
package of workshops lasting 1½ hours, complemented by 45-minute bite-size
sessions. Each event is timetabled for several different days and times over the
course of a week, with typically 4–6 events each day. Topics include open access,
keeping up to date, measuring performance, copyright, mind mapping and
collaboration tools. The whole programme is advertised via a colourful printed
leaflet with online bookings and further materials within the Skills Plus gateway.

⚠ To think about
However worthy the less tangible outcomes of such sessions might be, you still
need a hook to attract the research community. They need to appreciate the
value of the workshop to themselves as individuals, so including practical skills
outcomes in addition is essential.

Consider whether subject-specific sessions for research groups might be more
successful than generic workshops open to all; perhaps discussions about
philosophical issues might be easier in smaller groups.

Gaining the support of senior researchers can also be invaluable, but in order
to do so you also need them to understand the bigger picture. Referring to
published models and research in the LIS field can help persuade researchers
that this is indeed a substantial offering worthy of consideration. Even just giving
research deans and organizers of postgraduate development programmes

copies of the *Informed Researcher* booklet can aid this discourse.

The environment in which such a session takes place can also affect the outcomes. If you wish the group to discuss issues and engage in meaningful conversations as well as practise skills, a room which offers more than just a computer cluster will be helpful.

References and further reading

Association of College and Research Libraries (2015) *Framework for Information Literacy for Higher Education*, www.ala.org/acrl/standards/ilframework.

Bent, M., Gannon-Leary, P., Goldstein, S. and Videler, T. (2012) *The Informed Researcher*, London, Vitae, www.vitae.ac.uk/researcherbooklets. (Accessed 25.5.15)

Bent, M. and Stubbings, R. (2011) *The SCONUL Seven Pillars of Information Literacy: research lens*, London, SCONUL, www.sconul.ac.uk/sites/ default/files/documents/researchlens.pdf. (Accessed 25.5.15)

InformAll (2014) *InformAll Criteria for Describing, Reviewing and Evaluating Courses and Resources*, https://www.informall.org.uk/education/informall-criteria/. (Accessed 4.1.16)

Lund University (2015) *Kick Start to Academic Life*, www.sam.lu.se/en/staff/ courses-for-phd-students-and-teachers/phd-courses/courses-autumn-2014/kickstart-to-academic. (Accessed 24.4.15)

Vitae (2012) *Information Literacy Lens on the Vitae Researcher Development Framework Using the SCONUL Seven Pillars of Information Literacy*, www.vitae.ac.uk/vitae-publications/rdf-related/information-literacy-lens-on-the-vitae-researcher-development-framework-rdf-apr-2012.pdf. (Accessed 1.6.15)

Acknowledgements

Helen Young, Loughborough University Library; Hanna Voog, Ann-Sofie Zettergren, Åsa Lundqvist, Social Science Faculty Library, Lund University and Department of Sociology, Lund University; Suzie Kitchen, Northumbria University.

10.2 Generic information literacy skills programmes

WHEN I ASKED for contributions for this book, by far the most common offerings related to aspects of information literacy (IL) for researchers. Many librarians have run researcher programmes on information skills in various guises for several years, whilst for others it is a relatively new experience. What is certainly the case is that there is a lot of attention being given to this aspect of the library/research interface, perhaps because it appears to be a reasonably easy area to address.

The previous Tip (10.1) addressed the differences between information literacy and information literacy skills, suggesting that a preferred approach is a more holistic offering which speaks to the needs for developing understanding and awareness as well as skills and competencies. This ideal may not always be attainable, either because of a lack of confidence of library staff in their ability to deliver it, or more likely because the opportunities and support to develop the programme may not exist within the organization or the library. If that is the case, a practical, generic IL skills programme for the research community is still a very welcome contribution. Topics might include: an introduction to the library and services for researchers, search strategies and techniques, subject specific resources and how to access them, keeping up to date, referencing, citation and attribution, social media, writing for publication and measuring impact, to name but a few common titles. Some libraries provide more specialized sessions, covering topics such as tools for collaboration and sharing, copyright and intellectual property, ethics and finding grey literature.

However, as has already been mentioned earlier in the book, researchers are not all the same and their needs vary depending on their experience, their background and their abilities, and so planning a generic programme of workshops aimed at researchers may not be as straightforward as it first appears. In addition, whilst creating and delivering a programme of workshops we also need to consider how we will measure their effectiveness in developing more able researchers. It's all very well having a smart shiny programme which looks good from the outside but how do you know it's really making a difference to the quality of research?

> 'I'm amazed at how few researchers know that they can create accounts, save strategies, etc. – once demonstrated they become very engaged.' (Annette Ramsden, University of Central Lancashire)

👍 Best for:

- designing information literacy skills workshop programmes for researchers.

★ Examples from practice

University of Central Lancashire (UCLan), UK
UCLan offers a series of conjoined skills workshops for postgraduate students

and research staff, organized via their Graduate Research Office. The three workshops are deliberately interconnected and participants are encouraged to attend all three, though this doesn't always happen. The workshops adopt a common theme (for example, fracking) and cover:

1   search strategies, resources, evaluation, reference management
2   the Scopus database, based on search strategies in session 1
3   the Web of Science database, as above but with comparison of results.

> 'They see the difference in results when using exactly the same search strategy and they get hands-on practice at using each resource.' (Annette Ramsden, UCLan)

University of Salford, UK
As well as doing subject-specific workshops the library at the University of Salford contributes specific skills sessions to a generic training programme for research staff and postgraduates – the SPoRT programme (www.pg.salford.ac.uk/pgr_training). The programme is run by the Academic Development Unit and staff from across the university contribute sessions, making the library a collaborative partner in delivery. The sessions are organized and mapped to the Researcher Development Framework (see Tip 3.3). Workshop titles run by library staff include 'Electronic resources for researchers', 'Arts databases for research', 'Googlescholar for research', 'Introduction to EndNote', 'Locating and using historical archives for research', 'Referencing and information ethics for research', 'Open access publishing' and 'E-theses, third party copyright and e-submission'.

⚠ To think about
Who are the researchers you want to attract?
   Can you differentiate the programme by discipline or experience or are you planning a 'one size fits all' agenda? If so, how will you deal with different demands within the workshop?

> 'We get a wide range of attendees with different levels of experience. We have no prior knowledge of the skills base until the session commences.' (Annette Ramsden, UCLan)

Having such a mixed group as described by Annette may dilute your message, as inevitably you won't be able to tailor the session to give relevant subject-specific examples. If this is the only opportunity you have, and in many cases it is likely to be, consider how you might deal with this.
   Without some subject focus, generic programmes run the risk of being bland and of interest to no one. Think through the kinds of examples which will

generate general interest, perhaps around research skills themselves (e.g. use of search engines versus databases), a topical or local issue (research into a local landmark), or a very general subject (chocolate).

Although you'll want to tailor your demonstrations and examples to the interests of attendees, unless you are experienced and confident, this approach can lead to difficulties. Plan how you will respond if a live search throws up unexpected results; can you turn this into a learning experience without becoming flustered? Have ready-made search strategies available so you can be sure to demonstrate all the points you want to make.

If you're dealing with a large, mixed group, creating a personal feel and engaging with individuals can be difficult. Try to team teach, so that one of you can help less experienced participants. Think about ways in which you can follow up generic sessions with a more personal experience.

References and further reading

Powis, C., Webb, J. and Blanchett, H. (2010) *A Guide to Teaching Information Literacy: 101 tips*, London, Facet Publishing.

Secker, J., Boden, D. and Price, G. (2007) *The Information Literacy Cookbook: ingredients, recipes and tips for success*, London, Chandos.

Acknowledgements

Annette Ramsden, University of Central Lancashire.

10.3 Online resources and programmes

NOT ALL TEACHING and learning for researchers can take place face to face and there are many good examples of online tools, programmes and resources. The benefit of an online tool is that it has the potential to be accessed by anyone at any time, can be studied at the learner's pace and can provide a mixture of information and interactivity. However, there is also more potential for misunderstandings and use of the tool relies on the motivation of the individual researcher. Online materials provided alongside face-to-face sessions provide the best of both worlds, but in reality this isn't always possible.

There are many examples of online information literacy materials aimed at the research community, so rather than starting from scratch to develop your own, you can save time by looking to see what is already freely available. In general, librarians are very generous and love to share, so for some generic aspects or approaches to information literacy, you may be able to link directly to the resource (with appropriate recognition, of course). In other cases, it may be possible to adapt the materials to your own circumstances, or simply to get ideas and inspiration from the content, design or presentation.

One of the dangers of creating online content is the temptation to sit back once it has been created and think that the job is done. Remember, however, that maintaining up-to-date online materials is essential if you wish to maintain credibility and the resource to be valued and used. If facts are even slightly outdated, if one link is broken, this will reflect on the whole resource and can influence researchers' perceptions of the usefulness of the content as a whole.

Many libraries have online learning materials for students, but in general these are focused on undergraduate learning. Repurposing this material and adding specific elements relating to researchers can be a quick and easy way to create tailored resources for researchers. Rather than working on a whole course, bite-size learning objects enable busy researchers to identify a specific information need and go straight to the relevant help.

🖒 Best for:

■ using or developing online information literacy skills materials for researchers
■ developing researchers' information skills.

★ Examples from practice

ResMap
ResMap, devised at Birmingham City University (BCU), UK, is an online tool designed to map the research journey for postgraduate and doctoral researchers. The site has been developed using LibGuides and comprises: a home page, getting started, literature review, methodology and data, evaluation, final steps, potential pitfalls, support and news. The site contains links to tip sheets and further information and

> 'is the first time that all of this information and support has been brought together in one easily navigable format.' (Jane Richards, BCU)

PILOT online information literacy course
PILOT is the Postgraduate Information Literacy Online Training course originally designed at Imperial College, London and modified by Marion Kelt at Glasgow Caledonian University (GCU), UK. It covers: sources of specialist information, aspects of the publication process, including open access publishing and institutional repositories, blogs, wikis and podcasts. The managing information unit gives information on bibliographic software, copyright, referencing and plagiarism.

'The original version of PILOT was designed as a sequential course, with the option of using individual units on a standalone basis. Users at GCU did not use it in this fashion, preferring to go directly to the short sections they needed at the time they were required. To cater for this, and to address the problems with the structure and navigation, lecturers were provided with a set of direct links to the most popular sections which were embedded into Blackboard modules by the librarian. This helped lecturers provide blended learning resources in their modules and allowed them to direct students to the appropriate sections as pre-work and back-up to library training and relevant modules.' (Marion Kelt, GCU: from the Information Literacy website, www.informationliteracy.org.uk/portfolio/ casestudy-pilot)

PILOT is available at www.gcu.ac.uk/library/pilot/ under a CC licence.

PhD on Track

PhD on Track is a website developed collaboratively by a group of Norwegian university libraries. Through a series of detailed web pages it guides new PhD students through the research process, starting with review and discover, through share and publish, to evaluation and ranking tools. PhD on Track is licensed under a CC BY-NC-SA licence.

Get Research Help

Get Research Help is a series of web pages from the library of the University of British Columbia in Canada. Although the early sections are aimed more at undergraduate level, much of the information is relevant for higher-level researchers too and they do include advice on publishing research. Licensed under a CC BY-SA licence.

Northumbria University, UK

Northumbria University Library developed a research skills section of their popular Skills Plus platform, grouping together learning objects specifically relevant to researchers and labelling them so that researchers will find them. In addition, by disaggregating information on several topics which was previously all located within one helpsheet (for example, the current awareness helpsheet includes information on TOCs, search alerts and RSS feeds) they have created a series of very short bite-sized learning objects. This enables researchers who are short of time to quickly locate specific learning objects, whilst maintaining the integrity of the pre-existing materials, which are still useful in teaching situations.

'We originally brainstormed ideas for bite-size learning objects and prioritized those where we didn't already have help or where it was hidden within a longer guide.' (Suzie Kitchen, Northumbria University)

⚠ To think about

When developing an online tool, try to involve the research community in its development, to ensure the content is relevant and the tone is appropriate.

> 'We worked closely with the research community in developing the tone and content and then asked the Postgraduate Network to evaluate it.' (Jane Richards, Birmingham City University)

Think about what the priorities are for your researchers and where they might be looking for extra support.

Consider where the online material is to be housed, as this will affect the kind of interactivity you can build in. Material held within a virtual research environment may allow for more explicit information, but the environment itself may also be a barrier to discovery or use.

How important is it to give the resource your own personal or institutional spin? Tailored information is much more attractive, as it is immediately relevant and applicable, and so providing a mix of generic and personalized resources might be an attractive option.

How will you maintain the resource? How frequently will it need to be updated? Is there a way in which you can design it to minimize maintenance? Do you have appropriate technical support to create the learning objects?

References and further reading

Get Research Help, University of British Columbia Library, http://help.library.ubc.ca.
PILOT, www.gcu.ac.uk/library/pilot.
PhD on Track, www.phdontrack.net/about-phd-on-track.
Research Skills, www.northumbria.ac.uk/researchskills.
ResMap (2015) http://libguides.bcu.ac.uk/resmap.

Acknowledgements

Jane Richards, Birmingham City University; Suzie Kitchen, Northumbria University Library.

10.4 Diagnostic tools

DESIGNING AN INFORMATION literacy programme for researchers involves not only planning the content but also understanding who your audience is, what their prior knowledge and expectations are and deciding an appropriate level of delivery. Diagnostic tools can help both the teacher and researcher in this process, providing practical information about participants to the teacher and managing expectations of the learner.

There has often been controversy over the usefulness of diagnostic tools in information literacy, given that it is difficult to assess behaviours and approaches in this way. However, it is possible to use diagnostic tools to check specific knowledge; for example, you can ask about awareness of specific resources or familiarity with referencing styles. In this way researchers can identify gaps in their knowledge and skills and teachers can assess the practical competencies in the class at the start of a workshop. Beginning a workshop with an activity that highlights common needs and interests is also a useful way of engaging the group and demonstrating that the information is going to be tailored to their specific requirements. As well as assessing specific skills and knowledge, diagnostic tools can also be used as a means of self-reflection and development by researchers, enabling them to plan their own learning path. For example, asking researchers to rate their understanding of different concepts, or to describe and explain their views on an information issue, can lead to discussion and raised awareness of some of the more complex aspects of the information world.

Diagnostic tools can be simple or sophisticated online quizzes, maybe a straightforward paper checklist or even an informal discussion which highlights key issues.

🖒 Best for:

- identifying gaps in knowledge
- raising awareness of information literacy concepts with researchers
- planning information literacy interventions for researchers.

★ Examples from practice

Warwick University
The masters skills programme at Warwick University in the UK includes a short, five-minute, 'Assess your skills' quiz which, through a series of simple questions, helps students identify gaps in their knowledge and suggest workshops they can attend to help fill the gaps. Cardiff University has a similar tool but it is only available behind their firewall.

POMP and ROMP, James Cook University, Australia
Jackie Wolstenholme, Research Services Librarian at James Cook University, used a simple before-and-after approach to collect evidence of learning in her workshops with researchers. Based on an accepted pedagogical approach called

One Minute Papers (OMP), which asks learners to identify the most important, confusing and interesting things they have learned, she developed POMPs – Polling One Minute Papers – and ROMPs – Reflective One Minute Papers. The link to the online POMP was sent to researchers prior to attendance, with a small number of questions all visible on one screen and filled in anonymously. The high 72.7% completion rate enabled library staff to identify learning needs of the participants before the session as well as to tailor the session to their specific needs. This had the added benefit of engaging the researchers with the session beforehand. A list of the questions asked in the POMP is provided in the appendix of the published article. After the session, researchers were encouraged to reflect on what they had gained from it by filling in a ROMP, a second online form. The response rate for ROMPS was smaller but they still provided valuable data for library staff, as well as encouraging the researchers to reflect on their development and to encourage deeper thinking about the topics covered. In addition the responses to POMPs and ROMPs can be used as evidence of the value the library has contributed to the research process.

Informed Researcher

The Vitae booklet *The Informed Researcher* (Bent et al., 2012) includes a self-reflective tool which is used at Newcastle University, UK, with research students at the start of their development programme. The tool asks researchers to rate themselves on a scale of 1 to 5 on how confident they are in their abilities in a range of common attributes. It is linked to the UK Researcher Development Framework, enabling researchers to link their information literacy development into the broader context of their development as researchers. The tool was adapted from this original document (see Figure 10.2), which is used at

Are you an Information Literate Researcher?
Read the behaviour and associated example and then give yourself an honest rating between 1 and 5. This is just for you to keep.

Score : 1= Poor 2= Fair 3= Good 4= Very Good 5= Excellent

Behaviour	Example	Rating
I analyse my information needs before I start looking for information	Defining keywords and phrases, using mind mapping techniques, talking to colleagues, finding background information	
I choose sources appropriately	Don't just use Google, but try different types of information such as books, newspapers, government reports, people, websites	
I can list the best databases to use for my research	Know what is available at Newcastle and elsewhere	
I can search for information effectively and efficiently	Using advanced features of search engines and databases, combining words, limiting searches	

Figure 10.2 *Discussion activity to develop reflective researchers (based on an original idea from Helen Blanchett) (Continued on next page)*

Behaviour	Example	Rating
I know how to ask questions to help me get information	Using appropriate language, saying things in a different way, listening skills	
I can gather brand new data when required	Designing and creating surveys, gathering data, carrying out interviews	
I know how to keep up to date with new information	Knowledge of the main information sources for your job/subject area	
I understand how to interpret information retrieved from different sources	Understand how search engines rank results, knowing how to select appropriate results from a database search, being able to sort results sensibly	
I understand that different sources provide different types and quality of information	Able to explain the differences between scholarly journals, professional journals and popular journals	
I am involved in communication networks in my research area	Knowledge of appropriate mailing lists, conference networks	
I evaluate the quality of the information I find	Using appropriate criteria such as currency, bias, authority to assess information	
I can understand the information I find, analysing and synthesizing appropriately.	Able to summarize, reword information, collate material from several sources. Know not to cut and paste!	
I recognize the legal and ethical implications of using other people's work	Understanding of copyright and plagiarism. Able to reference material correctly	
I think about what I am doing in my search strategy and make changes as a result	Reflect on what works and change habits as a result	
I am aware of the scholarly communication debate	Able to explain why there is a movement to encourage publication in open access titles	
I understand the different types of publication and how to identify the best sources to read and to publish in	Able to explain peer review process for journals. Know how to find impact factors	
I understand the role of digital repositories	Knowledge of local and national repositories and how to access them	
I understand how to disseminate the results of my research effectively	Know key journals and how to publish in them. Can explain alternative dissemination options	
I know how to write in a way which is appropriate for my intended audience	Understanding of different writing styles and methods of conveying information	
I am aware of the social implications of my research activities	Understanding of how your research will contribute to society	

Figure 10.2 *Continued*

Newcastle University Library to encourage researchers to be reflective and to identify specific things they want to learn more about.

⚠ To think about

Don't just use a diagnostic tool for the sake of it. Plan what you or the researchers will be able to do with the results. Think of ways in which you can build upon the answers or highlight specific issues which merit a deeper consideration. How will researchers' answers help you in planning a workshop or, for the researcher, in developing themselves as more informed researchers?

References and further reading

Bent, M., Gannon-Leary, P., Goldstein, S. and Videler, T. (2012) *The Informed Researcher*, London, Vitae, www.vitae.ac.uk/researcherbooklets. (Accessed 18.4.15)

Warwick University (2015) *Student Careers and Skills: masters skills programme*, www2.warwick.ac.uk/services/scs/skills/msp. (Accessed 18.4.15)

Wolstenholme, J. (2015) Evidence based Practice Using Formative Assessment in Library Research Support, *Evidence Based Library and Information Practice*, **10** (3), 4–29, https://ejournals.library.ualberta.ca/index.php/EBLIP/article/view/24066.

Acknowledgements

Newcastle University Library; Helen Blanchett, Jisc.

10.5 Making an impact workshops

WHEREVER A RESEARCHER is based, at whatever level they are working, their ultimate aim is to answer a research question, discover something new and add some value to the research in their discipline. In order to achieve this, some form of dissemination is inevitable and in the main this still revolves around some form of scholarly communication. With well over 1 million articles published each year, making sure your work is noticed and doesn't fall through the cracks is bound to exercise the minds of many researchers. Workshops focused around advice on increasing visibility and reaching a wider audience will therefore inevitably attract interest amongst researchers at all levels. Similarly, once published, finding out that someone is reading your work, perhaps building on it or learning from it, is immensely satisfying at a personal level for all researchers. More pragmatically, in countries that operate some kind of research evaluation exercise, such evidence is crucial both to acquire future funding and to maintain employment.

In general, the library element of these specific workshops can be very practical and skills-based; making impact workshops cover providing advice on how to identify journals in which to publish, explaining the pros and cons of impact factors and enabling researchers to find information on the publication process. Certainly in the UK, where there is a clear imperative for open access publishing in order to qualify for inclusion in the next Research Excellence Framework exercise, there is less need for OA advocacy amongst senior researchers; emphasis has shifted to advice on the process, and practical provision to facilitate it by providing institutional repositories. Amongst more junior researchers, as well as perhaps older, less active writers, however, open access advocacy is still a vital part of such activity (see Tip 10.7) and can easily be factored into a skills-based workshop.

👍 Best for:

- increasing research visibility
- ensuring researchers understand issues surrounding copyright and open access
- helping researchers understand the publication process.

★ Examples from practice

Loughborough University, UK
Figure 10.3 is an example of a workshop planning document from Loughborough University.

Search engine optimization
One librarian in the Netherlands uses aspects of search engine optimization when talking to researchers about maximizing their impact.

> 'I explain that there are ways they can help their articles to be higher up the results list. Rather than inventing a snappy title for the article they should make sure it (the title) includes all the keywords people might be searching for. They should also take the time to create a really good list of alternative keywords and include that in the article too, maybe at the end of the abstract if that's allowed. I explain that articles with citations are good because then publishers can create links between articles and that also helps. They should make sure that they also add keywords to images and where they can, include links to other places, as all this will boost SEO.' (Librarian, Netherlands)

The Informed Researcher @ Newcastle University
The Science Liaison Team at Newcastle University in the UK runs workshops for both research staff and students focusing on pre- and post-publication concerns, such as identifying appropriate journals in which to publish, measuring personal

Workshop Title	**Increasing the visibility of your research – Academic and Research Staff**		
Presenter	Helen Young (h.young@lboro.ac.uk); Christine Hallam (c.hallam2@lboro.ac.uk)		
Topic			
	Room	Date	Time
	Library Seminar Room 2	Wednesday 2nd April	10.00-12.00pm
Length	2 hours		
Min/Max Numbers	Max 23		
Target Audience	Academic and Research Staff (Not PGRs)		
Blurb	Whilst you pride yourself on producing high quality research, are your research outcomes reaching the widest possible audience? Demonstrating the impact of your research is increasingly important for receiving funding, but to create an impact, it must first of all be noticed. This session will examine the various tools and services that are available to help you raise the visibility of your research outcomes, as well as discussing the benefits and challenges of this approach. The session will enable you to identify the most appropriate strategy for your own subject area.		
ILOs	Participants will have the opportunity to: • Reflect on their current dissemination strategy • Identify and test profile tools, such as Google Scholar Profile and Researcher ID • Examine other proven techniques for raising the visibility of research, e.g blogs, Twitter, e-mail signatures.		
Other Instructions			
Joining Instructions			

Figure 10.3 *Skills-based workshop planning document, Loughborough University (reproduced with permission)*

and article impacts and all aspects of copyright, open access and intellectual property. In addition to the workshop illustrated in Figure 10.4, material is available on a LibGuide: http://libguides.ncl.ac.uk/impact.

⚠ To think about

When venturing into the realms of providing advice on the publication process, it can be immensely helpful if you have personal experience of the process to

---

SAgE Postgraduate Researcher Development Programme. Part 1: Unlocking your research 1: Pre-publication – where to publish for maximum impact
How do you get your first article published? Which route should you choose? What do people mean by Open Access? Why do authors need to think about copyright and other ethical concerns? This workshop will explore traditional and new routes to publishing and discuss some of the issues involved. It will explain what is meant by Open Access publishing and show you how you can use Open Access tools to publish your research.

Figure 10.4 *Informed Researcher workshop, Newcastle University*

bring. If you haven't published yourself, consider inviting a senior researcher to the session to talk about their experiences. Asking the group at the start of the session who has already had material published is also useful, as well as encouraging participants to share their own experiences; it can break down any 'you and them' barriers and help the session to feel more like a shared experience. However, be alert to the fact that some inexperienced researchers may have inadvertently been encouraged to publish with a fraudulent or predatory publisher (see Tip 8.14); you'll need to deal with such discoveries very sensitively.

In addition, if there are teams within the library who deal with specific aspects of the publication process, such as the repository and open access compliance, explore how you can develop a joint workshop with them, integrating their expertise with yours. Not only will this provide a better experience for the researchers involved, it makes the delivery a more pleasant and satisfying experience.

Acknowledgements

Helen Young, Loughborough University; Jenny Campbell, Newcastle University.

10.6 Writing workshops (see also Tips 8.12 and 8.15)

A MAJOR ACTIVITY for most researchers is writing, whether it be a thesis, research report, journal article, book or some other means of disseminating the outcomes of their work. It is often taken for granted that anyone who is in a research position will have experience and skills at writing, but this may not be the case. Certainly many postgraduate students struggle with developing arguments or with rewriting information for different genres and even more senior researchers don't always have the necessary skills or, crucially, the time and motivation to gather their work together as a formal output.

As librarians, although we are comfortable with advising on referencing and citation, we may feel less comfortable about getting involved with the writing process itself, but even so there are ways in which we can facilitate it. The library is a neutral central space in which to run writing activities and so, rather than running workshops ourselves, perhaps we can plan and organize them, inviting relevant experts to provide the content. A series of writing for publication workshops might cover topics such as writing abstracts, how to review articles, dealing with procrastination and writer's block and specific requirements of key publishers, as well as lighter topics such as blogging about your research or writing for a non-academic audience.

Consider inviting publishers to come and talk about what they look for when work is submitted or find out if any researchers within your organization are journal editors and ask them to give a more personal view of what that involves. Perhaps postgraduate students who are ready to submit their thesis would be willing to chat to those just starting out about what they learned about writing. This kind of event could be run as an informal discussion or panel, enabling participants to submit questions and for the panel to prepare answers.

👍 Best for:

- encouraging researchers to write
- demonstrating the library's role in the writing process
- engaging with researchers at all stages of their research journey.

★ Examples from practice

Write here, write now! Writing Development Centre, Newcastle University, UK

Although housed within the Library, the Writing Development Centre at Newcastle has its own identity. The purpose of the WDC is to encourage students to learn to write for an academic audience. Whilst key for most undergraduates, the service also provides useful workshops for postgraduate students, as evidenced by the summer Write Here, Write Now workshops, which are based on similar, student-led meetings at Cambridge University (http://schreiberin.de/writers):

> . . . many of us find that lots of unstructured time is harder to work with, with no other commitments to break up the day or week, and little reason to do today what can be put off till tomorrow. It can be a struggle to find the motivation to work productively over the summer, and to develop a routine which will help you keep going. Writing can

also be a solitary practice, and if there are no peers around to support us, cheer us on and keep us on track, we can start to flag. Those of us who encounter issues like writer's block, perfectionism, procrastination or loss of focus or motivation in the course of our writing can feel particularly isolated during the summer.

The WDC will be running regular **Write Here, Write Now!** sessions over the summer. There aren't formally taught workshops – they are simply a space during the day in which to sit down with others and create a productive and encouraging environment in which to get some focused work done. The sessions are facilitated by the WDC tutors, but our role is simply to get you writing with a few quick warm-up exercises, and then to give you the space to write, together with others who are similarly focused. The WDC tutors will also be hosting writing clinics following these sessions, for quick queries and consultations alongside our usual **tutorials** which are still available over the summer.

Taken from the WDC blog at https://blogs.ncl.ac.uk/academicskills

Proofreading and peer review

One library encourages postgraduate students to attend peer-review and proofreading workshops:

'We run the workshops several times a year because you never know when students will start to write up their work. They have to bring some of their writing with them and agree to share it with a colleague. To begin with we have an open discussion about the importance of proofreading and being consistent in their writing and then we move on to explain more about the peer review process, how it works and what reviewers are looking for. We always ask a senior academic to come along to talk about their experiences and that really helps, because they can give examples of good and bad articles they've reviewed in the past.

Then we give out some simple guidelines for reviewing and ask the students to swap their work with a neighbour, preferably someone working in a similar field. They have half an hour to start reviewing the work and then they feedback to the author about what they've read. Sometimes it can get a little emotional but we are on hand to diffuse any awkwardness and it really does get them engaged. Quite often they agree to buddy up and keep commenting on the work in the future, so it can act as the start of a little self supporting community.' (Librarian, Australian university)

⚠ To think about

It is worth taking some time to discover what other activities relating to writing are taking place across the university. Often small-scale seminars are held within departments or faculties and there may be scope for suggesting they are offered to a wider audience. The library's role may simply be to gather this information together and present the opportunities to researchers in a more coherent way.

Consider attending workshops yourself as a participant, learning alongside other researchers. This will not only help you to develop your own writing abilities but should give you a deeper understanding of the challenges and concerns faced by the research community.

References and further reading

Corbyn, Z. (2008) PhD Students Need Help Developing a 'Writing Voice', Educationists Say, *Times Higher Education*, 25 September, www. timeshighereducation.co.uk/news/phd-students-need-help-developing-a-writing-voice-educationists-say/403658.article. (Accessed 12.3.15)

Acknowledgements

Helen Webster, Newcastle University

10.7 Open access workshops

AS PART OF their contribution to the wider scholarly communication debate, open access workshops usually comprise both an advocacy section, explaining to participants the underlying ethos of the open access movement, and a practical section, describing how to make work available in open access form, although this will vary depending on the audience. The potential audience will affect the way in which the session can be advertised to researchers; with mandates for OA now driving research submissions in the UK, many researchers are much more aware of what OA is and just require practical help in navigating the university systems. However, mandates also mean that some researchers may never grasp the wider implications of OA and follow the practical route from necessity rather than belief that it is a better approach. Librarians therefore need to tread a careful path between advocating the underlying concepts of OA and providing practical information to smooth the submission process.

The plethora of systems involved in making material open access can be very confusing for researchers, as they need to navigate their way through their organization's arrangements, as well as those of the publishers. Perhaps there are different databases for housing different types of media, data may be dealt with differently from written material, and there may be duplication in the way output is being recorded by different sections. Each publisher will have different requirements and rules too. The library can clearly play a part in helping researchers surmount some of these obstacles, but ultimately a more coherent approach by the whole institution is needed.

In addition, care must be taken to explain to researchers how open access resources affect them as consumers of information – why, for example, they find so much material through Google Scholar. This is all part of developing information literate researchers who understand how the information world works, what their responsibilities are and hence how open access can help increase the visibility of their work.

There are many good examples of open access-related workshops available online and more are appearing regularly, so only a few are highlighted below.

🖒 Best for:

- helping researchers understand why they need to publish their output in open access format
- assisting researchers through the process of open access publishing.

★ Examples from practice

Loughborough University, UK
This workshop (Figure 10.5) addresses both ethical and practical issues surrounding the open access debate.

SPARC open access workshop materials
SPARC Europe is a high-level policy body that engages with the European Commission, the European Parliament, universities and university associations to develop and argue the case for policies that further stimulate a more open and accessible Europe. In addition, it has developed a set of tools to help researchers and their organizations push forward the open access agenda. The 'How open is your research?' visualization tool enables organizations to visualize how open they are in the ways they manage and disseminate research output. The Open Access Citation Advantage Service provides evidence in the form of case studies to demonstrate whether open access articles are more highly cited. The SPARC website also links to many other open access resources.

University College Dublin (UCD), Ireland
Julia Barrett, Research Services Manager at UCD, has been addressing the complexities of open access in the humanities in her talks to research staff. She has identified some differences between humanities and sciences which are a useful starting point for debate with the humanities community. The following points are taken from one of her slide presentations to researchers and serve to initiate conversations around the kinds of issues humanities researchers might raise.

Workshop title: Open access – why is it important to me?

Course outline: The open access publishing movement has been growing in influence in the scholarly communications process in the UK for a number of years. As many funders and universities now mandate publishing using an open access route for certain publication types, it is becoming impossible to ignore it. This session will explain what open access is and how it impacts on research practice and dissemination.

Target audience: Mid-career and experienced PGRs, especially those intending to undertake a career in academia.

Outcomes: Participants will be able to:
1. Recognise the drivers behind the open access publishing movement
2. Identify the two main routes to open access (green and gold)
3. Discuss the benefits and challenges of publishing via the open access routes
4. Identify the key aspects of effective file management
5. Recognise how open access can benefit you as disseminators and consumers of research outputs
6. Identify the tools for open access at Loughborough University, e.g. the Institutional Repository
7. Identify where to go for help and support at Loughborough
8. Meet and network with other PGR students from across campus

Additional information: This session is recommended for all mid-career and experienced postgraduate research students and relates to the Researcher Development Framework's Domain D2 – Communication and dissemination.

Figure 10.5 *Open access workshop at Loughborough University (reproduced with permission)*

When considering the differences between Open Access in the Humanities compared to the Sciences we need to be aware that in the Humanities:

- monographs and book chapters remain important outputs
- national/language specific research is common
- integrity of the text is crucial
- there is often greater inclusion of third party material within published work – copyright issues
- there is less grant- and project funded research
- there are many more independent scholars
- there is less collaborative research.

Julia Barrett, UCD

⚠ To think about

Consider how best you can blend the ethical and pragmatic aspects of open access into a workshop which will be attractive to the research community. Is open access as a topic worthy of a workshop in its own right, or is it better to weave information about it into workshops on finding information and on writing for publication? As many universities have a very specific open access agenda, perhaps a combination of the two approaches will be most successful, enabling you to demonstrate to the organization that the library is the 'go-to' place for open access information.

Think about linking a series of workshops to International Open Access week (www.openaccessweek.org); this will give you an opportunity to highlight activities taking place elsewhere and helps place your own offering into a wider context.

References and further reading

Crossick, G. (2015) *Monographs and Open Access. A report to HEFCE*. [Online.] Available at: https://www.hefce.ac.uk/media/hefce/content/pubs/ indirreports/2015/Monographs,and,open,access/2014_monographs.pdf. (Accessed 28.7.15)

Jisc open access website, www.jisc.ac.uk/open-access.

SPARC, 'How open is your research?' visualization tool, http://sparceurope .org/howopenyourresearchis. Open Access Citation Advantage Service, http://sparceurope.org/oaca. The main SPARC website includes many useful resources and links, http://sparceurope.org.

Acknowledgements

Helen Young, Loughborough University; Julia Barrett, University College Dublin.

10.8 Workshops on ethics, licences and contracts

As **WITH MANY** of the higher-level topics that libraries can offer in a workshop programme for researchers, concerns such as ethical issues, intellectual property and a better understanding of licences and contracts need to be addressed at both a practical and a deeper level. For example, librarians know well that we can explain how to reference correctly; this is a skill and as long as the rules are followed a positive outcome is guaranteed. However, certainly at undergraduate level and, disappointingly, at postgraduate and even senior researcher level, there can be limited understanding of why this process needs to be followed and what the underlying ethics of citation and plagiarism are all about.

Workshops addressing these less tangible areas therefore need to be designed so that both the skills and the deeper understanding can be developed together. This can be challenging; as we have already observed, running skills workshops is much easier, both in terms of delivery and in attracting an audience. You may question whether changing mindsets is even our role: surely providing the information to enable people to make their own decisions is as far as we should go? I believe that librarians do have a responsibility here; we have a key part to play in developing information literate researchers and without tackling these issues we will have failed to deliver.

However, we do need to balance ideology with realism. Few researchers will have either the time or the inclination to attend a sermon, so finding ways to weave messages in amongst more practical advice is often the best approach. One way to do this is to use personal stories, either by collecting examples from the media, using your own experiences or inviting other researchers to share their own story.

Sessions also need to be marketed carefully to attract participants. Although an understanding of ethics in relation to topics such as copyright and re-use of data, as well as issues of intellectual property, plagiarism, licences and contracts are all essential for being a successful researcher in the 21st century, such topics are unlikely to attract a wide audience unless you can demonstrate their immediate value to an individual. The University of Minnesota, for example, advertises tutorials focusing on authors' rights, backed up by a comprehensive web page, www.lib.umn.edu/scholcom/manage-your-rights.

Data ethics are becomingly increasingly high profile and this may be an area in which library staff have less experience. However, we can still direct researchers to advice and resources to help, such as the excellent information provided by the Digital Curation Centre (www.dcc.ac.uk) and the UK Data Archive (www.data-archive.ac.uk/create-manage/consent-ethics).

Ethics relating to the use of social media is a growing area which also needs to be addressed and might well deserve a separate workshop.

🖒 Best for:

- raising awareness of ethical issues
- ensuring researchers comply with copyright and licensing demands.

★ Examples from practice

Publisher contracts

A librarian from the UK explains how she uses copies of contracts:

> 'I've written a few things myself and over the years I learned to be a little more careful of what I signed in terms of my own copyright. I made some silly mistakes to begin with. I bring my own contracts along to show people and confess where I went wrong – that

seems to make it more memorable and they really relate to it. More recently, I started asking some of the more senior researchers if they have examples of contracts they would be prepared to share and especially if it's something they regret.' (UK librarian)

Loughborough University, UK

Figure 10.6 illustrates the contents of Loughborough University's workshop on copyright.

⚠ To think about

Consider what issues need to be addressed and look at ways of weaving aspects

---

Workshop title: Copyright and your thesis

Target audience: This course is designed for early and mid-career PGRs.

Course outline: This course explains how and why all PGRs must comply with UK copyright law when writing and submitting their thesis. It will also highlight the importance of retaining your own copyright when publishing your research outputs.

Outcomes: Participants will be able to:
1. Recognise why it is important to think about copyright when producing research outputs
2. Identify some basic facts of UK copyright and how it directly relates to your thesis
3. Recognise the importance of complying with UK copyright law both in your thesis and other publications
4. Consider how and when to seek copyright permission
5. Recognise the need to retain copyright when publishing
6. Identify where to go for further help about copyright whilst at Loughborough
7. Meet and network with other PGR students from across campus

Additional information: This session is recommended for all early and mid-career postgraduate research students and relates to the Researcher Development Framework's Domain C1 – Professional Conduct and Domain D2 – Communication and dissemination.

Figure 10.6 *Copyright workshop at Loughborough University (reproduced with permission)*

---

of them into existing workshops, as well as perhaps designing a more specific session. Repetition of such important issues is no bad thing.

Try to devise titles which explain how the workshop will benefit the attendees individually.

This is an area which many of us may shy away from, as it's difficult to be sure you are sufficiently knowledgeable to deliver a comprehensive workshop. However, these kinds of questions will inevitable be raised in workshops on social media and writing for publication, for example, so if you can develop a baseline knowledge, you will at least be able to suggest more expert sources. When dealing with issues of ethics and the legal niceties of contracts, it's important not to raise expectations or put yourself in the position of an expert, unless this is your role, of course. All you should be aiming to do is to raise awareness of the possible pitfalls and suggest different approaches individuals might adopt in order to mitigate the effects. Consider how you can strike a balance between facilitating useful, relevant discussion and providing accurate information.

References and further reading

Bent, M. and Gannon-Leary, P. (2007) *Being an Information Literate Researcher: tips for avoiding plagiarism*, Newcastle, Jisc Plagiarism Advisory Service, http://nrl.northumbria.ac.uk/1392. (Accessed 12.3.15)

Collins, E., Milloy, C. and Stone, G. (2013) *A Guide to Creative Commons for Humanities and Social Sciences Monograph Authors*, Jisc, http://issuu.com/carenmilloy/docs/cc_guide_for_hss_monograph_authors_/1. (Accessed 7.9.15)

University of British Columbia, Canada, has created a useful guide to Creative Commons licences and how to apply them, http://copyright.ubc.ca/guidelines-and-resources/support-guides/creative-commons.

Acknowledgements

Helen Young, Loughborough University.

10.9 Social media workshops

AS THE USE of social media has become ever more pervasive, many librarians have added an element of social media to their information literacy workshops. In broad terms, social media refers to web-based services in which the content is created by the users of the service. Information generated using social media tools is, by its very nature, fairly short and often transitory but nevertheless, such interfaces are increasingly being used by researchers to network, discuss topics, generate and consume information.

There is such a plethora of tools available, with more being developed all the time, that it can be difficult to devise a workshop on this topic which delivers meaningful content.

'. . . my aim is to provide a general overview, focusing on the issues to consider (what's good about it; what do you need to think about) rather than detailed nuts and bolts (e.g. how to

set up a Twitter account, what retweet means). This is mainly because there are just too many social media tools to go into any depth, and most are technically fairly easy to use anyway. What's more difficult is using them effectively and choosing the most suitable one for your requirements.' (Lucy Keating, Newcastle University)

Although social media seems to be omnipresent, in academic life many people, including librarians, do not use it at all, while others may have dipped their toes into Facebook or Twitter purely for social reasons. Overcoming their reluctance to recognize an academic value in such tools is often the first barrier to overcome when offering workshops and, if you're a reluctant user yourself, changing your own working practices to accommodate social media will be the first hurdle.

'I try to be fairly practical and non-evangelical – I am enthusiastic, but at the same time, I know it's not for everyone.' (Lucy Keating, Newcastle University)

The first thing to consider is whether to offer a separate workshop focusing solely on social media, or whether to recognize where the tools can be integrated into existing content, for example as an information source in information retrieval workshops, or as a metrics tool in impact sessions. A dual approach is often the most effective: mentioning social media in other workshops can encourage researchers to attend a more specific session as well. *Social Media: a guide for researchers* (Cann, Dimitriou and Hooley, 2011) summarizes some of the criticisms which have been levelled at social media by researchers and academics who fear that the quality of public and academic discussion and debate is being undermined. There are concerns especially over privacy and misuse of information and personal data as well as opinions about the trivial nature of a lot of the interactions, not least the lack of any kind of peer-review filter or value labels. 'For researchers, putting your professional life online can feel exposing, particularly if you express opinions and ideas that have not been subject to the normal process of peer review' (Cann, Dimitriou and Hooley, 2011).

⚐ Best for:

- ■ engaging researchers with social media as a way of increasing the visibility of their research and making connections with other researchers.

★ Examples from practice

Using social media in your research workshops

Lucy Keating, one of the liaison librarians at Newcastle University in the UK, has been running workshops on social media for several years, both as part of the researcher development programme and as standalone sessions. Figure 10.7 shows two of the slides used in the workshops. Taking a general overview approach, Lucy also aims to include real life examples of how researchers are using different tools:

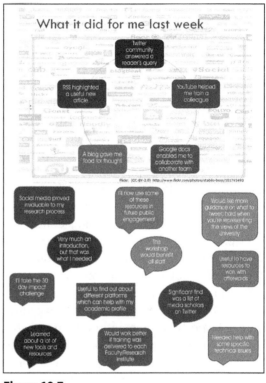

> 'This is because when you're confronted with a shiny new tool, it can often be tricky to work out how you would find a use for it. So hopefully this helps give people ideas and make decisions for themselves.' (Lucy Keating, Newcastle University)

Her workshops cover concerns the group has about using social media in research, such as too much choice, volatility, plagiarism, ethics, time consumed and use by peers; potential benefits, such as

Figure 10.7
Slides from social media workshop (© Lucy Keating, reproduced with permission)

high, measurable impact, interactive, collaborative, free and fun and tools for networking and collaborating, sharing, engagement and impact, widgets and metrics. The responses from participants have been very positive. The workshops are supplemented by an online guide, http://libguides.ncl.ac.uk/socialmedia.

Develop your own profiles on some social media platforms

> 'It's always easier to talk about tools and resources that you use yourself and over the years I have created my own personal profile on several platforms, such as Academia, ResearchGate and Google Scholar, to name just a few of the more common examples. I'm fortunate in having a few publications that I can add, so that I'm able to talk at first hand

about how I use them and what I like about them. I'm able to show e-mails I've received from other researchers, requests for my publications and even just the alerts from Academia telling me when people have searched for me using a search engine. As well as demonstrating the tools themselves from a personal perspective, it does help to lend some credibility to our workshops.' (UK librarian)

⚠ To think about

Having the appropriate skills to deliver an effective workshop may be your biggest challenge. As new tools are appearing all the time it's difficult to stay up to date with all the different choices. Think about how you might collaborate with colleagues, both in the library and elsewhere in the university, to help each other learn about new developments. Perhaps there are social media enthusiasts working in other sections of the library who might be persuaded to come along to a workshop to help facilitate it or to talk about how they use it. Does your library have a social media team who might contribute? Hearing about personal stories is a very powerful learning aid.

Find out which researchers in your organization are already active on social media and see what they are doing. Contact them to ask if you can use them as examples, or even better invite them to come along and talk about what they do and why it works for them. Maybe you can video them discussing how a social media tool has contributed to their research.

Consider how you can use social media as a tool in your own teaching, perhaps by encouraging participants to contribute via a virtual whiteboard, a blog or by posting comments on Twitter as the session progresses.

Is social media now too amorphous and intangible to be successfully tackled in a short workshop? How might you integrate elements of social media into the workshops you currently deliver?

Reflect on the best way to target your research community – discipline-specific workshops will enable you to show very relevant examples of how social media is being used by their peers.

Social media are changing and developing all the time so it can be difficult to keep up to date with new tools and resources. The Jiscmail Social Media News mailing list is a useful way for researchers and librarians to share information about the latest platforms for use by academics in their professional lives.

References and further reading

Andy Miah maintains a useful list of social media tools for academia on his blog:
  www.andymiah.net/2012/12/30/the-a-to-z-of-social-media-for-academics.

Cann, A., Dimitriou, K. and Hooley, T. (2011) *Social Media: a guide for researchers*, London, Research Information Network.

Jiscmail Social Media News mailing list, https://www.jiscmail.ac.uk/.

Minocha, S. and Petre, M. (2012) *Handbook of Social Media for Researchers and Supervisors: digital technologies for research dialogues*, London, Open University and Vitae, www.vitae.ac.uk/vitae-publications/reports/innovate-open-university-social-media-handbook-vitae-2012.pdf/view. (Accessed 31.7.15)

10.10 Bibliometrics workshops

IN AN EARLIER tip, I concluded that research is 'a process of investigation leading to new insights, effectively shared'. Assessing impact is about checking whether that sharing has been effective and one way to do that is to use a variety of bibliometric tools and measures. Bibliometrics are currently much more useful in STEM subjects; they are very hard to find consistently for arts and humanities disciplines. Nevertheless, many researchers are now being judged on such quantitative measures for job progression and security, as well as formal research assessment and evaluation exercises, and it's important that we, and they, understand what such metrics convey, when to use them and how to find them.

Assessing or measuring impact workshops are an increasingly common offering from libraries, often reinforced by detailed online guides. A workshop frequently covers the different ways in which impact can be measured at journal, article and individual level, looking, for example, at counting views and downloads, specific citation counting and the more sophisticated bibliometrics tools.

There is a wide range of bibliometrics tools currently available, measures such as journal impact factors and the h-index to name just a couple, and new ones are being developed all the time, so it is difficult to keep up to date on them all, let alone expect researchers to have either the time or inclination to do so themselves. Many researchers will be content with understanding the most common measures, but a few may wish to delve more deeply. Even if you don't plan to cover less common metrics in your workshops, it is helpful to at least be aware of what they are and what they do and to have some links prepared to help you answer a more complex query with confidence.

It is increasingly common for libraries to have a specific bibliometrics position within the team and this can be a great advantage. Such a person will be skilled in the use of a wide range of tools and able to answer even the most complex queries. Beware, however, of going into too much depth;

remember that you are not training the research group to become bibliometricians; they will often only be interested in how to apply the techniques to their own situation and too much detail can be offputting.

Alternative metrics (altmetrics) harvest data from a wide variety of less formal sources and, as mentioned in Tip 8.21, are becoming increasingly common, so including information about them in bibliometrics workshops can attract researchers who are interested in new ways of measuring impact. Example of altmetrics data displaying in traditional printed journals, use of the proprietary altmetrics toolbar and discussion amongst the group of the pros and cons of such metrics can add an interesting dimension to an otherwise fairly dry workshop.

👍 Best for:

- helping researchers understand the role of metrics in demonstrating the impact of their work
- raising awareness of issues surrounding the use of metrics to measure research effectiveness.

★ Examples from practice

The Informed Researcher@Newcastle University

As mentioned in Tip 10.5, the Science Liaison Team at Newcastle University runs workshops for both research staff and students focusing on pre- and post-publication topics. The 'measuring your impact' workshop encourages researchers to explore different quantitative measures such as citation counting, journal impact factors and the h-index. They discover how to track citations and analyse citation patterns and think about the relevance of 'views', 'downloads' and 'citations' in terms of their research impact. By comparing these with alternative metrics and discussing other more subjective aspects of impact, as well as disciplinary differences, the researchers are better able to understand how to apply bibliometric data to their own situation.

Resources to support these workshops can be found at http://libguides.ncl.ac.uk/impact and slides from the workshops are available on SlideShare (search Newcastle University impact).

⚠ To think about

Delivering bibliometrics workshops can be daunting. Ensure that you understand how all the different tools work and what the differences are and don't be afraid to admit your level of expertise; relax and work alongside the researchers to find solutions. You'll often find an experienced researcher in the group who is prepared to share his or her own experiences and this can add an extra, personal dimension to the workshop. If you have your own research history, demonstrating your own bibliometric profile makes the message much more memorable, too.

Set out expectations clearly beforehand, explain which tools and techniques you plan to cover and which are outside the scope of the session.

If you are talking to a mixed group of researchers, don't focus on solely scientific researchers; be aware that artists, humanities staff and even social scientists may not have a recognizable, quantitative metric available – metrics are based in the main on the Web of Knowledge, Scopus and Google Scholar, and so are dependent on the sources indexed in these resources. Google Scholar often returns better results for non-scientists.

References and further reading

MyRI, www.ndlr.ie/myri is an excellent open access toolkit that provides resources to supplement bibliometrics workshops.

Oxford Internet Institute, University of Oxford *TIDST: Toolkit for the Impact of Digitised Scholarly Resources*,
http://microsites.oii.ox.ac.uk/tidsr/welcome. (Accessed 24.4.15)

Acknowledgements

Newcastle University Library.

10.11 Workshops alerting to fraudulent publishing practices and misleading metrics (see also Tip 8.14)

MOST RESEARCHERS ARE now aware of the need to publish in reputable journals and they are increasingly learning to look for journal impact factors and other metrics as an indication of quality. However, as few are cognizant of the dangers of fraudulent publishers (see Tip 8.14), even fewer understand the next layer of deceit which is developing around misleading and bogus metrics. Library staff can raise awareness of such activity in workshops with researchers.

> 'We have a duty to protect and inform our new researchers of being careful with their work and their copyright.' (Jessica Eustace-Cook, Dublin)

This can be a sensitive area; if an inexperienced researcher has inadvertently already published in a questionable journal they may initially be very proud of their publication and may only realize their error during the workshop or discussion. If you realize the situation before the researcher, you'll need to find a tactful way of alerting them to the situation without embarrassing them before the rest of the group.

Some predatory publishers invent an impact factor and attach it to their publication and this will mislead some unwary authors, but it is relatively easy to check that this is fraudulent. The explosion of predatory publishers has led to a parallel development of websites purporting to provide legitimate metrics data for these less credible journals. As the publishers of the predatory journals are rarely able to gain recognition in the recognized journal ranking systems these websites, for a fee of course, award bogus impact factors to low-quality journals. This can help the journal to appear to be legitimate, especially as the companies have names such as Global Impact Factor, Journal Impact Factor from the Global Institute of Scientific Information and Universal Impact Factor.

As this is a delicate subject, introducing it as a topic for discussion in a face-to-face workshop may be the best way to raise awareness amongst researchers of the potential pitfalls, as it's easier to describe real examples and you may find members of the group prepared to share their own experiences.

👍 Best for:

■ ensuring authors are aware of publishing pitfalls.

★ Examples from practice

An anecdote

'In a recent workshop on making an impact with your research aimed at postgraduate research students I asked how many of the group had already published an article. Three of the twelve students proudly responded positively and we chatted about the publication process. Two of the three seemed surprised when I mentioned that the peer review process can be lengthy and frustrating and said that their articles had been accepted within two weeks of submission. After the class, I asked them to show me their publications, which they were very pleased to do, one student explaining that he was confident that it was a reputable publication as he had paid several hundred pounds for open access and the journal had a Global Impact Factor. He was very upset when we investigated further and showed that the GIF is a bogus metric and that the so called quality journal was in fact a fairly slick predatory publisher.' (UK librarian)

Example of an e-mail recently received by a librarian

Personal details have been removed from the e-mail exchange shown in Figure 10.8, but it serves as an example of the common messages received by researchers. What advice would you have given this senior lecturer?

>>———Original Message———-
>>From: [lecturer]
>>Sent: 09 February 2015 15:20
>>To: [librarian]
>>Subject: advice on publisher/The Nature of Shipbuilding Competitiveness
>>
>>Dear [librarian]
>>
>>Sorry to disturb – I was just wondering whether you know the company
>below? It is clearly a fishing e-mail but I am actually in process of writing a book and
>will need a publisher at some point. Is it common for publishers to approach people in
this way?
>>With thanks in anticipation and best regards
>>
>>[name]
>>Senior Lecturer
>>School of Marine Science and Technology
>>
>>From: [name]
>>Sent: 09 February 2015 15:14
>>To:
>>Subject: The Nature of Shipbuilding Competitiveness
>>
>>Dear Mr. [name]
>>Recently, in the electronic archive of the University of [name]
>>we have found an interesting research on "The Nature of Shipbuilding
>>Competitiveness".
>>We consider this particular topic may be of interest to a wider audience,
>>therefore, I would like to inquire about an eventual publication. In this
>regard, may I kindly ask if the above-mentioned work is authored by you?
>>
>>Perhaps you may come back to us with a confirmation, at your earliest
>>convenience, and we will be glad to provide further details on our offer. We
>>would be particularly interested in an expanded version of your research-
>>work, to publish it in the form of a book.
>>
>>Thank you for your time Mr. [name] and I am looking forward to hearing
>>from you!
>>
>>—
>>Kind regards/FreundlicheGrüße
>>
>>[name]
>>Acquisition Editor
>>
>>[publisher]
>>

Figure 10.8 *Example of a publisher approach by e-mail*

⚠ To think about

Predatory publishers mainly (but not always) target new, less experienced researchers, playing to their need to find a foothold on the publication ladder. Once someone has been deceived it can be difficult to admit, so careful handling of the situation is needed.

Plan how you will deal with the discovery of a deception within a class situation, so that individuals aren't embarrassed.

This is a growing industry which preys on unwary, inexperienced authors. How can you raise awareness of the pitfalls amongst researchers during a workshop?

Further reading

Beall, J. (2015) *Scholarly OA: misleading metrics*,
   http://scholarlyoa.com/2013/08/06/bogus-impact-factor-companies.
   (Accessed 18.4.15)

10.12 Research data management workshops

TIP 8.10 ADDRESSES definitions of data and data handling, discussing the different ways in which the terms can be interpreted, and 8.11 considers data management plans in general. The open access movement has raised awareness of the importance of making research data accessible; not only is it essential to demonstrating the integrity of the research, it fulfils the ethical requirement for the data, as well as the written output, to be openly available. Funders are increasingly mandating open access data and research data management (RDM) plans as a condition of funding, so researchers can no longer ignore these requirements.

Given these imperatives for transparency of research data and the concomitant need for researcher development, how then can librarians contribute to RDM workshops? Some universities do not recognize RDM as a role for the library and have separate research offices or technical units managing the data storage solutions. There is certainly a need for a robust technical infrastructure, which arguably sits more appropriately with an IT service. Other organizations situate data management solely within the library, or, more commonly, as collaboration between several sections.

Coming from a technical perspective, the aim of RDM workshops is often on purely practical concerns; focusing on precise skills or detailed instructions on how to manage specific kinds or formats of data. As librarians, we have skills in managing metadata which are easily transferable to data curation. Additionally, the traditional liaison librarian role lends itself well to the advocacy aspect of RDM. According to Brown, Bruce and Kernohan (2015) 'the data equivalent of subject or liaison librarians – "blended individuals" who will be data specialists – will need appropriate career structures of their own.'

Whether as a fully fledged data management librarian, or in a more traditional subject awareness-raising role, therefore, there is clearly a place for librarians in contributing to RDM training. You may wish to consider whether it is feasible to blend aspects of RDM into your existing workshops, either directly, if you have the knowledge to do so, or merely by alluding to it as an essential additional skill and by signposting to other, more expert sources of help.

⚑ Best for:

- helping researchers understand issues of data management.

★ Examples from practice

Digital Curation Centre

The Digital Curation Centre in the UK provides training materials for repurposing and re-use as part of its DC101 tutorial. Topic areas include:

- conceptualizing data
- creating or receiving data
- appraising and selecting data
- ingesting data
- preserving data
- storing data
- access and re-use.

In addition, material is available specifically aimed at librarians (see References below).

FOSTER

The FOSTER portal is a European Union e-learning platform which houses a growing collection of training materials on all aspects of open science. It includes resources as well as information about events taking place around Europe and is constantly being added to.

MANTRA

Developed at the University of Edinburgh, UK, MANTRA is a free, non-credit, self-paced course designed for postgraduate students, early career researchers and more senior academics, which provides guidelines for good practice in research data management. It enables users to identify themselves and suggests how the tutorials will be useful:

Career Researcher
MANTRA is for you if you want to reflect on your current research data management (RDM) practice, and devise or revise plans for future research projects and funding bids.

3 things you might want to use MANTRA for:

— Reflect on your current data management practice or develop research data management plans.
— Browse through the content and work on the units that are more relevant to you.
— Use specific content as reference resources and to evaluate your own practice.

We recommend that you start exploring: Data management plans

MANTRA website

Access the materials at http://datalib.edina.ac.uk/mantra. Within the MANTRA portal you will also find a handy DIY RDM training kit for librarians.

⚠ To think about

The curation of research data requires very specific skills, as well as additional knowledge and expertise. Are these skills which all librarians should expect to have in future, or should they be the province of a new breed of data librarian?

Not all libraries have the capacity, or the will, to expand their services in this way. However, there is a growing expectation from the research community that we will be able to help, so think carefully about any statements you may wish to make about what you can offer:

> '. . . and we used to have a sentence on our research support pages that just said they (researchers) should consider what they did with their data and to ask us for help, or something along those lines. It resulted in all kinds of queries we just didn't feel capable of answering, so in the end we took it away altogether.' (European librarian)

If you can't call upon a research data specialist, as a generalist be realistic about what you can offer. With such good online training resources available, you don't need to reinvent them, but you may need to adapt them to be relevant to your own institution. This doesn't necessarily mean you have to actually adapt them, as this UK librarian explains:

*'I've found the MANTRA materials incredibly helpful. I'm not at all an expert in all this [RDM] stuff, but I do think it's important to make sure all our researchers are aware of it. So I started a workshop called 'managing research data, some things to think about' and, basically, I've just swiped some of the stuff from the DCC so that I've got a few introductory slides. I'm very upfront about not being an expert and saying we are going to have a discussion about how all this will work for us here . . . then I actually work through the first bit of the MANTRA unit on DMPs on the big screen and we watch a couple of their videos and have a bit of chat about it. Thankfully it's all got CC licences so I don't feel too bad about just re-using it. It's all quite relaxed and informal, more about sharing experiences than me teaching them. I can show them where to find practical help on our website too, so they do go away with some practical info and they can follow through the rest of the course in their own time. It's a bit of a get-out, I know, but it's all I feel able to do at present.'
(UK librarian)*

Alternatively, can you collaborate with staff in other sections of the library or organization to run some joint workshops, sharing expertise and learning from each other at the same time? As a minimum, organizing and hosting workshops within the library, even if they are delivered by experts from elsewhere, will both increase your own knowledge and raise the visibility of the library.

Consider whether the workshops need to be discipline-specific. Arts and humanities researchers are more likely to have a lot of qualitative data, whereas science data is more usually quantitative. If it needs different kinds of curation it may be more attractive to the research community to attend more tailored workshops.

References and further reading

Australian National Data Service (2014) *Publishing and Sharing Sensitive Data*, http://ands.org.au/guides/sensitivedata.html. (Accessed 4.8.15)

Brown, S., Bruce, R. and Kernohan, D. (2015) *Directions for Research Data Management in UK Universities*, http://repository.jisc.ac.uk/5951/4/JR0034_RDM_report_200315_v5.pdf. (Accessed 28.4.15)

Digital Curation Centre resources for librarians: www.dcc.ac.uk/rdm-librarians.

FOSTER, www.fosteropenscience.eu/foster-taxonomy/research-data-management.

MANTRA portal, http://datalib.edina.ac.uk/mantra; MANTRA training kits for librarians, http://datalib.edina.ac.uk/mantra/libtraining.html.

SECTION 11

Bibliography

At the end of each tip you will find any specific citations referred to in that tip, along with additional relevant further reading. This bibliography includes all the citations and further reading, together with some more general references which may be of interest.

Akers, K. G., Sferdean, F. C., Nicholls, N. H. and Green, J. A. (2014) Building Support for Research Data Management: biographies of eight research universities, *International Journal of Digital Curation*, **9** (2), 171–91.

Allan, B. (2013) *The No-Nonsense Guide to Training in Libraries*, London, Facet Publishing.

Anderson, R. (2011) The Crisis in Research Librarianship, *Journal of Academic Librarianship*, **37** (4), 289–90.

Archinfo (2014) Available at www.archinfo-richview.com/index.html. (Accessed 1.5.15)

Association of College and Research Libraries (2015) *Framework for Information Literacy for Higher Education*, www.ala.org/acrl/standards/ilframework.

Australian National Data Service (2014) *Publishing and Sharing Sensitive Data*, http://ands.org.au/guides/sensitivedata.html. (Accessed 4.8.15)

Australian National Data Service (2015) *What is Research Data?*, http://ands.org.au/guides/what-is-research-data.html. (Accessed 4.8.15)

Ayob, A., Rahman, H. A. and Sendut, P. H. (2010) Effectiveness of Libraries in Supporting Researchers' Information Needs: the impact of a digital library, unpublished paper delivered at the National Seminar on Information Technology in the Library, 3–5 August 2010, Bayview Hotel, Penang, Malaysia.

Ball, A. (2012) *Review of Data Management Lifecycle Models*, http://opus.bath.ac.uk/28587/1/redm1rep120110ab10.pdf. (Accessed 1.5.15)

Barker, A. (2015) The Liverpool Scene – University Library and University Press as Partners, *SCONUL Focus*, **63**, 18–20.

Barnett, D. and Heath, F. M. (2013) *Research Library 21st Century*, Hoboken, NJ, Taylor & Francis.

Beall, J. (2015) *Beall's List*, http://scholarlyoa.com/publishers. (Accessed 8.1.15)

Beall, J. (2015) *Criteria for Identifying Predatory Publishers*, https://scholarlyoa. files.wordpress.com/2015/01/criteria-2015.pdf. (Accessed 8.1.15)

Beall, J. (2015) *Scholarly OA: misleading metrics*, http://scholarlyoa.com/2013/08/06/bogus-impact-factor-companies. (Accessed 18.4.15)

Beard, C. and Bawden, D. (2012) University Libraries and the Postgraduate Student: physical and virtual spaces, *New Library World*, **113** (9/10), 439–47.

Bell, D. (2015) *Read for Research* blogpost, Citylibresearchers blog, https://citylibresearchers.wordpress.com/2015/04/24/read-for-research-campaign-at-city-university-london-library. (Accessed 25.4.15)

Bent, M. (2004) ResIN: Research information at Newcastle University Library, *SCONUL Focus*, **32**, 28–30.

Bent, M. (2008) *Information Literacy Landscape*, Moira's Info Lit Blog, www.moirabent.blogspot.co.uk/p/information-literacy-landscape.html. (Accessed 24.5.15)

Bent, M. and Gannon-Leary, P. (2007) Being an Information Literate Researcher: tips for avoiding plagiarism, Newcastle, Jisc Plagiarism Advisory Service, http://nrl.northumbria.ac.uk/1392. (Accessed 12.3.15)

Bent, M., Gannon-Leary, P., Goldstein, S. and Videler, T. (2012) *The Informed Researcher*, London, Vitae, www.vitae.ac.uk/researcherbooklets. (Accessed 25.5.15).

Bent, M., Gannon-Leary, P. and Webb, J. (2007) Information Literacy in a Researcher's Learning Life: the 7 ages of research, *New Review of Information Networking*, **13** (2), 81–99.

Bent, M. and Stubbings, R. (2011) *The SCONUL Seven Pillars of Information Literacy: research lens*, London, SCONUL, www.sconul.ac.uk/sites/default/files/documents/researchlens.pdf. (Accessed 4.1.16)

Bewick, L. and Corrall, S. (2010) Developing Librarians as Teachers: a study of their pedagogical knowledge, *Journal of Librarianship and Information Science*, **42** (2), 97–110.

Black, B., Connell, T., Dotson, D., Efkeman, T., Leach, B., Mandernach, M. and Reese, T. (2013) *Research Commons Task Force Findings and Recommendations*, http://library.osu.edu/staff/administration-reports/RCTFReport.pdf. (Accessed 27.5.15)

Blummer, B. and Kenton, J. (2012) Best Practices for Integrating E-books in Academic Libraries: a literature review from 2005 to present, *Collection Management*, **37** (2), 65–97.

Boadi, B. Y. (2006) Income-generating Activities: a viable financial source for African academic libraries?, *The Bottom Line*, **19** (2), 64–77.

Bourg, C., Coleman, R. and Erway, R. (2009) Support for the Research Process:

an academic library manifesto, www.oclc.org/content/dam/research/
publications/library/2009/2009-07.pdf?urlm=162924. (Accessed 27.5.15)

Bradbury, K. and Weightman, A. (2010) Research Support at Cardiff
University Library, *SCONUL Focus*, **50**, 65–70.

Brewerton, A. (2013) *RLUK: Redefining the Research Library Model: workforce
survey findings*, www.rluk.ac.uk/strategicactivity/strategic-
strands/redefining-research-library-model/. (Accessed 4.1.16)

Brown, A. (2013) *Library Publishing Toolkit*, IDS Project Press.

Brown, J. M. and Tucker, C. (2013) Expanding Library Support of Faculty
Research: exploring readiness, *Portal*, **13** (3), 283–99.

Brown, S., Bruce, R. and Kernohan, D. (2015) *Directions for Research Data
Management in UK Universities*, https:/www.fosteropenscience.eu/
sites/default/files/pdf/1240.pdf. (Accessed 4.1.16)

Bruce, C. (1997) *The Seven Faces of Information Literacy*, Adelaide, Auslib Press.

Bruce, C., Edwards, S. and Lupton, M. (2006) Six frames for Information
Literacy Education: a conceptual framework for interpreting the
relationships between theory and practice, *ITALICS*, **5** (1), 1–18.

Burrows, T. and Croker, K. (2012) Supporting Research in an Era of Data
Deluge: developing a new service portfolio within Information Services
at the University of Western Australia, paper presented at VALA, 6–9
February, Melbourne, Australia, www.vala.org.au/vala2012-
proceedings/vala2012-session-1-burrows. (Accessed 12.3.15)

Cameron, W. B. (1963) *Informal Sociology: a casual introduction to sociological
thinking*, New York, NY, Random House.

Candela, L., Castelli, D. and Pagano, P. (2009) On-demand Virtual Research
Environments and the Changing Roles of Librarians, *Library Hi Tech*,
27 (2), 239–51.

Cann, A., Dimitriou, K. and Hooley, T. (2011) *Social Media: a guide for
researchers*, London, RIN.

Carlson, J. and Kneale, R. (2011) Embedded Librarianship in the Research
Context: navigating new waters, *College and Research News*, March, 167–70.

Carlson, J. and Yatcilla, J. K. (2010) The Intersection of Virtual Organizations
and the Library: a case study, *Journal of Academic Librarianship*, **36** (3), 192–
201.

Carroll, D. (2011) Fostering a Community of Scholars at the University of
Warwick: the Wolfson Research Exchange, *New Review of Academic
Librarianship*, **17** (1), 78–95.

Christensen-Dalsgaard, B. (2012) *Ten Recommendations for Libraries to Get
Started with Research Data Management*, The Hague, Liber Working Group
on E-Science/research data management, http://libereurope.eu/wp-content/
uploads/The%20research%20data%20group%202012%20v7%20final.pdf.
(Accessed 24.5.15)

CILIP (2014) *Research Data Management Briefing Paper*,
www.cilip.org.uk/sites/default/files/documents/Research%20data%20ma
nagement%20briefing%20July%202014_0.pdf. (Accessed 27.5.15)

Cole, E. (2015) *Embedding ORCID Across Researcher Career Paths: final project summary*, https://orcidnorthumbria.wordpress.com. (Accessed 17.7.15)

Collins, E., Milloy, C. and Stone, G. (2013) *A Guide to Creative Commons for Humanities and Social Sciences Monograph Authors*, Jisc,
http://issuu.com/carenmilloy/docs/cc_guide_for_hss_monograph_
authors_/1. (Accessed 7.9.15)

Cooke, L. (2011) Evaluating the Impact of Academic Liaison Librarians on Their User Community: a review and case study, *New Review of Academic Librarianship*, **17** (1), 5–30.

Coonan, E. and Secker, J. (2011) *A New Curriculum for Information Literacy (ANCIL)*, http://newcurriculum.wordpress.com. (Accessed 10.1.13)

Coonan, E. M. (2011) Navigating the Information Landscape, *The Serials Librarian*, **61** (3–4), 323–33.

Corbyn, Z. (2008) PhD Students Need Help Developing a 'Writing Voice', Educationists Say, *Times Higher Education*, 25 September,
www.timeshighereducation.co.uk/news/phd-students-need-help-
developing-a-writing-voice-educationists-say/403658.article.

Corrall, S. (2010) Educating the Academic Librarian as a Blended Professional: a review and case study, *Library Management*, **31** (8/9), 567–93.

Corrall, S. (2014) Designing Libraries for Research Collaboration in the Network World: an exploratory study, *Liber Quarterly*, **24** (1), 17–48.

Corrall, S., Kennan, M. A. and Afzal, W. (2013) Bibliometrics and Research Data Management Services: emerging trends in library support for research, *Library Trends*, **61** (3), 636–74.

Corrall, S., Kennan, M. A. and Salo, D. (2013) Research Know-How for Research Support Services: preparing information specialists for emerging roles, *Proceedings of the American Society for Information Science and Technology*, **50** (1), 1–4.

Corrall, S. and Lester, R. (2013) The Researcher's View: context is critical. In Watson, L. (ed.), *Better Library and Learning Spaces: projects, trends and ideas*, London, Facet Publishing, 183–92.

Cox, A., Verbaan, E. and Sen, B. (2012) Upskilling Liaison Librarians for Research Data Management, *Ariadne*, **70**,
www.ariadne.ac.uk/issue70/cox-et-al. (Accessed 27.5.15)

Cox, A., Verbaan, E. and Sen, B. (2014) A Spider, an Octopus, or an Animal Just Coming into Existence? Designing a curriculum for librarians to support research data management, *Journal of eScience Librarianship*, **3** (1). Available at doi:10.7191/jeslib.2014.1055. (Accessed 21.10.15)

Cox, A. M. and Pinfield, S. (2013) Research Data Management and Libraries: current activities and future priorities, *Journal of Librarianship and Information Science*, **46** (4), 299–316.

Cox, J. (2010) Academic Libraries in Challenging Times, *An Leabharlann: the Irish Library*, **19** (2), 7–13, http://aran.library.nuigalway.ie/xmlui/bitstream/handle/10379/1412/JohnCoxArticle.pdf?sequence=1.

Cozzens, S. E. (2007) Death by Peer Review? The Impact of Results-Oriented Management in U.S. Research. In Whitley, R. and Gläser, J.(eds), *The Changing Governance of the Sciences: the advent of research evaluation systems*, Dordrecht, Springer, 225–42.

Crossick, G. (2015) *Monographs and Open Access: a report to HEFCE*, www.hefce.ac.uk/media/hefce/content/pubs/indirreports/2015/Monographs,and,open,access/2014_monographs.pdf. (Accessed 28.7.15)

Crotty, D. (2014) Altmetrics: Mistaking the Means for the End, *The Scholarly Kitchen*, http://scholarlykitchen.sspnet.org/2014/05/01/altmetrics-mistaking-the-means-for-the-end. (Accessed 1.5.14)

Cuillier, C. and Stoffle, C. J. (2011) Finding Alternative Sources of Revenue, *Journal of Library Administration*, **51** (7–8), 777–809.

Daniels, W., Darch, C. and de Jager, K. (2010) The Research Commons: a new creature in the library?, *Performance Measurement and Metrics*, **11** (2), 116–30.

Dewey, B. (2010) *Transforming Research Libraries for the Global Knowledge Society*, Elsevier Science, http://NCL.eblib.com/patron/FullRecord.aspx?p=1582337.

Dewey, B. I. (2004) The Embedded Librarian, *Resource Sharing & Information Networks*, **17** (1–2), 5–17.

Digital Curation Centre (2015) *What is Digital Curation?*, www.dcc.ac.uk/digital-curation/what-digital-curation. (Accessed 29.3.15)

Directory of Open Access journals, http://doaj.org.

Dixon, D. (2014) Complementary Skills, Resources, and Missions: best practices in developing library-press collaborations, Poster presented at the Library Publishing Forum, Kansas City, MO, 2014, doi: http://dx.doi.org/10.7710/2162-3309/lpf.1005.

Drewes, K. and Hoffman, N. (2010) Academic Embedded Librarianship: an introduction, *Public Services Quarterly*, **6** (2–3), 75–82.

Drummond, R. and Wartho, R. (2009) RIMS: the Research Impact Measurement Service at the University of New South Wales, *Australian Academic & Research Libraries*, **40** (2), 76–87.

Duhon, L. (2015) *How to Write a Book Review (for Librarians)*, http://libguides.utoledo.edu/write_a_review. (Accessed 21/7/15)

Elsevier (2015) *Publishing Campus*, www.publishingcampus.elsevier.com. (Accessed 8.5.15)

Engeström, Y., Kaatrakoski, H., Kaiponen, P., Lahikainen, J., Laitinen, A., Myllys, H., Rantavuori, J. and Sinikara, K. (2012) Knotworking in Academic Libraries: two case studies from the University of Helsinki, *Liber Quarterly*, **21** (3/4), 387–405.

Engineering and Physical Sciences Research Council (2015) *Research Data: scope and benefits*. Available at: https://www.epsrc.ac.uk/about/standards/researchdata/scope/. (Accessed 21.10.15)

Enright, S. (2015) Supporting Researchers with a Research Information Management Platform, *SCONUL Focus*, **63**, 24–33.

European Commission Expert Group on Assessment of University-Based Research (2010) *Assessing Europe's University-Based Research*, EUR 24187 EN,. Brussels, http://ec.europa.eu/research/science-society/document_library/pdf_06/assessing-europe-university-based-research_en.pdf. (Accessed 15.5.15)

European Universities Association (2015) *EUA'S Open Access Checklist For Universities: a practical guide on implementation*, www.eua.be/Libraries/Publications_homepage_list/Open_access_report_v3.sflb.ashx.

Exner, N. (2014) Research Information Literacy: addressing original researchers' needs, *Journal of Academic Librarianship*, **40** (5), 460–6.

Fallon, H. (2010) And So It Is Written: supporting librarians on the path to publication, *Journal of Library Innovation*, **1**(1), 35–41.

Fallon, H. (2010) *Academic Writing Librarians* blog. Available at http://academicwritinglibrarian.blogspot.co.uk/ (Accessed 21.10.15)

Fletcher, J. and Drummond, R. (2015) *Providing Research Support: a practical guide for academic and research libraries*, Chandos Information Professional Series, London, Chandos.

Freeman, G. T. (2005) The Library as Place: changes in learning patterns, collections, technology and use. In *Library as Place: rethinking roles, rethinking space*, Council on Library and Information Resources, www.clir.org/pubs/reports/pub129/freeman.html.

Gannon-Leary, P. and Bent, M. (2008) A Destination or a Place of Last Resort? The research library of the future, its users and its librarians, *Library and Information Research*, **32** (101), 3–14.

Gannon-Leary, P. and Bent, M. (2010) Writing for Publication and the Role of the Library: 'Do have a cow, man!' ('Don't have a cow, man' – Bart Simpson), *New Review of Academic Librarianship*, **16** (1), 26–44.

Gannon-Leary, P., Bent, M. and Webb, J. (2007) Developing and Managing Effective Library and Information Services to Support Research and Researchers, University of Northumbria Performance Measures Conference, South Africa.

Gannon-Leary, P., Bent, M. and Webb, J. (2008) Researchers and Their Information Needs: a literature review, *New Review of Academic*

Librarianship, **13** (1), 51–69.

Gannon-Leary, P., Fontainha, E. and Bent, M. (2011) The Loneliness of the Long Distance Researcher, *Library Hi Tech,* **29** (3), 455–69.

Garside, J., Bailey, R., Tyas, M., Ormrod, G., Stone, G., Topping, A. and Gillibrand, W. P. (2015) Developing a Culture of Publication: a joint enterprise writing retreat, *Journal of Applied Research in Higher Education,* **7** (2), 429–42.

Gordon, R. S. (2004) *The Librarian's Guide to Writing for Publication,* Lanham, MD, Scarecrow Press.

Gumpenberger, C., Wieland, M. and Gorraiz, J. (2012) Bibliometric Practices and Activities at the University of Vienna, *Library Management,* **33** (3), 174–83.

Hall, B. (2015) Getting to Know Our Researchers and Understanding Their Needs, *SCONUL Focus,* **63**, 45–7.

Hall, H. (2010) Promoting the Priorities of Practitioner Research Engagement, *Journal of Librarianship and Information Science,* **42** (2), 83–8.

Hall, L. W. and McBain, I. (2014) Practitioner Research in an Academic Library: evaluating the impact of a support group, *Australian Library Journal,* **63** (2), 129–43.

Hansson, J. and Johannesson, K. (2013) Librarians' Views of Academic Library Support for Scholarly Publishing: an every-day perspective, *Journal of Academic Librarianship,* **39** (3), 232–40.

Harris, M. R. (2005) The Librarian's Roles in the Systematic Review Process: a case study, *Journal of the Medical Library Association,* **93** (1), 81–7.

Hicks, D., Wouters, P., Waltman, L., de Rijcke, S. and Rafols, I. (2015) Bibliometrics: The Leiden Manifesto for research metrics, *Nature,* 520 (7548), 429–31, www.nature.com/news/bibliometrics-the-leiden-manifesto-for-research-metrics-1.17341.

Hofer, A., Brunetto, K. and Townsend, L. (2013) A Threshold Concepts Approach to the Standards Revision, *Communications in Information Literacy,* 7 (2), 108–13, www.comminfolit.org/index.php?journal=cil&page= article&op=view&path%5B%5D=v7i2p108.

InformAll (2014) *InformAll Criteria for Describing, Reviewing and Evaluating Courses and Resources,* https://www.informall.org.uk/education/informall-criteria/. (Accessed 4.1.16)

Jaguszewski, J. M. and Williams, K. (2013) *New Roles for New Times: transforming liaison roles in research libraries,* Washington, DC, www.arl.org/nrnt.

Jilovsky, C. and Genoni, P. (2014) Shared Collections to Shared Storage: the CARM1 and CARM2 print repositories, *Library Management,* **35** (1/2), 2–14.

Jisc (2015) *Institutions and Managing Research Data,*

www.jisc.ac.uk/guides/research-data-management. (Accessed 1.9.15)

Jisc (2015) Open access website, www.jisc.ac.uk/openaccess.

JiscInfoNet (2014) *Implementing a Virtual Research Environment*, www.jiscinfonet.ac.uk/infokits/vre. (Accessed 5.5.15)

Kenney, A. (2014) *Leveraging the Liaison Model: from defining 21st century research libraries to implementing 21st century research universities*, www.sr.ithaka.org/blog-individual/leveraging-liaison-model-defining-21st-century-research-libraries-implementing-21st. (Accessed 25.5.15)

Kesselman, M. and Watstein, S. (2009) Creating Opportunities: embedded librarians, *Journal of Library Administration*, **49** (4), 383–400.

Kocevar-Weidinger, E., Benjes-Small, C., Ackermann, E. and Kinman, V. R. (2010) Why and How to Mystery Shop Your Reference Desk, *Reference Services Review*, **38** (1), 28–43.

Kramer, B. (2013) *Using Refworks for Systematic Reviews*, www.slideshare.net/bmkramer/usingrefworksforsystematicreviewssept2013. (Accessed 24/3/15)

Kroll, S. and Forsman, R. (2010) *A Slice of Research Life: information support for research in the United States*, www.oclc.org/content/dam/research/publications/library/2010/2010-15.pdf. (Accessed 4.1.16)

League of European Research Universities (2012) *Research Universities and Research Assessment*, www.leru.org/index.php/public/publications/category/position-paper/. (Accessed 4.1.16)

Lee, S. H. (2012) *Digital Information and Knowledge Management: new opportunities for research libraries*, Hoboken, NJ, Taylor & Francis.

Lewis, M. (2010) Libraries and the Management of Research Data. In McKnight, S. (ed.), *Envisioning Future Academic Library Services: initiatives, ideas and challenges*, London, Facet Publishing, 145–68.

Lowry, C. B., Adler, P., Hahn, K. and Stuart, C. (2009) *Transformational Times: an environmental scan prepared for the ARL Strategic Plan Review Task Force*, Washington, DC, www.arl.org/focus-areas/statistics-assessment/1203-transformational-times-an-environmental-scan-prepared-for-the-arl-strategic-plan-review-task-forceVooyy-mLSUk. (Accessed 2.5.15)

Luce, R. E. (2008) A New Value Equation Challenge: the emergence of eresearch and roles for research libraries. In Council on Library and Information Resources (ed.), *No Brief Candle: reconceiving research libraries for the 21st century*, Washington, DC, Council on Library and Information Resources, 42–50.

Lund University (2015) *Kick Start to Academic Life*, www.sam.lu.se/en/staff/coursesforphdstudentsandteachers/phdcourses/coursesautumn2014/kickstarttoacademic.(Accessed 24.4.15)

MacColl, J. (2010) Library Roles in University Research Assessment, *LIBER*

Quarterly, **20** (2), 152–68.

Martin, J. (2013) Refreshing Information Literacy: learning from recent British information literacy models, *Communications in Information Literacy,* **7** (2), 114–27.

McBain, I., Culshaw, H. and Walkley Hall, L. (2013) Establishing a Culture of Research Practice in an Academic Library: an Australian case study, *Library Management,* **34** (6/7), 448–61.

McCluskey, C. (2013) Being an Embedded Research Librarian: supporting research by being a researcher, *Journal of Information Literacy,* **7** (2), 4–14.

McGowan, J. and Sampson, M. (2005) Systematic Reviews Need Systematic Searchers, *Journal of the Medical Library Association,* **93** (1), 74–80.

McNamara, D. and Core, J. (1998) *Teaching for Learning in Libraries and Information Services: a series of educational workshops: the EduLib Project and its teaching materials,* Hull, EduLib Project.

McPhie, J. and Wannerton, R. (2014) Marketing Our Collections, *SCONUL Focus,* **61**, 39–41. (Accessed 8.5.15)

Mercer, H. (2011) Almost Halfway There: an analysis of the open access behaviors of academic librarians, *College & Research Libraries News,* September, 443–53.

Meyer, E. and Land, R. (2003) *Threshold Concepts and Troublesome Knowledge: linkages to ways of thinking and practising within the disciplines,* Edinburgh, www.ed.ac.uk/etl/docs/ETLreport4.pdf.

Minocha, S. and Petre, M. (2012) *Handbook of Social Media for Researchers and Supervisors: digital technologies for research dialogues,* London, Open University and Vitae, www.vitae.ac.uk/vitae-publications/reports/ innovate-open-university-social-media-handbook-vitae-2012.pdf/view. (Accessed 31.7.15)

Mullins, J. L., Rust, C., Ogburn, J. L., Crow, R., Ivins, O., Mower, A., Nesdill, D., Newton, M. P., Speer, J. and Watkinson, C. (2012) *Library Publishing Services: strategies for success: final research report (March 2012),* SPARC, http://docs.lib.purdue.edu/purduepress_ebooks/24.

National E-Science Centre (2012) *Defining e-Science,* www.nesc.ac.uk/nesc/define.html. (Accessed 2.5.15)

National Information Standards Organization (2013) *NISO RP152013: Recommended Practices for Online Supplemental Journal Article Materials: a recommended practice of the National Information Standards Organization and the National Federation of Advanced Information Services,* Baltimore, MD, NISO, www.niso.org/apps/group_public/download.php/10055/ RP152013_Supplemental_Materials.pdf. (Accessed 17.7.15)

Neway, J. (1985) *Information Specialist as Team Player in the Research Process,* Westport, CT, Greenwood Press.

Parker, R. (2012) What the Library Did Next: strengthening our visibility in

research support, *VALA 2012*, Melbourne, Australia, www.vala.org.au/
direct-download/vala2012-proceedings/435-vala2012-session-1-parker/
file. (Accessed 4.1.16)

Perkins, D. (1999) The Many Faces of Constructivism, *Educational Leadership*,
57 (3), 6–11.

Pickton, M. (2015) *Research Support Hub*, http://Researchsupporthub.
northampton.ac.uk. (Accessed 25.5.15)

Potter, N. (2012) *The Library Marketing Toolkit*, London, Facet Publishing.

Potter, N. (2015) The Library Marketing Toolkit,
www.librarymarketingtoolkit.com. (Accessed 25.5.15)

Powis, C., Webb, J. and Blanchett, H. (2010) *A Guide to Teaching Information
Literacy: 101 tips*, London, Facet Publishing.

Price, G. (2014) Library as Publisher: capacity building for the library
publishing subfield, *Journal of Electronic Publishing*, **17** (2),
www.infodocket.com/2014/05/27/new-article-library-as-publisher-
capacity-building-for-the-library-publishing-subfield. (Accessed 25.5.15)

Proquest (2015) *Ulrichsweb: Global Serials Directory*.
Available at: www.ulrichsweb.com/. (Accessed: 21.10.15)

Puente, M. A. (2010) Developing a Vital Research Library Workforce,
Research Library Issues: a bimonthly report from ARL, CNI, and SPARC,
272, 1–6.

REF (2014) *REF 2014*, www.ref.ac.uk/about. (Accessed 15.5.15)

Reimer, T. (2014) *Imperial College London ORCID Project*, London,
https://www.imperial.ac.uk/research-and-innovation/support-for-
staff/scholarly-communication/orcid/project. (Accessed 25.5.15)

Reimer, T. (2015) *Imperial College London ORCID Project*, https://repository.
jisc.ac.uk/5876/1/Imperial_College_ORCID_project.pdf. (Accessed
30.4.15)

Research Information Network (2006) *Researchers' Use of Academic Libraries
and Their Services*, www.rin.ac.uk/system/files/attachments/Researchers-
libraries-services-report.pdf. (Accessed 4.1.16)

Research Information Network (2010) *Research Support Services in UK
Universities*, London, http://soas.ac.uk/careers/earlycareerresearchers/
file69090.pdf. (Accessed 4.1.16)

Research Information Network (2011) *The Role of Research Supervisors in
Information Literacy*, www.rin.ac.uk/our-work/researcher-development-
and-skills/information-handling-training-researchers/research-superv.
(Accessed 1.6.15)

Research Information Network (2011) *The Value of Libraries for Research and
Researchers: a RIN and RLUK report*, www.rluk.ac.uk/wp-content/uploads/
2014/02/Value-of-Libraries-report.pdf. (Accessed 24.4.15)

Research Libraries UK (2012) *Reskilling for Research*, www.rluk.ac.uk/wp-content/uploads/2014/02/RLUK-Re-skilling.pdf.

Research Libraries UK (2012) *Value and Impact,* www.rluk.ac.uk/
strategicactivity/strategic-strands/redefining-research-library-
model/foundations/impact/. (Accessed 16.7.15)

Richardson, J., Nolan-Brown, T., Loria, P. and Bradbury, S. (2012) Library
Research Support in Queensland: a survey, *Australian Academic &
Research Libraries,* **43** (4), 258–77.

San Francisco Declaration on Research Assessment (2012),
www.ascb.org/dora. (Accessed 4.1.16)

Schloegl, C. and Stock, W. G. (2008) Practitioners and Academics as Authors
and Readers: the case of LIS journals, *Journal of Documentation,* **64** (5),
643–66.

SCONUL (2015) *Research Data Management: briefing for library directors,*
www.sconul.ac.uk/sites/default/files/documents/SCONUL%20RDM%20
briefing.pdf. (Accessed 23.4.15)

Secker, J., Boden, D. and Price, G. (2007) T*he Information Literacy Cookbook:
ingredients, recipes and tips for success,* London, Chandos.

Sferdean, F. (2014) *Research Lifecycle Model at UM,* https://mlibrarydata.
wordpress.com/2014/02/28/research-lifecycle-model. (Accessed 1.5.15)

Shumaker, D. (2012) *The Embedded Librarian: innovative strategies for taking
knowledge where it's needed,* Medford, NJ, Information Today.

Smallwood, C. (2009) Librarians as Writers, *American Libraries,* **40** (6/7), 54–7.

Smallwood, C. (2010) *Writing and Publishing: the librarian's handbook* (ALA
Guides for the Busy Librarian), Chicago, American Library Association.

STAR METRICS (2015) *Science and Technology for America's Reinvestment*
(STAR), www.starmetrics.nih.gov. (Accessed 25.5.15)

Steiner, A., Thomas, J. A. and Thompson, E. E. (2012) Supporting Research
at QUT: a tale of three librarians and a Creative Industries super-faculty,
Arts Library Society Australia & New Zealand Conference (ARLIS/ANZ
2012), 6–8 September 2012. National Gallery of Victoria, Melbourne, VIC,
http://eprints.qut.edu.au/54208/2/54208.pdf. (Accessed 25.5.15)

Taylor, C. (2015) *Research Data Management: briefing for library directors,*
www.sconul.ac.uk/sites/default/files/documents/SCONUL%20RDM%20
briefing.pdf.

Taylor-Roe, J. (2014) Introducing PDA into an Academic Library: natural
evolution or reckless abandon?, PowerPoint,
http://library.bcu.ac.uk/squaring/taylorroe.pdf (Accessed 5.5.15)

Tenopir, C. (2015) *Librarians Do Research Too,* Elsevier,
http://libraryconnect.elsevier.com/sites/default/files/LC_Tenopir_Libraria
ns_Do_Research_Too.pdf.

Tenopir, C., Birch, B. and Allard, S. (2012) *Academic Libraries and Research
Data Services: current practices and plans for the future,* An ACRL White

Paper (4), www.ala.org/acrl/sites/ala.org.acrl/files/content/publications/
whitepapers/Tenopir_Birch_Allard.pdf.

Texas A&M University Libraries (2015) *ORCID and Other Researcher
Identifiers: ORCID integration,* http://guides.library.tamu.edu/content.
php?pid=553864&sid=4564757. (Accessed 16.4.15)

Ubogu, F. and Van den Heever, M. (2013) Collaboration on Academic
Research Support among Five African Universities, *Qualitative and
Quantitative Methods in Libraries* **2**, 207–19.

UKSG (2014) *Webinar on the Library as Publisher,*
www.uksg.org/libraryaspublisher. (Accessed 28.7.15)

UNESCO (2013) *The UNESCO Global Media and Information Literacy (MIL)
Assessment Framework: country readiness and competencies.* [Online.]
Available at: http://unesdoc.unesco.org/images/0022/002246/224655e.pdf.
(Accessed 30.7.15)

University of Leicester (2015) *Make your Publications Open Access.* Available
at: http://www2.le.ac.uk/library/for/researchers/publish/open-access.
(Accessed 21.10.15)

University of Melbourne (2005) Policy on the Management of Research Data
and Records. Available at: www.unimelb.edu.au/records/pdf/research.pdf.
(Accessed: 21.10.15)

University of Waterloo Library (2015) *Calculate Your Academic Footprint,*
http://subjectguides.uwaterloo.ca/content.php?pid=84805&sid=2787897.
(Accessed 8.4.15)

Vaughan, K. T. L., Hayes, B. E., Lerner, R. C., McElfresh, K. R., Pavlech, L.,
Romito, D., Reeves, L. H. and Morris, E. N. (2013) Development of the
Research Lifecycle Model for Library Services, *Journal of the Medical
Library Association,* **101** (4), 310–14.

Vitae (2010) *Researcher Development Framework,* www.vitae.ac.uk/
researchers-professional-development/about-the-vitae-researcher-
development-framework. (Accessed 4.1.16)

Vitae (2012) *Information Literacy Lens on the Vitae Researcher Development
Framework Using the SCONUL Seven Pillars of Information Literacy,*
www.vitae.ac.uk/vitae-publications/rdf-related/information-literacy-
lens-on-the-vitae-researcher-development-framework-rdf-apr-2012.pdf.
(Accessed 4.1.16)

Vitae (2015) *Realising the Potential of Researchers,*
www.vitae.ac.uk. (Accessed 12.5.15)

Warr, R. B. (1983) Bibliometrics: a model for judging quality, *Collection
Building,* **5** (2), 29–34.

Webb, J., Gannon-Leary, P. and Bent, M. (2007) *Providing Effective Library
Services for Research,* London, Facet Publishing.

Wenger, E. (1998) *Communities of Practice: learning, meaning and identity,*

Cambridge, CUP.

Whitchurch, C. (2009) The Rise of the Blended Professional in Higher Education: a comparison between the United Kingdom, Australia and the United States, *Higher Education*, **58** (3), 407–18.

Wiklund, G. and Voog, H. (2013) It takes Two to Tango: making way for relevant research support services at Lund University Libraries, *Sciecom Info*, 1 [Online.] Available at: http://journals.lub.lu.se/index.php/sciecominfo/article/view/6125. (Accessed 21.10.15)

Wilsdon, J. et al. (2015) The Metric Tide: Report of the Independent Review of the Role of Metrics in Research Assessment and Management, doi:10.13140/RG.2.1.4929.1363.

Witt, M. (2012) Co-designing, Co-developing, and Co-implementing an Institutional Data Repository Service, *Journal of Library Administration*, **52** (2), 172–88.

Wolstenholme, J. (2015) Evidence Based Practice Using Formative Assessment in Library Research Support, *Evidence Based Library and Information Practice*, **10** (3), 4–29, https://ejournals.library.ualberta.ca/index.php/EBLIP/article/view/24066.

Wubbels, T. (2007) Do We Know a Community of Practice When We See One?, *Technology, Pedagogy and Education*, **16** (2), 225–33.

Wusteman, J. (2008) Editorial: Virtual Research Environments: what is the librarian's role?, *Journal of Librarianship and Information Science*, **40** (2), 67–70.

Wusteman, J. (2009) Virtual Research Environments: issues and opportunities for librarians, *Library Hi Tech*, **27** (2), 1–6.2), 67–70.

Wusteman, J. (2009) Virtual Research Environments: issues and opportunities for librarians, *Library Hi Tech*, **27** (2), 1–6.

Index